A GUIDE TO ENGLISH LITERATURE

A GUIDE TO ENGLISH LITERATURE

K.M. Jan
Shabnam Firdaus

ATLANTIC
PUBLISHERS & DISTRIBUTORS (P) LTD

Published by

ATLANTIC

PUBLISHERS & DISTRIBUTORS (P) LTD

7/22, Ansari Road, Darya Ganj,
New Delhi-110002
Phones : +91-11-40775252, 23273880, 23275880, 23280451
Fax : +91-11-23285873
Web : www.atlanticbooks.com
E-mail : orders@atlanticbooks.com

Branch Office
5, Nallathambi Street, Wallajah Road,
Chennai-600002
Phones : +91-44-64611085, 32413319
E-mail : chennai@atlanticbooks.com

Printed in India at Nice Printing Press, A-33/3A, Site-IV, Industrial Area, Sahibabad, Ghaziabad, U.P.

PREFACE

Literature is the response of the writer to life in the verbal symmetry of art. Criticism interprets and evaluates literature revealing the beauty of art which the reader might have otherwise missed. The essays included in *A Guide to English Literature* were written separately by the authors in pursuit of their study of English literature. Later they conceived the idea that the writings might be compiled in the form of a book for the benefit of the students of English literature in general and particularly for those pursuing English literature at the Honours and the Postgraduate level.

The book deals with the novels—Ernest Hemingway, *A Farewell to Arms,* Thomas Hardy's *Far From the Madding Crowd, The Mayor of Casterbridge* and *Tess,* Emily Bronte's *Wuthering Heights,* E.M. Forster's *A Passage to India,* Virginia Woolf's *To the Lighthouse* and Mulk Raj Anand's *Untouchable.* The various aspects of the novels—theme, title, characterisation and narrative techniques have been thoroughly discussed.

In the same way, the book throws light on the plays of Shakespeare, "Macbeth," "Othello," "Twelfth Night," Marlowe's, "Dr. Faustus," "Edward II" and Shaw's "St. Joan."

In the field of English poetry, we have taken up for discussion John Milton's "Lycidas," "The Paradise Lost," "Pope's Epistle to Dr. Arbuthnot" and "The Rape of the Lock," Keats's "The Eve of St. Agnes," Dryden's "Mac Flecknoe," Coleridge's "The Ancients Mariner," "Metaphysical Poetry," "Wordsworth as a Poet" and Eliot's "The Wasteland."

We hope the book will prove useful for those who are genuinely interested in English literature and at the same time for the students who have taken up English literature as a subject for higher studies. The nature of the book leaves little scope for originality yet personal perceptions and analysis may be perceptible at places.

K.M. JAN
SHABNAM FIRDAUS

CONTENTS

Preface *v*

1. *A Farewell to Arms* by Hemingway 1
2. *The Mayor of Casterbridge* by Hardy 15
3. *Far From the Madding Crowd* by Hardy 31
4. *Wuthering Heights* by Emily Bronte 43
5. *A Passage to India* by E.M. Forster 58
6. *Tess* by Hardy 75
7. *To the Lighthouse* by Virginia Woolf 81
8. *Untouchable* by Mulk Raj Anand 85
9. *Macbeth* by Shakespeare 94
10. *Othello* by Shakespeare 109
11. *Dr. Faustus* by Marlowe 122
12. *Edward II* by Marlowe 130
13. *Twelfth Night* by Shakespeare 141
14. "Lycidas" by Milton 153
15. *The Paradise Lost* by Milton 161
16. *Rape of the Lock* by Pope 164
17. *Epistle to Dr. Arbuthnot* by Pope 172

18. *The Eve of St. Agnes* by Keats 178

19. *Mac Flecknoe* by Dryden 191

20. *The Ancient Mariner* by Coleridge 196

21. *St. Joan* by Bernard Shaw 203

22. Metaphysical Poetry 214

23. Wordsworth as a Poet 224

1

A Farewell to Arms by Hemingway

Ernest Hemingway is a modern American novelist. The polarities of love and war constitute the fictional microcosm of Hemingway. Though he evokes the scene of the place in the precise, hard but transparent language he also creates the romance of the meaning through his use of symbols. He conveys by implications his essential meaning. He is not a symbolist writer in the tradition of Kafka. It is something foreign to his art as Hemingway has not written allegories.

The very first paragraph of the novel, *A Farewell to Arms* is symbolic. The passage presents a house in a village that looks across the rivers and plains to the mountains: "There are pebbles and boulders, dry and white in the sun." The peace of the village is disturbed by the march of the troops. The dust lies in the air and the falling leaves are powdered under the feet of the marching troops. The natural calm of the village returns as the troops pass away in their march ahead. It suggests by implications the disturbance of natural life of the village and the effect of war on the rhythm of the natural life of the people. Hemingway retains the objective surface which is pregnant with the resonance of suggestiveness as well. It is against his bare, hard prose that certain images come to acquire the force of the symbol.

The novel is set in the background of rivers, mountains and plains. Rain too occurs and becomes a pervasive symbol in the novel. The first chapter of the novel refers to the death of thousands by cholera during the rains and since then rain is associated with doom or disaster. After his recovery in the hospital in Milan, Frederic Henry is separated from his beloved, Catherine Barkley by the sudden arrival of the midnight train in the rain. There is also the subtle use of the suggestive power of the weather in the novel in the passage. Frederic Henry and Catherine discuss their flight to Switzerland "Switzerland is down the lake — we can go there. That will be lovely."

It was clouding over outside and the lake was darkening (Quoted from *A Farewell to Arms*).

The last line foreshadows in terms of the symbol of the weather the fate of the lovers in Switzerland, as the rain is associated with doom and disaster.

There are two memorable scenes in the novel when it is not raining. They are associated with peace and love. In the beginning the priest describes his home in the Abruzzi Mountains "where man may love God without feeling foolish and where spring was the most beautiful in Italy." The second scene is associated with the life of Catherine and Frederic at the chalet in the sweet Alps where their love in the clear winter sunshine is soaring into the idyll.

Yet there is distinction between the big rain which symbolises the general destruction of war and the small rain which is associated with spring rain that regenerates life. It is raining when Henry is dreaming of his return from Milan. His dream slightly alters the medieval lyric, "Christ that my love were in my arms and I in bed again. That my love Catherine. That sweet love Catherine down might rain. Below her again." Henry through the lyric involves the western wind that will bring the renewal of his love and life. The poet of the medieval lyric must be aware of the symbol of Christ as the gentle rain falling on the earth in spring to make it fertile and green again. Catherine replaces Christ in the altered lyric of the dream "That my sweet Catherine down might rain." Here gentle rain is associated with the regenerating force of spring. Henry wakes up, he is faced with the deluge and war that washes off the resistance of the Italian army.

Set against war, "home" emerges as the most powerful

symbol in the novel. War represents all that is not home and negative, hateful and undesirable in life. "Home" represents all that is not war and is positive loving and desirable in human life. In a world torn by war the word "home" which recurs in the novel acts like a refrain and acquires an emotional force. When Henry goes back to the front after his idyllic love in the hospital, he admits, "It did not feel like home-coming." He remembers, "We felt very happy and a little time our room felt like our own home the same way." Henry who is homeless in war finds his home in the love of Catherine. He leaves war for it but his home ends for him as Catherine Barkley dies in childbirth.

At this point Hemingway compares life to the struggle of ants on the smouldering log which flashes across the mind of Henry:

> Once in camp I put a log on the top of the fire. It was full of ants. And as it commenced to burn the ants swarmed out and went forward torwards the centre where the fire was; then turned back and ran towards the end. When, there were enough on the end they fell off into the fire. I remember thinking at the time it was the end of the world.

Here there is the fusion of the idea and the image and the emotional force of the idea is intensified by the shock supplied by the image. Henry builds his home like the ants on the burning log and thus the end is predictable. When the Hemingway sensibility works at its highest point it works upon an immediate objective level which translates ideas into concrete things. His images immediately evoke the idea associated with it. The symbols of the mountains and the plains which have been dealt with at the same length by Carlos Baker do not become symbols by the same criterion in the novel.

CHARACTER OF FREDERIC HENRY

Frederic Henry is the central character in Ernest Hemingway's novel, *A Farewell to Arms.* He is an American citizen and a student of architecture in Italy. He joins the Italian army as an ambulance driver. The change of profession reflects the fact that he was detached from his former professional concerns. He seeks to relieve his emotional restlessness by joining the world of violence. Perhaps he wants to get the full feel of life in the presence of death. The war seems no more dangerous to him than "war in the movies." But his romantic ideas of war are shattered by his wounding. Earlier he had thought that there is danger to ambulance drivers but "I know I would not be killed. Not in this war." But the things turn out differently. Frederic Henry rejects the glory of wars which the recruiting posters proclaimed by appealing emotionally to the words "sacred, glorious and sacrifice." He thinks he has seen "nothing sacred and the things that, were glorious had no glory and the sacrifices were like the stockyards at Chicago if nothing was done with the meat except to bury it." With this realization and confronted with an illogical and unjust execution of the officers at bridge who had got separated from their regiments, Frederic Henry deserts war.

Frederic Henry drinks and visits bawdy houses. It is with this motive that he pays his first visit to Catherine Barkley in the British hospital. He knows that he does not love Catherine Barkley nor he has any idea of loving her. It is like a game of bridge in which he said things instead of playing cards. On being slapped for kissing her, though he is angry yet certain seeing it all ahead like the moves in a chess game. It is only after he is wounded and hospitalized in Milan that he realises he is in love with Catherine.

From the haunting loneliness, Frederic Henry learns the value of togetherness as if the woman Catherine were the missing half of the entity which he was meant to be. He felt very happy "and in a little time the room felt like our home. My room at the hospital had been our home." When he goes back to the front he admits that "it did not feel like home-coming." Before being injured, he feels quite at home in barracks. When in love, Henry begins to see his situation in a new light. He goes through a process of de-massification. He is no longer an insignificant part of the whole or a well-oiled piece of machinery that obeys the button which some unknown operator works. Now he is a unique, important individual who has got a point of view through being in love and which is fully his own. Now he sees war from this angle. For him his private army which includes his beloved and himself has a more immediate reality than the army to which he belongs. Earlier he did not worry death in war. But now it appears as a threatening force that will take away all that he values. It disrupts peace and chance of domestic happiness and makes more urgent the note of transiency which is a threat to his love. Frederic Henry through love learns the meaning of life, the value of his existence.

Like Catherine, he too suffers from a paranoid fear of a threat of vague, hostile forces that would destroy their happiness. But he is different from Catherine also. For Catherine a vitalizing relationship like love has it own sanction. She asks, "What good would it do to marry now? We are really married. I could not be any more married. You are my religion. You're all I have got?" But Henry has his faith in formal religion. He is much more anxious about the absence of marriage ceremony than Catherine. When the child is born dead, he was disturbed because it had not been baptised. In spite of all this, Frederic Henry finds solace and comfort in his relationship with Catherine. His religious sensibility does not inhibit his participation in his joys of life.

Frederic Henry's days with Catherine in Switzerland are characterised by a real idyllic calm and serenity. The element of conflict is completely absent. He senses its precariousness. His view of man and the world seems pessimistic. At one point in the novel, he tells Catherine "You always feel trapped biologically." Frederic Henry's obsession with death and his view of life in this perspective seem to be those of Heminway himself as Frederic Henry is the objective correlative for Hemingway's own biographical involvement with the first world war and Catherine partly resembles Agnes von Kurowsky, the American nurse who was his beloved.

To Frederic Henry man who is biologically trapped appears like ants on a burning log which annihilates them. Catherine, the warm reality of Henry's love turns into a statue with her death which implies the end of his private world for which he had signed a private peace. There is a sense of deep loss as Frederic Henry bids farewell to the statue that now Catherine has come to be. He feels this is "the end of the trap. This was what people got for loving each other." It confirms his belief in a world hostile to the aspirations of the individual. He says, "You did not know what it was about. You never had time to learn. They threw you and told the rules and the first time they caught you off base they killed you."

Frederic Henry is trapped between love and death. Though biologically trapped, he together with Catherine achieves a kind of immortality in love. Frederic Henry is the projection of Hemingway himself to a great extent. It is on account of the strength of the biographical or personal details of the author's own life behind the character that Frederic Henry emerges as a living, throbbing and life-like character.

CHARACTER OF CATHERINE

Hemingway's novel, *A Farewell to Arms* unfolds a unique vision which is composed of antonyms — war and love. War stands for the negative, destructive forces at work and love is the nourishing elixir of life in the background of the first world war which is the background of the novel. Catherine Barkley represents love, the creative impulse of life which becomes a more urgent note in the perspective of war.

It is the surgeon, Rinaldi who, at first, talks to Henry about Catherine Barkley and takes him along with himself to see Miss Barkley. It is evident that Miss Barkley prefers Henry to Rinaldi. Since then Henry takes care to see her frequently. She is a British nurse in a hospital at Gorizia in Italy. She is tall, blonde, has tawny skin and gray eyes. She was engaged to a man for eight years. He was killed in war the previous year. She was going to cut off her beautiful hair from grief when he died. Hence she is crazy when she meets Henry. She feels a gap, a psychological void which Henry comes to fill up. It is obvious that she needs psychological support. She keeps with her the rotten stick of her fiance as a memento before she meets Henry. Thus she is in a mental state of readiness to respond to Henry. Frederic Henry at first takes his relationship with Catherine Barkley lightly. He treats her in the same way as he treats other British girls on the front. He neither loves Catherine nor has any idea of loving her. For him it is a game like bridge in which you say things instead of playing cards. It is the personality of Catherine that compels him to recognise his real self. She is not some *harum-scarum* woman. She is interested in living a dignified life. Though she is a nurse, she does not like the nurse's evening-off aspect of life. She slaps Henry when he wants to kiss her. She is not a flirt but one for whom love is religion.

There is a sharp difference between the personality of Catherine and Henry. Frederic Henry has a religious sensibility. From time to time he is perturbed by the thought that they have not gone through the rituals of marriage. He insists on it repeatedly. He is also anxious that the child born to Catherine is not baptised. But Catherine does not believe in religion. At the hospital of Switzerland, she gets the fact registered that she believes in no religion. Unlike Henry she is not at all concerned that they have not performed the rituals of marriage. Her consciousness is uninhibited. She thinks freely in a completely untraditional manner. She is bold in her attitude and perfectly sincere and truthful. She does not believe in formalities but in the essential spirit. When Henry insists on marriage, she replies, "What good would it be to marry now? We are really married and could not be any more married."

Catherine's religion is love which needs no sanction of traditional religion. For her, love implies complete fusion of two individuals into a union in which separate identities lose their existence and are merged completely. Catherine does not consider herself as a separate identity. She tells Henry, "I want what you want. There's not any separate me any more. Just what you want." The heroine of "For whom the Bell Tolls" also seeks a union with the hero and she feels she does not stand apart as a separate entity. Catherine shares this *attitude* with her. She worries only being sent away from Henry who is her "religion" and all she has got. Henry also finds home in the love of Catherine. He has a sense of home where Catherine is. Whether it is a room in a hotel or at the hospital he feels like home in the presence of Catherine. This is why when he goes back to barracks, it did not feel like home-coming. Like Henry, she suffers from paranoid fears. Even when they are together, they feel alone against the world. She is at one time prophetic in her fear "I am afraid of the rain because sometimes I see myself dead in it" and it is really raining when she dies.

Catherine is unconventional in her approach to life. She remains a very sweet, lovable feminine character, the symbol of love and life as opposed to war, the negation of life. She absorbs all the interest and attention of Henry. Such a powerful and magnetic person she is, when she dies, Henry loses his world of love reminding Wordsworth's line in the poem "She dwelt among the Untrodden Ways": "and o! The difference to me" suggesting a world of difference that takes place with her death.

Q. Justify the title of the novel, *A Farewell to Arms.*

Q. Discuss the theme of the novel, *A Farewell to Arms.*

Q. Discuss the polarity of love and death in *A Farewell to Arms.*

Answer

The polarity of love and death is an organising image in the novels of Ernest Hemingway. This pattern is further emphasized in the war novels. *A Farewell to Arms* is no exception. The perspective of war is, no doubt, a result of Hemingway's biographical involvement with it. The experience lived through the world war I created in Hemingway the need to write about it creatively.

War appears as more than the simple background for a love story. It echoes concerns of Hemingway about death which is a functional element in connection with the central theme of the novel, the precariousness of life which makes it all the more precious. The beauty of life is in its very transitoriness but it is the presence of love which reveals this beauty to the full.

The central character of the novel is Frederic Henry. It is through his eyes that we follow the course of events in the novel. When we first see Henry, he is already involved with the war. But he does not seem to have any reason for it. "I don't know", he told the head nurse in Milan hospital when he was asked the reason why he joined the Italian army. "I was in Italy," he adds, "I speak Italian." But these explanations do not make his motive more understandable. As an American he has no particular duty towards Italy nor there is any compulsion from any quarter to join the army against his wish. Henry seeks to relieve his emotional restlessness. It is the only cause for this adventure. It is like a need of getting as close to death as possible to get the full feel of life. Otherwise, Frederic Henry was a student of architecture. The change of activity implies Henry's detachment from his former professional concerns and a desire for involvement with the deadly world of men at war. He joins war with utter disregard for what may happen to him as an individual. It is only when love appears in the form of his relationship with the hospital nurse, Catherine that he feels the need of questioning intellectually what he is doing. When Frederic Henry goes back to the front after idyllic love in hospital, he admits that "it did not feel like home-coming." This reference to home reflects the fact that he now knows what a home feels like. Before being injured, he felt at home in barracks. Henry in love begins to see his situation in a new light. He goes through a process of demassification. He is no longer an insignificant part of the whole or "a well-oiled piece of machinery that obeys the button which some unknown operator works." Now he is a unique important individual who faces life from a perspective which is peculiarly his own.

From the haunting loneliness, Frederic Hênry learns the value of togetherness as if the woman, Catherine were the missing half of an entity which he was meant to be. "We could feel alone when we were together, alone against others." The lovers, Henry and Catherine become like an army against the dangers of the outside world. Now Henry understands the real meaning of life, the value of his own existence. For Henry, the private army of his has a more immediate reality than the army to which he belongs. He has no regard for the abstract notions of duty, glory and honour like Jordan in "*For Whom the Bell Tolls.* Frederic Henry signs a separate peace for a haven of love and life, leaving behind the man he had been in the war front of Italy.

Love, there, appears as the involvement with life as opposed to death which means the suppression of life. Love gives Frederic Henry the reason for being alive. Death is a threatening force which takes away from him that he now sees as valuable. Death which, at first, appeared a real possibility but did not worry Frederic Henry very much takes on a more palpable reality as the novel progresses and appears as the end of everything desirable. It is then that life instincts manifest themselves in full force. These life instincts which are related not only with love but with the drives associated with self-preservation overcome death instincts and Henry feels saved through love. But the irony of this salvation is that at the climax of their happiness Catherine Barkley dies in childbirth which destroys the perspective of life which Frederic Henry has come to enjoy. It is comparable to the death of Jordon in *For Whom the Bell Tolls.* The sad joke comes as a final comment on the ultimate meaning of the experience of living. The very brevity of life increases its value and its precarious character increases its significance.

The intensity of life involved in the experience of love reflects itself not only in the release of all tensions but also death of the individual self through its becoming one with the other person. The identity of each lover disappears and both merge into a special entity that is more than the sum of its parts "Oh darling I want you so much I want to be you, too" says Catherine. It is a kind of relationship to which all other religious or otherwise considerations are irrelevant. Catherine says, "What good would it do to marry now [...]? I could not be any more married. You are my religion. You are all I have got." The priest says to Henry, "When you love, you wish to do things for. You wish to sacrifice. You wish to serve." This is the direction which Frederic Henry's life takes after finding a home in Catherine's love. But the death of Catherine brings it to a close. "It was like saying good bye to a statue" (dead Catherine), says Frederic Henry. But they achieve a kind of eternity and immortality in love in the face of death. To the mind of Frederic Henry, this panorama of death is relation to life presents the image of the swarm of ants on the burning log which annihilates them completely. It is a polarity in which man is inevitably involved and through which he tries to emerge as he fights against a mighty opponent, time. "Always at my back I hear/Time's winged chariot hurrying near" that Henry quotes is the basic concern of the novel. Through Frederic Henry, Hemingway stresses the aspects of human condition that he sees as most relevant in man's relation with his destiny. Torn between mortality and immortality, the Hemingway's hero discovers in love the inevitability of death and the real value and beauty of love in the face of death. Death is less final, less negative when the dying hero or the heroine has truly loved and been loved.

The title of the novel, *A Farewell to Arms* is significant. The arms are both, the weapons of war as well as the embrace of the beloved. Man is biologically trapped in the dialectics of life and death. His immortality can only consist in the assertion of immortality in the creative act like love which makes life meaningful in this background.

Discuss the prose style of Hemingway with reference to *A Farewell to Arms*

Ernest Hemingway's prose style is the product of his creative vision in the novel. He writes about rough things like fishing, horse-race, boxing and war. This is the external surface of his novel. His prose takes on its character from the subject matter of his writing. But the hard objective surface conceals beneath it a lyrical vision of life. His novels deal with war and love at the same time. They constitute the polarities of the novel and create a rich complex prose style.

Hemingway has a strong sense of fact, place and scene. He maintains complete objectivity, for example in the opening passage of the novel, *A Farewell to Arms*:

> "Troops went by the house and down the road and the dust they raised powdered the leaves of the trees. The trunks of the trees too were dusty and the leaves fell early that year and we saw the troops marching along the road and the dust rising and leaves, stirred by the breeze, falling and the soldiers marching and afterwards the road bare and white except for the leaves."

Hemingway evokes the place and the scene with a strong sense of fact. The prose acquires a hard precision and rich concreteness. Words are like window-panes. They do not stand between the reader and the meaning. Hemingway's eye for the particulars rather than the general and the abstract lends the necessary concreteness to the passage. The various clauses of the sentences are compound rather than complex, joined by the conjunction "and." This structure imparts a complete objective flow to actions, their sequence by allowing equal opportunity to each element in the scene to make its impression. The rhythm of the passage is really the rhythm of the action. The prose is hard, bare, concrete and precise. This is the peculiar Hemingway prose. It is the result of a careful attention to the act of verbal selection. Hemingway once said that he wished if he could, "to strip language clean to lay it bare down to the bones." He realized that our words from loose using have lost their edge. Hence he corrected, substituted, and recorrected his words till they could economically bear the burden of the experience. Thus he expunged the words that were irrelevant and achieved a transparent concreteness in his expressions.

No doubt, Hemingway retains the objective surface but it is pregnant with the resonance of suggestiveness as well. It is against his hard and bare prose that the passages of lyrical beauty acquire significance.

"We felt very happy and in a little time the room felt like our own home. My room at the hospital had been our home in the same way."

These are the words of Frederic Henry in *A Farewell to Arms*. The word "home" comes to acquire a symbolic significance. Against Henry's homelessness in war, "home" which is very much associated with the personality of Catherine and which acts like a refrain in the novel gathers a symbolic emotional force. Hemingway's strong sense of fact, place and scene does not prevent him from catching in words the mental processes of the character at the highest dramatic point. Though speculation by the author or the character is kept to the minimum, when it occurs, it acquires greater force in contrast with the pervasive, hard, bare, precise style of Hemingway. Frederic Henry's mental processes are registered with as much fidelity as possible:

"There's just a child that has to be born. It makes trouble and is born and then you look after it and get fond of it may be. What if she should die? She cannot die. But if she should die? Hey, what about that? What if she should die?" In the midst of his speculation about child birth, the sudden popping up of the question. "What if she should die?" and its reiteration at short, frequent interval reveals a mind obsessed with the fear of death of Catherine and the consequent loss. The subjective emotion is presented with its full force as in a stream-of-consciousness novel.

The prose of Hemingway at its best gives a sense of depth and moving on different levels. Hemingway says, "It is the kind of writing that can be done, if anyone is serious enough and has luck. There is fourth and fifth dimension that can be gotten." He achieves his concentrated effects through the use of literary allusions as well. Critics have recognised lines from poems as part of his prose passages. One obvious example is "But at my back I always hear/Time's winged chariot hurrying near" just at the high point when the lovers are abruptly separated by the arrival of midnight train in rain. The literary allusion points up the time-haunted consciousness in a novel where living is fighting against the enemy of man, "time."

Hemingway goes beyond the ordinary dimension of prose exposition and description and gets the full impact of the emotional experience.

When Hemingway's sensibility functions at its highest point; it works upon an immediate objective level which translates ideas into concrete things. Life is a baseball game where each error is punished by death or compared to the struggle of ants on the burning log, "once in camp I put a log on top of the fire and it was full of ants. As it commenced to burn the ants swarmed out and went first towards the centre where the fire was; then turned back and ran towards the end. When there were enough on the end, they fell off into the fire [...]. I remember thinking at the time that it was the end of the world."

We are aware of the double implications, the idea and the image, and the emotional force of the idea is intensified by the shock supplied by the image. This is the form of Hemingway's understatement. Hemingway by the power of his written words makes us hear, makes us feel before all to makes us see. By this means he is able to transfer to his reader the true essence of the way it was. The power of his writing derives from its tough exterior but also from its tender spots of sensibility. The passages of muted lyricism provide a measure and a meaning to the tough exterior. They are rare and brief but achieve a special resonance by being sounded against a hard, polished surface of his typical prose. Hemingway's achievement lies in the successful blend of his two styles.

2

The Mayor of Casterbridge by Hardy

Hardy's view of life is usually classified as pessimism. Some have preferred to classify it as deterministic, fatalistic, agnostic etc. Hardy wanted it to be described as meliorism. The difference between pessimism and meliorism is the following. Pessimism believes that everything in the world has a tendency to become evil and that the end of all our efforts is dark. On the other hand meliorism believes that though the opportunities for happiness are limited we can make them more enduring by adapting ourselves to the existing circumstances of life with the help of wisdom and knowledge. Despite Hardy's intention, his works go in the direction of pessimism.

Hardy's philosophy of life consists of the following:

1. Pessimism at times having something of meliorism
2. Fatalism
3. Nature as a hostile or indifferent force though occasionally sympathetic
4. Love which usually promises hope ends in despair.

The Mayor of Casterbridge like other novels of Hardy, illustrates this view well.

The novel manifests the feeling that man is an alien in the universe which is possibly hostile and certainly indifferent and the conviction that he will have to make sense of it himself if any sense is to be made at all, the necessity of taking an attitude even though it may be logically senseless.

The life of Henchard is a series of defeats, some deserved and some undeserved. Susan's life is even more pathetic. The same can be said of Giles, Tess, Marty South and Clym Yeobright. The concluding lines of the novel are "Happiness was but an occasional episode in a general drama of pain." The concluding line of "Tess" is "Justice was done and the president of the immortals, in Aeschylean phrase, has finished his sport with Tess."

Hardy believed that evil is both external and internal. By the external evil, he meant our environment, including circumstances, chance and coincidence, and society. By the internal evil, he meant the unbriddled instincts and emotion *eg.* love and sex, greed and ambition, jealousy and hatred etc.

Fate. Other novels of Hardy show only fatalism but *The Mayor of Casterbridge* assigns a great importance to human action as well in the determination of our life. Giles, Tess, Marty South and Clym suffer without committing any sin or guilt. But Henchard is partly sinning and partly sinned against. There is a tragic flaw in the character of Henchard as it is in Othello, Lear or Macbeth. It is the eruption of the irrational and absurd in human affairs as the modern existentialist would view it. There is the same weak sediment lodged in Henchard's unconscious. It takes his moral being out of focus in a few befuddled moments. Further, it is his own error that in a fit of whim or pride, he dismisses a wise manager like Farfrae and also restrains his relations with Elizabeth Jane. In this blunder he loses in three ways. He creates his own formidable rival who defeats him in business as well as in love. He gives him a chance to come in contact with Lucetta. He also darkens the chances of Elizabeth Jane.

But fate is also against him when he amends for his injustice to Susan, fate should have spared him. By honouring Susan and Elizabeth Jane he gives a proof of his conduct and integrity. But for it he gets punishment instead of reward. Susan dies while Lucetta marries Farfrae.

Farfrae also prospers by dint of his character, his business acumen and dealings. But how can we explain the suffering of Susan and Jane? What sin or crime they have committed?

Nature. In Hardy Nature is generally blind or hostile. Weather gods favour Farfrae and disfavour Henchard without any justification. In *Woodlanders* Giles shows his character by offering his only room to Grace when benighted. A heavy downpour worsens the condition of the already worsening Giles and he dies.

Love. Almost all the heroes and heroines of Hardy look to love for peace and happiness. It does give satisfaction but only in the beginning. Soon it leads to complications which make the lover suffer. It is Henchard's love for Susan that deprives him of happiness that he might have got from Lucetta. It is being broken in love that breaks Giles.

After all, Hardy shows that by suffering and wisdom we can make the limited opportunities more enduring. Jane often says that she does not want to be effusive on happy occasions. They may invite the wrath of fate. The contrast between Henchard and Farfrae shows that unbriddled emotion may lead to disaster even though the heart may be good.

AS A TRAGEDY

Thomas Hardy has written tragic novels. His concept of fate manifested through his novels has affiliations with the Greek writers of tragedy rather than with Shakespeare. Hardy's novels like George Eliot are expression of determinism but in his novel, *The Mayor of Casterbridge*, fatalism has been transferred from the outside to the inside. Hardy comes very close to Shakespeare here. Other heroes of Hardy like Giles Winterborn, Diggory Venn, Tess, Gabriel Oak are destroyed by the "unforeseen powers." But the tragedy of Hardy in *The Mayor of Casterbridge* emanates from the character also.

Hardy has created a fully tragic character like Shakespeare's in the form of Henchard. Henchard's sale of his wife in a fit of intoxication at Wessex fair constitutes the tragic error. His wife and onlookers remind him again and again of what he is going to do. But he does not listen. A self-destructive energy drives him to this act. The prolonged consequences of this act which go beyond the control of Henchard result in his tragic suffering.

Henchard would have lived the ordinary life if a hay-trusser, had not the event of the sale of his wife given a violent twist to his life. He becomes a teetotaller, great as "the Mayor of Casterbridge" and fit for a fall after this rise. The coincidences and chance happenings that occur in the life of Henchard are all direct or indirect consequences of this act. They remind him repeatedly of this act and determine his fate.

Susan, the wife of Henchard sold away at Weydon Prior eighteen years ago also reappears just at the time, Henchard is on the point of marrying Lucetta, his beloved. He returns to his forsaken wife as it is his first, duty to attend her. Thus his love for Lucetta is doomed by his original sin. After the death of Susan, Henchard asks Elizabeth Jane to take his name as she is his daughter. He explains things to her in the background of the past. The same night when he breaks the seal of the letter of his dead wife, he learns that his Elizabeth Jane had died and the present one is the daughter of Newson. Next day he has to retreat from Elizabeth Jane whom he had approved so warmly. The death of his own daughter, the birth of Newson's daughter, who acquires the same name may be a chance occurrence. But his suffering and a sense of alienation on the discovery of the real parentage of Elizabeth Jane results indirectly from the sale of his wife at Weydon fair.

After the death of Susan, Lucetta comes to Casterbridge in the hope that she will be able to marry Henchard. In the meanwhile, Henchard dismisses his wise manager, Farfrae on flimsy grounds. He thus creates his own formidable rival who defeats him in business. By restraining his relationship with Elizabeth Jane he allows him a chance of coming in contact with Lucetta and winning her heart. Henchard, thus, creates in Farfrae not only a rival in business but also in love who defeats him in both. The appearance of the furmety woman, the witness of Henchard's sale of his wife in the court, the day Henchard acts as a magistrate can be attributed to chance. But her charge against Henchard of the sale of his wife which Henchard publicly accepts harks back to his original sin. This incident of the furmety woman results not only in his loss of reputation but sends Lucetta into a hurriedly arranged marriage with Farfrae in order to avoid marriage with a reckless character like Henchard. Henchard in this way fails to marry his old beloved and save himself, from bankruptcy.

Henchard sells his wife. He thus strikes at the most intimate human relationship. Quite naturally his tragedy is the tragedy of alienation. His wife is dead. His beloved has married his rival. He is left alone with Elizabeth Jane whom he had treated cruelly. But she takes care of Henchard. Henchard treats her as a valuable possession as he is alienated from every one else. He lies to Newson when he comes to enquire about his daughter. When Newson reappears and he feels unable to keep his secret, he leaves Casterbridge the way he had come some twenty-five years ago. When he comes back to ask for forgiveness of Elizabeth Jane and presents a gift on her marriage, she rejects him. Henchard dies in complete alienation from the whole world except his old servant, Abel Whittle whom he had treated severely.

Character is destiny in *The Mayor of Casterbridge.* Immoderation is the keynote of Henchard's character. His sale of his wife in intoxication, his unusually warm intimacy with Farfrae and his equally strong hatred against him point in the same direcion. His immoderation in drinking at fair leads him to commit the tragic error of the sale of his wife. On the consequences of this act he has no control. All the chance happenings are connected with this event as the original sin causes the fall of Adam. The consequences of Henchard's sale of his wife hunt him down to his complete tragic alienation.

The act of Henchard emanates from his own character. Its consequences like furies in the Greek tragedy bring about his fall.

Write a note on the treatment of the rustic life in *The Mayor of Casterbridge.*

Hardy's novels deal with the rustic life. The region where he locates his stories is called Wessex. The characters of his novels are countryside people. Farmers, shepherds, thatchers and hay-trussers move in the rural world of Wessex. *The Return of the Native, Woodlanders, Far From the Madding Crowd* and *Tess* all belong to this world. Hardy chooses to deal with life in town in *The Mayor of Casterbridge.* The events in the novel take place in the village of Weydon Priors and Casterbridge in upper Wessex. But the town of Casterbridge is ultimately bound up with the rural agricultural England.

Casterbridge, though a town, in the words of Hardy "was the complement of rural life around it, not its urban opposite." It was a place deposited in the black upon a cornfield. There was no suburbs in the modern sense or transitional intermixture of town and down. It stood with regard to the wide fertile land adjoining clean cut and distinct, "like a chessboard on a green tablecloth." This vivid description of the town in terms of the simile "like a chessboard on green tablecloth" projects the intimate link of the town with its green agricultural landscape around. The geographical location of the town determines its rural roots. The trades and professions carried on in Casterbridge are dependent on the agricultural villages around it. The business of the town is concerned with buying and selling farm animals and produce. The bustle of the weekly market is the centre of the town's life where shops sell tools and implements for agricultural and pastoral life. Hardy comments, "Casterbridge was in most respects, but the pole focus or nerve-knot of the surrounding country life." In spite of the fact that Casterbridge is a town, its milieu is composed of the same rustic concerns. "After mid summer they watched the weather cocks as men waiting in ante-chambers watch the lackey. Sun elated them, quiet rain sobered them, thorny weeks of watery tempest stupefied them. That aspect of the sky which they now regarded as disagreeable they then beheld as maleficent." Since the business of Casterbridge depends on the agricultural produce, the people of Casterbridge hope from, and fear the weather as the village people.

Michael Henchard, the principal figure of the novel has a rural background. He is a poor hay-trusser. He comes to the town of Casterbridge, becomes a corn-merchant and finally the Mayor of Casterbridge. Farfrae is a Scot who is on his way to America in the pursuit of his ambition. But he stays in Casterbridge and becomes a corn-merchant and finally the mayor of the town. Henchard and Farfrae are both migrants to Casterbridge. They illustrate the historical process of exodus from the country to the town, rise to wealth and prosperity which the country life would have no scope for. Michael Henchard's final ousting by a younger, ambitious rival, Farfrae becomes an individual tragedy and part of the history of the human generations, the younger replacing the older.

The migration of Henchard and Farfrae also suggests the gradual decay of the established ways of the country life. The first two chapters of the novel which are not located in Casterbridge but in the purely rural background portray the well-established ways of living in Weydon Priors with its fair of animals, tents of furmety and other entertainments to which are attracted the people of the neighbouring villages. The furmety woman presided over her tent, sells furmety and ale. But later the novel shows the impact of the industrial revolution which in its process was destroying the old, agricultural England. The people unadaptable to change, like the furmety woman, have to lose their job. Others learn new skills or like Henchard exploit their knowledge of agriculture in a new business situation. The corn laws of 1815 kept the price of corn artificially high. Thus farmers and merchants like Henchard dealing in corn rose easily to prosperity. But the failure of Henchard in business can also be attributed to his bad calculation of weather. Thus though Casterbridge is a town, the milieu remains rustic.

Hardy's treatment of the rustic life in *The Mayor of Casterbridge* is of a writer who has the first hand experience of the village life. He seems to have observed the decay of the established village life with the advent of the industrial revolution and the mechanical process. In this novel, Hardy captures the phase of transition through which Wessex or the rural England had to pass.

LUCETTA

Though Elizabeth Jane is the heroine of the novel, *The Mayor of Casterbridge,* Lucetta plays an important role in the novel. Lucetta presents a sharp contrast with Elizabeth Jane as Henchard is a foil to Farfrae. While Elizabeth Jane suffers without having committed a sin or crime, Lucetta suffers partly for her weaknesses and partly for the circumstances.

Lucetta was the daughter of a military officer. She really belonged to Bath but had spent her life in Jersey. Her aunt Templeman had died leaving her a rich legacy behind. We do not know much about her past, except that once she was staying at Jersey at a boarding house where she met Henchard who had fallen ill. She nursed him to health but grew so intimate with him that there was a scandal in the town. Henchard came back with a promise to marry her. When Henchard was on the point of marrying her, his long forgotten wife reappeared and this prospect was over.

Lucetta came to town after the death of Henchard's wife in order to marry Henchard. There was no hindrance in the way as she had succeeded to fortune. She no longer bore warm allegiance which characterized her in their first acquaintance yet he had a conscientious wish to bring about her union with him. But Lucetta lacked constancy. Her character had the quality of fickleness. By informing Henchard of her arrival in the town through a letter, she quickened his feeling towards herself. But she was completely indifferent to him, when he paid his visit because she had already met-Farfrae. She felt no moral binding to Henchand. She rejected the objection of Elizabeth Jane that she was dissolved from all vows by the return of the other woman and that it was a new courtship.

Unlike Elizabeth Jane Lucetta was a coquette. When Farfrae met her by chance, for the first time, she persuaded him to stay and talk to her by lying and carried on her conversation with him. She took care to heighten her natural attraction when she was preparing to receive Henchard. But the hyperborean crispness, strigency and charm of Farfrae of a well-braced musical instrument made him attractive to her. She had perceived in him the curious double strands in the thread of life, the commercial and the romantic which represented the two aspects of his personality though she fell deeply in love with Farfrae, she was no simpleton.

Lucetta is shrewd and calculating. Her interest in the company of Elizabeth Jane was not a pure case of sympathy for a girl who was neglected by her father. She had wanted to provide an excuse for Henchard to visit her house. Later when her affection is engaged by Farfrae she wants to use Elizabeth Jane as a watch dog to keep off her father as there was no love lost between the two. Though Lucetta felt deeply in love with Farfrae and was all tenderness of for him, she could not extend the ordinary courtesy of entertaining. Henchard as a visitor, when he came to her on reading her letter. Even when Henchard forces her into the promises of marriage, she does so only to deceive him. Lucetta lacks a moral vision. She lacks the ability to adhere to principles except that of selfish interest. We can only forgive Lucetta for claiming Farfrae as her husband in spite of the mutual affection between Elizabeth Jane and Farfrae because she was not aware of it.

Lucetta lacks self-confidence and is therefore secretive. She had not the courage and honesty to confess her past to Farfrae. She kept her secret to herself. She avoided the presence of Henchard when he is employed at her farm to escape the disclosure of her past which she badly dreaded. She implored Henchard not to take revenge on her when she found him in such a mood. She clandestinely wrote a letter to him. Finally she succeeded in persuading him against such an act. Unlike Elizabeth Jane she was always elusive. She wrote love letters to Henchard who did not use it against her. But the bundle of letters came to the hands of an unscrupulous character who arranged the skimmity-ride in the town. Lucetta had formed the habit of writing letters from her loneliness. It finally landed her in difficulties. She could not recover from her shock of skimmity-ride and died.

Lucetta was a coquettish woman who thrived on her charm. She was shrewd and calculating also. For her charm had great importance than principles. She was always hankering after fascination and her imagination. But she was foolish as well, as she could easily get attracted to anybody unthoughtfully and later rescinded her step. She is full of charm, vitality and complexity. But her lack of courage to face the facts, brings about her tragic death. Lucetta has some affinity with Eustacia Vye of "The Return of the Native."

CHARACTER OF FARFRAE

Farfrae is one of the very important characters in Hardy's novel, *The Mayor of Casterbridge.* He is not the hero but he provides a contrast to the central character of the novel. He embodies certain qualities of character in contrast with those of Henchard that lead him to inevitable success. Farfrae impresses us as the best example of a successful man in this business world.

Farfrae is an outsider to Casterbridge as Henchard is. He is a Scotchman. Like Henchard, he enters Casterbridge as an ambitious young man. He intends to go to America in search of a career. He is persuaded by Henchard to stay on and become his partner in business. Farfrae has a peculiar knack for business. He exhibits administrative and executive abilities in the management of Henchard's business. The success of Henchard's business depends on his exceptional skill when Henchard managed business, everything depended on his memory and tongue. Under the able administration of Farfrae letters and ledgers took the place of tongue and memory. He was quite steady, cautious and alert Henchard admires his skill and befriends him to the point of telling the secrets of his past life.

Farfrae offers a sharp contrast with the character of Henchard. Farfrae is cool; calculated and cautious. His steps are measured and balanced. He is an extrovert. On the other hand, Henchard is rash, immoderate, foolish and introvert. Whereas Henchard in egotistic and obstinate, Farfrae is pragmatic and modest. He has an innate sense of business, whereas Henchard rises to that height by the sheer power of will which he later comes to lose. Farfrae's sense of enterprise is reflected in his introduction into Casterbridge a machine for sowing seeds which is only mocked at by Henchard. Farfrae is modern and progressive while Henchard stands for orthodox ways of doing things.

Though Farfrae is a level-headed, ambitious young man who leaves his native country to make his fortune, there is also a strong romantic element in him. He sings beautifully and puts much feeling into his songs. He is able to charm the audience with his thrilling voice. When he meets Lucetta, his enthusiasm is immediately kindled and he is soon fascinated by her. His transference of love from the simple, homely Elizabethan Jane to the dazzling Lucetta was also due to his romantic nature.

Farfrae has a steady temperament. He is modest and patient and very temperate in his conduct. It is on account of the qualities of his character that he rises as a corn factor and later becomes the Mayor of Casterbridge. He is a man of principle. He does not stoop to gain success in the field of business. Though Henchard dispensed with his services, he employs no underhand method to compete with Henchard in business. He refuses to entertain the old customers of Henchard because he does not want to take business from his hands. He does not forget that once they were friends and Henchard has been kind to him. He modestly accepts it in the presence of his customers. Naturally he is kind and considerate to Henchard. When Henchard has gone bankrupt, Farfrae invites Henchard to stay on in the same house which has now passed into his own hands. He asks Henchard to take possession of anything in the house that he likes most. He tries to secure a shop for Henchard in order to set him up in business and start a fresh life. But he gives up the idea when he learns that Henchard harbours inimical feelings towards him. But later he induces the town council to secure for him a shop for marketing seeds and roots. He shows great delicacy in his treatment of Henchard. He avoids any impression of his triumphing over a fallen rival.

Out of his liberal and generous spirit he has earlier helped Henchard in curing grown corn. Only at the time of welcoming the royalty he is rough with Henchard. But Henchard is himself to blame for this.

Farfrae is a decent man. He becomes a rival of Henchard in love without knowing. When he marries Lucetta, he has great regard for her feelings. When he marries Elizabeth Jane, his regard for her feelings is equally strong. He agrees to her request to search for Henchard and takes great pain.

Farfrae shows Henchard's faults. He shadows him in business and in love replacing him as cornfactor and Mayor and winning and marrying both the women he loved in the days of his prosperity. His success reflects Henchard's failure.

Sketch the character of Elizabeth Jane

Elizabeth Jane is the heroine of Thomas Hardy's novel, *The Mayor of Casterbridge*. She is the typical figure of Hardy's fictional world. Like Giles, Tess, Marty and Clym Yeobright, she suffered without committing any sin or crime. She acts as a mouthpiece for Hardy's philosophical thoughts on life. Through her we are made to see the proportion of gaiety and pain that interweave the fabric of human life. Her last comment on life, in fact, is Hardy's view of life that informs the fictional vision of Hardy's novels.

Elizabeth Jane was the daughter of Newson, the sailor. After the disappearance of Newson she lived with Henchard as her mother married him. For the first time, she was in prosperity. Though she was rapidly becoming good-looking and comfortably circumstanced, she did not make a fool of herself by dress. But the reasonableness of almost everything that Elizabeth did was nowhere more conspicuous than in the question of clothes. She refrained from bursting out, like a water-flower and clothing herself in puffings and kinck-knacks. Her triumph was tempered by circumspection.

Moderation was the keynote of Elizabeth Jane's character. She was drawn to Farfrae since she had seen him singing at King's Arms.

She felt a spiritual kinship with Farfrae. She admired the serious light in which he looked at serious things. She thought he felt exactly as she felt about life and its surroundings that they were a tragical rather than a comical thing. That one could be gay on occasions, moments of gaiety were interludes, not part of the actual drama. She responded well to the admiration and interest of Farfrae. She was so much attached to him that with the dismissal of Farfrae as the manager of Henchard, she had anxiety to know if Farfrae was going away from the town. Her heart fluttered to think of it. She felt her heart going out to him. But as was her wont, she would say, at the same time, to herself that such dreams were not for her.

Elizabeth Jane was a sober character. She was thoughtful. She was never gay or demonstratively happy like Gabriel Oak in *Far From the Madding Crowd.* Whenever she was about to touch the extreme point, her thoughts immediately moved in the opposite direction to retain the balance that characterized her personality. One day when she dressed herself in an unusually beautiful dress, everybody was attracted. She felt for the first time, she was admired so much. But the next moment her usual fear of exaggerated appearances engendered a deep sadness. She thought there was something wrong in all this. If people knew how an unfinished girl she was that she could not talk Italian or use globes or show any of the accomplishment, they learnt at boarding schools, people would despise her. Her mind then turned to buying of grammar books, dictionaries and a history of all the philosophies.

Elizabeth Jane had a pessimistic bent of mind. She had always the field mouse fear of the coulter of destiny despite fair promise which is common among the thoughtful who had suffered early from poverty and oppression. Like Oak, she thought she would not be too gay. It would be tempting to providence to hurt mother and her and afflict them agonies as he used to do. She had learnt the lesson of renunciation and was familiar with the wreck of wishes as with the diurnal setting of the sun. As soon as her attachment to Farfrae grew to a point, she was asked by Henchard not to see Farfrae again.

In spite of her wishes to the contrary, she exhibited complete obedience and discipline. Later she left Henchard's house to live with Lucetta and Henchard withdrew his restriction on her meeting with Farfrae. But when Farfrae paid his first visit, he came in contact with Lucetta. Lucetta felt attracted to him and married him. Elizabeth Jane bore all this calmly and quietly. When Henchard declared that she was his daughter, she was ready to take up his sirname. The next she called him father warmly only to meet a cold response as he had known through his wife's letter that she was Newson's daughter. Her response is that she left the house of Henchard with his permission as she did when Farfrae, her old lover had married Lucetta.

Elizabeth Jane had a sensitive and tender sensibility. Notwithstanding that cold response of Henchard in the past, her filial affection for him was intact, she believed. She was deeply attached to Henchard as a daughter. But she knew he had deceived her about her parentage and lied to her father. She reacted with an equally strong feeling of hatred against Henchard. She could not understand the motive of Henchard behind this action. She was incapable of forgiving him and rejected him when he paid his visit on her wedding day. Her heart softened only when she came to know the goldfinch in the cage he had brought but could not present as a gift. She regretted for misunderstanding him in his last visit. She set out to find him out. But it was too late. He was already dead, quite broken-hearted, when she could find him.

Elizabeth Jane's path of life had a brief sunshine of happiness after her marriage with Farfrae. She had a calm and serene life. She had learnt the secret of making endurable the limited opportunities of life. Hardy describes his philosophy of life not as pessimism but meliorism and Elizabeth Jane like Oak in *Far From the Madding Crowd* is the best example of meliorism. Though the panorama of life occasioned her reflection that happiness was but an occasional episode in a general drama of pain, she had learnt the art of making the best of the little opportunities of life. The sufferings of the heroine of *The Mayor of Casterbridge,* like other heroes and heroines of Hardy are not on account of some fault of her own but for the fact that she lived in a world hostile to her dreams.

THE PLOT CONSTRUCTION IN MAYOR OF CASTERBRIDGE

Thomas Hardy was an architect. He exhibits the same art in his plot construction. Unlike stream of consciousness writers whose plots are very slight, the plots of Hardy's novels are massive and carefully built. *The Mayor of Casterbridge* has also a well-built plot which, like other novels of Hardy, is designed to project Hardy's view of human life.

The Mayor of Casterbridge is subtitled, "the tragic story of a man of character." Quite naturally the novel follows the rise and fall of the central character, Henchard. The plot of the novel can be divided into four stages. The first stage consists of the first two chapters when Henchard sells his wife and is engaged in the futile search for his wife. The second stage begins with the chapter 3 and ends with the fourteenth. It depicts Henchard as a prosperous cornfactor and Mayor of Casterbridge. There is a gap of eighteen years between the second chapter and the third chapter. At this stage, his long sold wife, Susan and his supposed daughter, Elizabeth Jane join him. The third phase runs from the fifteenth chapter to fortieth chapter which portrays the decline of Henchard. His wife dies. He fails to marry his beloved, Lucetta on account of his slackness, loses in business and becomes bankrupt. The last phase of the novel shows Henchard in utter despair at the prospect of losing Elizabeth Jane, the only earthly bond that he has been able to retain, his exile from Casterbridge and his tragic death.

Casting a critical glance at the plot of *The Mayor of Casterbridge* one is aware of the improbabilities that take the form of coincidences and chance happenings in the novel. They seem to be deliberately contrived to point up the irony of fate in the novel. The long sold and almost forgotten wife, Susan reappears just at the time when Henchard is on the point of marrying his beloved, Lucetta. The day Farfrae arrives at King's Arms, Henchard is presiding at a function as the mayor of the town.

Bad corn is mentioned. Farfrae knows how to change bad corn into good one. He stays on at the request of Henchard but later he becomes his rival both in love and business. The same day Susan, with her daughter arrives at Casterbridge and stays at the same inn. Elizabeth Jane meets Farfrae in the form of a waiting maid. The girl is later presented to the world as the daughter of the Mayor. After the death of his wife, Henchard tells Elizabeth Jane that she is his daughter and she agrees to take his name. The same day he opens the sealed letter of his wife to learn that Elizabeth Jane is not his daughter but Newson's. Henchard has remarried his wife in order to conceal his past. But the day he acts as a magistrate, the furmety woman enters the court and reveals the whole secret. At this Lucetta hurriedly marries Farfrae and Henchard fails to repair his fortune with a wealthy marriage.

There are a lot of improbabilities as Hardy's plot abounds with coincidences and chance happenings. But in spite of those improbabilities, Hardy emerges as an excellent artist. The coincidences and chance happenings demonstrate that man is a toy, a plaything of hostile forces that inevitably lead to his destruction. But in *The Mayor of Casterbridge* as in the novels of George Eliot, fatalism is transferred from outside to inside. Henchard's immoderation and egotism play an important role in his ruin. But even they are overshadowed by "the persistence of unseen powers" which defeat him at every turn. The plot projects Hardy's philosophy. Hardy is not an observer of men and women in the society like Meredith. He is a novelist of human condition and his plot is subordinated to the philosophical idea in the novel.

3

Far From the Madding Crowd by Hardy

Thomas Hardy is not a writer of social comedy like Jane Austen and Meredith. Thomas Hardy is a philosophical writer. His plot-construction, characterization and all other elements of the novel present a philosophical world view. His characters are not particular individuals but man himself and the circumstances, woven around him illustrate his existential condition. In the novels of Hardy man appears against a background of alien, indifferent and hostile universe where all his efforts for happiness come to a dark end. Hardy's novels seem to present a pessimistic view of life but Hardy prefers to call it meliorism. Meliorism implies the principle of making the most of the little opportunities of happiness that life offers.

The very title of the novel, *Far From the Madding Crowd* is ironical. The novel mingles pathos with happiness setting the principal characters into a measure of chastened happiness but with the marked stress on furious passions, thwarted purposes and shattering griefs which are the realities behind the idyllic calm of the pictorial scene. The second chapter of the novel contains the pictorial description of Norcombe Hill. Gabriel Oak who is not much sensitive to nature is "impressed with the speaking loneliness of the scene or rather with the complete abstraction from all its compass of the sights and sounds of man. Human shapes interferences, troubles and joys were all as if they were not and there seemed to be on the shaded hemisphere of the globe no sentient being save himself." The pictorial invocation of the face of nature suggests that the stage is not limited to the little corner of Wessex and that in the localised passions and conflicts man is to be seen fighting with his destiny.

Thomas Hardy's view of life is fatalistic and deterministic. He finds the force and malevolence of fate both in the external circumstances as well as the internal, irrational stuff that man is made of. In *The Mayor of Casterbridge* Henchard is more sinned against than sinning, yet his immoderate character is as much responsible as the coincidences and chance happenings. Hardy comes very close to the Greek tragic vision where man is a mere puppet in the hand of fate but in some of his novels the character of the protagonist is also responsible for his destruction. The mainspring of the action or plot of the novel is the character of the Bathsheba. She was a capricious woman. It is her capriciousness that creates the necessary web in which Gabriel Oak and Boldwood are caught. She plays the role of a coquette. She stops Gabriel Oak to tell him she has no lovers. When his interest in her is aroused, she rejects him. She writes a valentine to Boldwood and disturbs his peaceful life. When he feels quite interested she marries Troy. The fickleness of Bathsheba accounts a good deal of frustration of Gabriel Oak and Boldwood and later for her own self. Thus love which promises to bring happiness and fulfilment in life in fact brings disappoint and frustration in the life of Oak, and Boldwood. They are not responsible for this as Giles, Marty South and Tess are responsible for their tragedy.

The malevolent nature of the universe is reflected in the chance happenings in *Far From the Madding Crowd*. They are all set against man's struggle for happiness as we see in the case of Henchard in *The Mayor of Casterbridge*. Oak's ewes run through a thicket and fall into a chalk pit. The savings of Oak's ten years' labour are brought to nothing. Later the fatalistic hostility can be seen in the fire that destroys the harvest of Bathsheba and the poisoning of the sheep in the clover field. Chance plays a greater role in the case of Boldwood when Bathsheba meets Troy all accidentally one night. If Troy had not come in Bathsheba's life, she would have probably married Boldwood. Then the sudden reappearance of Troy at Christmas party when she was to declare her engagement deprives Boldwood of his happiness. Boldwood shoots Troy and goes to jail. Fanny Robin's life is even more pathetic. Like Giles, Tess and Marty South fate seems to have played trick on Fanny Robin. Her mistake between All St.'s Day and All Soul's Day and Sergeant Troy's infinite postponement of the marriage fall in the category of chance happening. But in the case of Oak we find both fate as well as character responsible for failure and success in life. In this respect he is very close to Elizabeth Jane of *The Mayor of Casterbridge.* Both illustrate Hardy's meliorism. Oak's life like Henchard's is a series of failures but he finally succeeds by the steadfastness of his character. Fate also helps Oak in the end as it helps Elizabeth Jane with the death of Lucetta. In the same way, with the death of Troy and imprisonment of Boldwood, the path is cleared for Oak's marriage with Bathsheba. As in the life of Elizabeth Jane "happiness was an occasional episode in a general drama of pain" for Gabriel Oak.

Discuss *Far From the Madding Crowd* as Tragi-comedy.

Thomas Hardy's novel, *Far From the Madding Crowd* is the story of Bathsheba as she occupies the central place in the novel. The other characters are Gabriel Oak and Sergeant Troy. The role of Sergeant Troy is very brief. All the three lovers revolve round the figure of Bathsheba. While Boldwood's story comes to an unhappy end, the story of Oak comes to a happy end. Hence *Far From the Madding Crowd* is a blend of tragedy, and comedy. While Boldwood is the hero of the tragedy, Gabriel Oak is the hero of the comedy.

There is irony in the very title of the novel. The novel mingles pathos with its opposite setting the principal characters into a measure of chastened happiness but with the main stress on furious passions and shattering griefs which are the realities behind the idyllic calm of the pictorial scene. Bathsheba who is at the centre of the tragi-comedy is described in the very first chapter of the novel: "She simply observed herself as a fair product of Nature in the feminine kind, her thoughts seeming to glide into far-off though likely drama in which men would play a part-vistas of probable triumphs — the smiles being a phase suggesting the hearts were imagined as lost and won." The introduction of Bathsheba Everdene suggests the kind of stuff we should expect in the novel. The mainspring of action is the character of the charming Bathsheba. She is a capricious woman. She stops Gabriel Oak on his way to tell him she has no lovers. She, thus, excites his interest in herself but only later on to reject him on the ground that she likes him but does not love him. It is her caprice that disturbs the peace of Boldwood in life by sending the valentine to him. When he feels quite interested, she marries Sergeant Troy. The fickleness of Bathsheba accounts for a good deal of frustration of Gabriel Oak and Boldwood. Hardy's comment that "women are never tired of bewailing man's fickleness in love, but they only seem to snub his constancy" is relevant here.

Like other novels of Hardy, the malevolent nature of the universe is reflected in the chance happening that are all set against man's struggle for happiness. Sometimes they threaten to destroy and sometimes they really strike. Shepherd Oak's ewes run through a thicket and fall into a chalk pit. The savings of Oak's ten years' labour are brought to nothing. He is ruined. A series of other accidents, the fire that destroys Bathsheba's harvest and the poisoning of the sheep in the clover field are fatalistic only in their cumulation. But more decisive in their consequence are the destruction of Oak's ewes, the valentine that Bathsheba sends to Boldwood and the sudden appearance and disappearance of Sergeant Troy from the scene. Fanny Robin's mistake between All Soul's Day and All St.'s Day and Sergeant's infinite postponement of the wedding also fall in this category.

The case of Boldwood, the traditional, calm self-disciplined bachelor, well-adjusted with his solitary life who is stung to infatuation by a woman's capricious blandishments also highlights, the malevolence of fate in the novel as the witches stir up the imagination of a Macbeth who was loyal to king Duncan of Scotland. Sergeant Troy is, above all, the agent of malevolence when Bathsheba gives in to his flatteries. When long supposed drowned, he returns to confound Boldwood as "The impersonator of Heaven's" persistent irony towards him and snatch his delight away, "Troy began to laugh a mechanical laugh. Boldwood recognised him now." Instead of focusing on the complications hinging upon Troy and Boldwood, Hardy relies on the fatalistic machinery. Troy disappears as suddenly as he had appeared on the scene. The personal tragedy of Boldwood is dragged in to clear the air, dissipate illusions and prepare the harmonious union of Oak and Bathsheba. The tragic catharsis is turned to the benefit of others.

After the sound and fury of passions, the disillusionment of Bathsheba with Troy, the tragedy of Boldwood leads to the happy union of Bathsheba and Gabriel Oak. It is safe to predict that Bathsheba will now prove a more suitable mate for Oak which she might have failed to do earlier. *Far From the Madding Crowd* bears some resemblance to the ending of *The Mayor of Casterbridge* where the novel almost simultaneously closes on the union of Elizabeth Jane and Farfrae as well as the tragedy of Henchard. The tragedy of Henchard weighs heavily on the consciousness of the reader like the tragedy of Boldwood also because he is the central figure of the novel and Elizabeth Jane is marginalised. But in *Far From the Madding Crowd*, Bathsheba is the central figure whose story ends with a happy union with Gabriel Oak. It is a tragi-comedy where Gabriel Oak like Elizabeth Jane in *The Mayor of Casterbridge* learns that happiness is but an occasional episode in a general drama of pain.

CHARACTER OF BATHSHEBA EVERDENE

Bathsheba Everdene is the heroine of the novel, *Far From the Madding Crowd* written by Thomas Hardy. She stands out among the heroines of Hardy for the combination of rare traits in her character. She is the epitome of her sex. She is narcissistic in her character and proud of her charms. At the same time she manages her farms successfully as a man.

Bathsheba is a womanly woman in full bloom and vigour. She is so attractive in her physical charms that she captivates a man immediately. Gabriel Oak falls in love with her at first sight and later Sergeant Troy gives up Fanny Robin in order to marry her. She has an impulsive nature. In the words of Hardy, she is "an Elizabeth in brain and Mary Stuart in spirit." She often performed actions of the greatest temerity with a manner of extreme discretion. She runs to stop Gabriel Oak who is going back to tell him that she has no lover in order to retain him as one. When Oak's interest in her is aroused and it finds expression in the form of marriage proposal, she rejects it on the ground, she likes him but does not love him. She sends a valentine to Farmer Boldwood and his peaceful solitary life is disturbed by his newly aroused interest in her. As Lucetta comes across Farfrae in *The Mayor of Casterbridge*, when she comes across Sergeant Troy by chance, she succumbs to the glamour of a townsman. Like Lucetta, she also marries Sergeant Troy clandestinely.

Bathsheba is a woman of independent nature and capable of strong hold on life on a footing equal to men. We gather this impression of Bathsheba from the way she handles the dishonest bailiff, her business transactions with men at corn-market and her confidence at the head of the table of the harvest festival. The outstanding strength of her personality is her capacity for her cool, confident demeanour after the shooting of Sergeant Troy. She does not faint at the incident and is in perfect control of the situation. Hence, there is substance in Hardy's describing her as "the stuff of which great men's mothers are made."

With all her independence and self-confidence, she is vulnerable to her feminine frailty. She is at once attracted to Sergeant Troy, though his behaviour is offensive. He appears admirable because he proceeds from the admiration of Bathsheba's person. Like most women, Bathsheba is incapable of judging the behaviour of men. She fails to discriminate between the surface glitter and the golden character of Oak. She falls an easy prey to Troy's shrewd flatteries on such occasions.

Like Lucetta, she has no time for moral considerations and judgment. The hold of Troy is so strong that all thoughts of Boldwood are driven away. She is swept away by her impulses.

She is a passionate woman. She is indignant and feels revulsion when she faces the truth of Troy's connections with Fanny Robin. It is more than Bathsheba can bear when Troy kisses the dead Fanny Robin. She forgets her indignation and revulsion in her wifely attachment to the husband and insists on her being kissed.

The mainspring of the action of the novel lies in the temerity of Bathsheba's character. It is also the source of all her troubles. In the words of Hardy, "Bathsheba, though she had too much understanding to be entirely governed by her womanliness, had too much womanliness, to use her understanding to the best of her advantage." Her fault lies in plunging into action without caring for the consequences. She jilts Boldwood in order to marry Troy. But later she has to regret her actions. In her disillusionment with Troy, she thinks of Oak and Boldwood in the light of old lovers and what life would have been with them as husbands. When Troy is supposed to be drowned, she considers the case of Boldwood by way of making amends to him for the past errors. But Troy reappears the night she is to be engaged to Boldwood. She comes to accept Gabriel Oak as her husband when her dream of a happy life with Troy and Boldwood has already receded.

The various incidents of farm life give form and shape to her relationship with Oak which is not rendered less intimate and binding for the little quarrels arising from his well-deserved reproofs. In fact, she needs him in business but it does not mean that she has no personal regard for Oak. When Gabriel Oak informs her of his proposed departure, Bathsheba was aggrieved at the withdrawal of Gabriel's hopeless love which she had grown to regard as her inalienable right for life. Bathsheba, in return, marries the only man who has proved her strength and fidelity during the peril and betrayals of love which she had experienced.

Bathsheba Everdene is quite an unconventional heroine of Hardy's novel. Her horse-riding with a touch of assurance, her explicit overtures to her lovers and her almost masculine handling of her business set her apart from the heroines of Hardy. She is a rash, hasty, impulsive and uncontrollable nature like Henchard. She also runs through her share of unhappiness like Henchard partly through her impulsive, hasty decision and actions and partly because of the malevolence of the universe which frequently appears in the form of chance happenings.

CHARACTER OF GABRIEL OAK

Gabriel Oak is the essential part of the rural setting of the Wessex life which is portrayed in Hardy's novel, *Far From the Madding Crowd*. As he worked on the farm on all six days of the week, he always appeared dressed in his old clothes. He wore a low crowned felt hat spread out at the base by tight jamming upon the head for security on high winds and a coat like Dr. Johnson's his lower extremities being encased in ordinary leather legging and boots emphatically large to reach foot. When Farmer Oak smiled, the corners of his mouth spread till they were within an important distance of ears, his eyes were reduced to chink, and diverging wrinkles appeared round them extending upon his countenance like the rays of the rising sun. He had reached the time of life at which "young" ceases to be the prefix of a man. He was at the highest period of masculine growth, for his intellect and emotion were clearly separated.

He is indispensable and characteristic figure in the pastoral landscape which forms the background of the novel. He is seen presiding at the sheep-washing by the pool in the meadows or at the sheep-shearing at the barns or lancing the wind-swollen sheep to save their lives. When it was not the sheep, it was the corn-ricks that claimed his anxious care. It was none else than Farmer to protect the barnful of wheat-ricks from the unruly storm in the night. Gabriel Oak is thus the product of the soil to which he belonged.

Oak was attracted to Bathsheba as a moth to light. He fell in love with Bathsheba at first sight and remained steadfast through the many ups and downs of life. It was Bathsheba who kindled his initial interest in her by calling on his way back home and telling that she had no lovers. He was unfortunate in that Bathsheba rejected him when he finally proposed to her. The moment Bathsheba rejected him, he had uttered these words "I shall keep wanting you till I die" and he kept the word. He belonged to the even tempered order of humanity and felt the secret fusion of himself in Bathsheba to be burning with a fine flame when she was gone away from Norcombe Hill. When he was reduced by an accident from a rich farmer to a poor man, he went in search of work in the direction where Bathsheba had been. When he found work in her farm, he was happy. He had no wish to converse with her. The thought that his bright lady and himself formed one group exclusively their own, containing no other in this world was enough. Even seeing her for the time effaced his perception of the great difference between seeing her and possessing her. Though small quarrels with Bathsheba marked his life there, his emotional attachment to her remained unchanged. He only said to himself, "I will help to my last effort the woman I have loved so dearly." He is unselfish and unpossessive in his love for Bathsheba. He is the antithesis of Sergeant Troy. He is the model of innocence, self-sacrificing spirit, honesty and loyalty and rural simplicity. But as he lacks outward glamour, he fails to impress Bathsheba. On the other hand, Troy, the choice of Bathsheba is urban, refined in manners but cunning, fickle and treacherously shrewd. As a lover, he was also different from Boldwood. There was a time Boldwood was completely far from the emotion of love. But when it got hold of him, he was fully under its grip. But the flame of love kept gently smouldering in Gabriel Oak. Boldwood reacted violently to the death of his hopes by killing Troy whereas Oak was liberal in his attitude to his rivals. He was satisfied even if not he but someone had become the object of Bathsheba's attention.

The most notable feature of his character was his gentleness and unselfishness which was natural to a shepherd with his regard for helpless animals. When he found his sheep dead at the foot of the hill, his first feeling was one of pity for the untimely death of the animals and their unborn lambs. The thought that animals were uninsured came only afterwards. It is no wonder that such a man watched over Bathsheba's interests as his own, cared more for her happiness than his own success.

Like Elizabeth Jane in *The Mayor of Casterbridge*, Oak was neither too happy in his happiness nor too sorry in sorrow. He exhibited a stoical response to the upheavals in life. He was as much resigned to the loss of Batsheba as to the loss of the sum of his capital with the destruction of his sheep. The way he had lived had accustomed him not to hope too much. So when Boldwood was overconfident of his success with Bathsheba, he advised him "not to be sure" and reminded that "There is many a slip between the cup and the lip:" He had lost the habit of becoming sure of things in life. But he had answered this life with assurance of the qualities of his character. He himself was as steadfast as the north star. It was his steadfastness, added to his competence that he was able to win the heart of the wayward Bathsheba. As in the life of Elizabeth Jane, happiness was but an occasional episode in a general drama of the pain of his life.

THE CHARACTER OF SERGEANT TROY

Sergeant Troy figures in Thomas Hardy's novel, "*Far From the Madding Crowd.*" He holds a distinct position in the novel for the conspicuous qualities of his character and the role he plays in the novel. Hardy depicts a universe which is evil in the sense that it mars the possibilities of human happiness. Sergeant Troy seems to be the possibilities of this evil in the world of "Far From the Madding Crowd."

Sergeant Troy a young slim, handsome rake in a military tunic was irresistibly debonair. He was a peculiar sort of person for whom memories are an encumbrance and anticipation a superfluity. He lived in the present and cared only for what was present before his eyes. Being entirely innocent of the practice of expectation he was never disappointed.

Sergeant Troy was a sensualist. He had no moral

considerations. He was inclined to extract the utmost pleasure from the passing moment. He was moderately truthful to men but to women he "lied like a Cretan." He was impulsive. He had strong bouts of impulsive moments and he got half the pleasure of feeling in being able to express it on the spur of the moment.

Troy was full of activity but his activities were less of a locomotive than vegetative nature. He was brilliant in speech but below commonplace in action. He had quick comprehension and considerable force of character. But his comprehension engaged with trivialities. He was well-educated for a member of the middle class family. He spokes fluently and unceasingly. He had the ability of being one thing and seeming another, for instance he could speak of love and think of dinner, call on the husband to look at the wife, be eager to pay and intend to owe. He was a male dissembler who with untenable fictions, charmed the female and acquired power reaching to extremity of perdition. Hardy identifies Sergeant with the devil, an emissary of the general malevolence when Bathsheba gives in to his early flatteries "the careless Sergeant smiled within himself and probably the devil smiled from a loop-hole in Tophet, for the moment was the turning point of a career."

Sergeant Troy is particularly attractive to the opposite sex. It is this aspect of his that Fanny Robin succumbs to his charms. He has also the gift of the gab. His imagination was fired by the presence of an attractive personality and language got tremendous power of weaving a magical spell on the fair sex. As he dazzled and enchanted Bathsheba by the miracles of his swordplay, by the quick keenness and flashing assault of his manner and speech that he won the heart of Bathsheba. His deformities lay too deep for a woman's eye, whereas the sterling qualities of Oak's character lay hidden beneath his unpolished rustic manners. There could be no other foil to the constant, slow, silent and unexpressive Oak than the dashing debonair Troy whose charms lay in his superficialities.

But Sergeant Troy is not without merit. He is adroit in the skill of swordplay. He wields the sword in a way no one can.

He has a fine skill of urbane conversation. He appears quite fair to Fanny Robin in the beginning. He stands before the whole congregation waiting for the bride who never comes. But as he lived in the present, the passing moment, he never afterwards cared to take care of his old beloved. He spurned the financial overtures of Boldwood for giving up Bathsheba for him. His motive was never commercial but instinctive.

After all is said and done, Sergeant Troy is a *deus ex machina*, a product of Hardy's machinery of crass casualty. He is brought in just to dash the hopes of Boldwood not once but twice and to pave the way for the happy reunion of Oak and Bathsheba to bring a happy ending to an otherwise tragic love story. Sergeant Troy's role resembles that of Alec in "Tess" as a malevolent force.

4

Wuthering Heights by Emily Bronte

Wuthering Heights is the masterpiece of Emily Bronte. It is unique in its conception and the power of execution. The technique employed by the novelist projects her vision adequately and powerfully. The technique of the novel is flawless from this point of view.

The novel, *Wuthering Heights* begins midway. Lockwood, a tenant at Thrushcross Grange pays a visit to Heathcliff, his landlord at Wuthering Heights and encounters a strange world there. As the first scene of a Shakespearean tragedy strikes the keynote of the play, *Wuthering Heights* in its first chapter plunges us into the action of the novel where we see through the eyes of Lockwood, the abnormally impolite conduct of Heathcliff, the appearance of the ghost of Catherine and Heathcliff calling upon her in the middle of the night at the window. It is a powerful opening as any of the Shakespearean tragedies. It, at once, keys up our mind to the level of intense spiritual drama that the novel presents and also brings to light that our ordinary expectations of a novel are not to be fulfilled. The novel could easily turn into a melodrama which it never does. There is also the influence of the novel of terror but it has been put to a brilliant use like the supernatural in the opening scene of *Macbeth.*

The reader fully identifies himself with Lockwood in this first visit to Wuthering Heights and his curiosity is also piqued like Lockwood's. Emily Bronte, like Joseph Conrad's *Lord Jim,* establishes the convention of flashback. Nelly Dean, the house-keeper at Thrushcross Grange and former maid-servant at

Wuthering Heights narrates the past in order to satisfy the curiosity of Lockwood and the voice of Lockwood fades into the voice of Nelly Dean. The voice of Nelly Dean also fades and we hear the voice of the protagonists through the novel. One of the purposes served by the complex method of narration is that the truth and authenticity of the incredible events and characters is fully established. Nelly Dean who has acted as a servant in the house and been a close observer of the action and confidante of Heathcliff, Catherine, Catherine Linton and Isabella stands spiritually outside it. She along with Lockwood is the narrator and acts as a chorus suggesting complete inadequacy of our normal expectations. We see the action of the novel through the eyes of Nelly Dean and Lockwood but the impression is so vivid that everything seems happening before our eyes. The plot is set in a series of scenes linked together by the briefest possible passages of narrative or explanatory comments.

The method of narration may be defined as "dramatic-pictorial." The natural surroundings of the locale of the novel are presented in the words of Lockwood:

> "'Wuthering Heights' is the name of Mr. Heathcliff's dwelling, Wuthering being the significant, provincial adjective describing the atmospheric tumult to which its station is exposed in stormy weather, one may guess the power of the north wind blowing over the edge by the excessive slant of a few stunted firs at the end of the house and by a range of gaunt thorns all stretching their limbs one way as if craving alms of the sun."

"Wuthering" is here defined in terms of storm a force that stunts the growth of plants and the way thorns are described there is hardly any distinction between man and nature. This symbol further extends to the natural energies of the human nature as well as repression and cruelty on the human plane. Nature imagery is the staple vehicle of the novel. It is invested with human attributes and *vice versa.* Heathcliff says, "He might as well plant an oak in a flower pot and expect it to thrive as imagine he can restore her to vigour in the soil of his shallow cares."

The entire novel has a poetic framework and imagery becomes the natural vehicle of expression. Like Shakespearean tragedy, *Wuthering Heights* acquires its poetic form and intensity from the speeches of the central characters in which the density of imagery defines the dominant passions of the characters. The speeches do not concentrate everything in themselves but spread their radiance through the entire novel. Catherine defines her relationship with Heathcliff with a terrible honesty:

> "My love for Linton is like the foliage in the woods, time will change it I'm well aware as winter changes the trees. My love for Heathcliff resembles the eternal rocks beneath, a source of little visible delight but necessary Nelly, I am Heathcliff."

There is a sense in which Heathcliff is Catherine herself and does not function as an independent character but as a projection of Catherine's own being. "He is that within her which is at one with the primary energies of nature, her deepest instinctive need" while her love for Linton is only superficial. Natural images are not part of the decoration but the essential part of the communication. In the same way, the calm and the storm which are the basic images of the novel are inseparable from the spiritual reality of the novel. The poetry of Hardy's novel is the poetry of the atmosphere but the higher flights of Emily Bronte's imagination are inherent in the structure of her drama. They express themselves in the turn which the plot takes. The images constitute the essential meaning of the novel. Thus, we find that Emily Bronte has forged a form which powerfully communicates the essential experience of the novel.

WUTHERING HEIGHTS AS A UNIQUE NOVEL

Emily Bronte produced a single novel, *Wuthering Heights* and became part of the history of English literature. It was so because it is a novel utterly unlike any other novel. The novel is unique in the way it has been conceived and composed. The novel derives its strength from the unique vision embodied as well as the way it has been projected in the form of the novel.

The description of the locale of Wuthering Heights on the first page of the novel is quite suggestive:

"'Wuthering Heights' is the name of Mr. Heathcliff's dwelling, 'Wuthering being a significant provincial adjective, descriptive of the atmospheric to which its station is exposed in stormy weather.' Pure bracing ventilation one must have there at all times indeed: one may grass the power of the north wind blowing over the edge, by the excessive slant of a few stunted firs at the end of the house; and by a range of gaunt thorns all stretching their limbs one way, as if craving alms of the sun."

The description makes it clear that in the world of "Wuthering Heights" there is no distinction between man and nature as the thorns have "limbs." They stretch their "limbs" and crave "alms of the sun." The powerful north wind stunts the growth and slants the firs. The same is applicable to the human world on the symbolic plane. Heathcliff's natural growth and development is stunted by Hindley and later that of Hareton by Heathcliff himself. Heathcliff also talks of Catherine in the shallow cares of Edgar Linton. He thinks of Catherine as an oak in a flower pot. The novel shows the effect of external forces on the natural growth of Heathcliff, Catherine and Hareton. Nor there is any distinction between the spirit of the dead and the alive as we find Heathcliff calling upon the spirit of Catherine after the dream of Lockwood. The dream is so concretely realized with the all its sensations that the authenticity of the experience is fully established and there seems to be little distinction between dream and reality.

The entire novel seems to have been conceived and composed on a different scale. The stormy heights of Wuthering Heights and the calm of Thrushcross Grange in the valley, the contrast of moonbeam and lightning, frost and fire foliage and rock underline the fact the novel is built on the clash of the opposite elemental forces. The structure of the novel is poetic and complex so that like a poem, it yields to several levels of interpretation. Derek Traversi puts forward a Marxist interpretation of the novel, others find it a spiritual drama, for example.

The concern of the novel is neither social, economic nor political. Nor it is a sentimental romantic novel. Therefore, the emotions and characters are not ordinary. None of the characters of the novel come closer to the characters of Jane Austen, Dickens, Mrs. Gaskell, Trollope, Thackeray, Meredith or Bennet. They are conceived on a different scale. They are charged with the extraordinary intensity of emotion. Heathcliff as his name indicates, is a combination of heath and cliff and is identified with the landscape of Wuthering Heights. He acquires almost a superhuman stature in the novel. He is compared by Walter Allen to a turbulent river whose natural course has been dammed which leads to the destruction of all that comes in the path. Catherine, though not superhuman, is extraordinarily in her peculiar conflict. She marries Edgar Linton but loves Heathcliff.

The theme of the novel is defined in terms of the images of the novel as in a Shakespearean tragedy. Catherine reveals her depth of emotion to Nelly Dean "My love for Linton is like the foliage in the woods, time will change it," I'm well aware, as winter change the trees. My love for Heathcliff resembles the eternal rocks beneath a source of little visible delight but necessary. Nelly, "I am Heathcliff."

The sense of fusion suggested by the sentence "Nelly, I'm Heathcliff" is a rare feat of linguistic and imaginative achievement. Catherine defines her passion in religious, though not in Christian terms: "I cannot express it; but surely you and everybody have a notion that there is, or should be an existence of yours beyond you. What were the use of my creation if I were entirely contained here?" Like a Shakespearean tragedy the theme of the novel is condensed and concentrated in the speeches of the principal characters. The novel acquires its intensity and clarity of vision from them.

Last but not the least, it is the unique narrative technique of the novel that renders nuances to the reader with all its shades and richness. The flash-back technique like "Lord Jim" of Conrad, the narration of the novel through two narrators Lockwood and Nelly Dean in which their voices disappear in different characters' voices bring the entire thing so concretely to the reader.

COMMENT ON THE IMAGES AND STRUCTURE OF *WUTHERING HEIGHTS*

Wuthering Heights is a novel *sui generis*. Emily Bronte is not philosophical like Hardy nor interested in the social comedy like Jane Austen. She is interested in projecting on to the canvas of the novel, her own inner conflicts. The images and structure of the novel reflect the nature of the experience.

Wuthering Heights is conceived and composed on a poetic scale. The nature of the conflict in the novel involves a contrast which is inherent in the images and structure of the novel. The pattern of images as well as their recurrence communicates the essential meaning of the novel. The basic pattern of imagery as established on the very first page of the novel in the adjective, "Wuthering" which is at the centre of the description of Wuthering Heights by Lockwood:

> "'Wuthering Heights' is the name of Mr. Heathcliff's dwelling, wuthering being the significant provincial adjective describing the atmospheric tumult to which its station is exposed in stormy weather. One may guess the power of the north wind blowing over the edge by the excessive slant of a few stunted firs at the end of the house and by a range of gaunt thorns all stretching their limbs one way as if craving alms of the sun."

"Wuthering" is here defined in terms of storm, tumult, exposure and the power that stunts the growth and produces excessive slant and a craving for warmth, health and natural growth. The way gaunt thorns are described, there is hardly any distinction between man and nature. The symbol further extends to the nature of the energies of human nature as well as repression and cruelty on the human plane. The other house, Thrushcross Grange unlike Wuthering Heights is situated in the leafy valley below associated not with storm but a calm which runs counter to all that "Wuthering Heights" stands for.

Nature imagery is the staple vehicle of the novel. It is invested with the human attributes and *vice versa*. The major themes of the novel are powerfully communicated through this kind of imagery. For example Catherine tells Nelly Dean, "Tell her what Heathcliff is an unreclaimed creature without refinement, without cultivation, an arid wilderness of furze and whinstone." Heathcliff's mode of reaction is similar "He might as well plant an oak in a flower pot and expect it to thrive as imagine he can restore her to vigour in the soil of his shallow cares." The image of the stormy wind stunting the growth of the gaunt thorns which was part of Lockwood's description of "Wuthering Heights" extends significantly into the plan of Heathcliff's revenge "We'll see if one tree won't grow as crooked as another in the same wind to twist it."

Wuthering Heights acquires its poetic form and intensity from the speeches of the central characters in which the density of imagery defines the dominant passions of the characters. The speeches do not concentrate everything in themselves but spread their radiance through the entire novel. Catherine defines her relationship with Heathcliff with terrible honesty: "My love for Linton is like the foliage in the wood, time will change it, I am well aware as winter changes the trees. My love for Linton resembles the eternal rocks beneath, a source of little visible delight but necessary. Nelly I am Heathcliff."

The symbolism which underlies the contrast between the two houses, "Wuthering Heights" and "Thrushcross Grange" runs throughout the novel. The contrast between "the foliage" and "the rocks" stands for the contrast between the superficial needs and the deepest necessity of Catherine's nature. Linton himself an inhabitant of "Thrushcross Grange" is the image of refined graces of civilization, while Heathcliff, a combination of heath and cliff represents the eternal necessity and demand of Catherine's nature. Her love for Linton is therefore only superficial while her love for Heathcliff comes from her deepest instinctive needs.

The novel is concerned with the elemental dichotomies that inform the universe, the two opposed principles represented by two houses, calm and storm, rock and foliage that pervade the structure of the novel. The children of one house cannot breathe in another's as Catherine Linton says of her relationship with Linton Heathcliff:

> "One time, however, we were near quarreling. He thought the pleasantest manner of spending a hot July day was lying from morning till evening on a bank of heath in the middle of the moors, with the bees humming dreamily about the bloom, the lark singing overhead and the blue sky and the bright sun shining steadily and cloudlessly. That was his most perfect idea of heaven's happiness, mine was rocking in a rustling green tree with a west wind blowing and the bright white clouds flitting rapidly overhead, and not only larks but throstles and black birds and linnets and cuckoos pouring out music on every side [...]. I said I should fall asleep in his and he said never breathe in mine."

The pattern of the imagery of the two houses is further extended into the story of the two generations. The wild, consuming passion of Heathcliff and Catherine in the first generation has been modified in the mild creative energy of the second generation where Hereton and little Cathy occupy the centre of the stage. They stand on the threshold of a rewarding fruitfulness. They are at peace with themselves and the world and leave "Wuthering Heights" for the use of such ghosts as choose to inhabit it. *Wuthering Heights* is a poetic novel. The form of the novel is determined as much by its plot as by its imagery. It is different from any novel of Jane Austen and Dickens.

Emily Bronte along with Charlotte Bronte stands apart from her contemporary novelists. Many of the great novelists of the nineteenth century like Dickens, Thackeray and George Eliot showed moral preoccupations and social interests. But a notable difference in imaginative quality separates the novel of Charlotte Bronte and Emily Bronte from those of the other great English novelists of the last century. The difference lies in the emotional intensity, the unique concentration upon fundamental human passions in a state of essential purity. Emily Bronte who is said to have maintained aloofness from the world at large, communicates her personal vision in *Wuthering Heights.*

Wuthering Heights has all the paraphernalia of a romantic novel. There are sentimental and melodramatic passages where the creative impulse is weak. The events described may strike an incredible at times. But these are not the characteristics of the novel. In *Wuthering Heights,* Emily Bronte's achievement lies in the transformation of romanticism through the operation of an intensely personal imaginative power. The character of the novel owe their existence not to the social and moral assumptions of the contemporary novel but from sources simpler and deeper than the traditional novel. The writing is differentiated from vague romanticism in the very opening description of Wuthering Heights where it rises to the deeply poetic reference to the image of "the range gaunt thorns all stretching their limbs one way as if craving alms of the sun." Lockwood's terrible dream is, similarly, marked by a unique immediacy in the description of physical pain "I pulled its wrist on the broken pane and rubbed it till the blood ran and soaked the bedclothes." Here Emily Bronte shows her capacity, to transform melodrama into an intensely personal creation, even the incredible acquires an immediate actuality.

The two themes of the novel, personal and social, stand in the closest relationship and define each other. The relationship between Heathcliff and Catherine Earnshaw which appears like a romantic passion is based on the recognition that the individual is not sufficient in himself or herself and that one needs contact with another existence for completion, "What were the use of my creation, if I were entirely contained here?" It is in this particular sense that she says, "Nelly, I am Heathcliff" and "If all else perished and he remained and I should still continue to be and if all remained and he were annihilated, the universe would turn a mighty stranger. I should not seem a part of it." Though Catherine is drawn to Edgar Linton who symbolises the graces of the civilized life, yet she compares her longing for Linton to "the foliage in the woods: time will change it, I'm well aware as winter changes the trees." She compares her love for Heathcliff to "the eternal rocks beneath, a source of little visible delight but necessary." The common sense of Nelly Dean which finds an echo in Catherine also that she can abandon the brutal Heathcliff for the socially acceptable match with the young, rich and attractive Edgar Linton is refuted by her own deeper self." "Heathcliff is more myself than I am. Whatever our souls are made of his and mine are the same; and Linton's is as different as a moon beam from lightning or frost from fire." There is a conflict between social considerations and spiritual yearnings with which Emily Bronte is concerned.

The contrast between Heathcliff and Edgar Linton further extends to the two houses, Wuthering Heights and Thrush-cross Grange. While Wuthering Height, is the incarnation of its owner, Heathcliff, with its savage surroundings and stormy heights, Thrushcross Grange answers to the character of its owner, Edgar Linton with social refinements and distinctions. The contrast is emphasized on the return of Heathcliff when, Catherine asks if she can bring him into the parlour. Edgar Linton is vexed and suggests the kitchen as "a more suitable place" for him. It is the expression of the world of social distinctions to which Edgar Linton belongs. Catherine puts herself in the same class as Heathcliff and instructs Nelly Dean to lay two tables — one for master and Isabella; the gentry and another for Heathcliff and herself being of the lower orders. It is this distinguished civilization of Lintons which drives Heathcliff on this path of destruction which brings him to his death. The novelist presents the consuming conflict or clash of the opposite impulses from which the novel derives its unique power. The focus of the novel, unlike any other contemporary novel of the nineteenth century, is on the fundamental human passions which run counter to the civilized social considerations. The artistic grandeur of the novel lies in its reticence rather than the resolution.

CHARACTER OF HEATHCLIFF

It is remarkable that Emily Bronte carved her name in the history of English literature by writing one single novel. The novel acquires its significance for its poetic imagery and the power of her characterisation that produced characters like Catherine and Heathcliff.

The setting of "Wuthering Heights" is set in Yorkshire moors. The figure of Heathcliff seems to rise from its landscape. Heathcliff seems to impersonate some natural force or energy as his name "heath" plus "cliff" suggests. It is also remarkable that his origin is unknown and he seems to merge with the landscape. Catherine asks Nelly Dean to tell Isabella "what Heathcliff is: an unreclaimed creature, without refinement, without cultivation: an arid wilderness of furze and whinstone." Heathcliff emerges as the most powerful character that the English novel produced. Later on he turns into a pitiless monster yet he commands the sympathy of the reader. In this feat Emily Bronte comes very close to Shakespeare in his creation of Macbeth who commands the sympathy of the reader after committing the murder of ki. g Duncan.

Our first strange but memorable encounter with Heathcliff takes place in the form of Lockwood watching Heathcliff in the middle of the night calling upon the spirit of Catherine at the window to come once more. Emily Bronte's power of actualizing even the incredible scene plays a great role in the creation of her character. Lockwood satisfies his curiosity by relation of the past by Nelly Dean and we see Heathcliff as a child who is brought by Mr. Earnshaw as a gipsy child from Liverpool. He becomes a playmate of Catherine and Hindley and gets emotionally attached to Catherine. A strong emotional trait manifests in his character from the very beginning. After Catherine is left with the Lintons, he meant to shatter the windowpane to smithereens if Catherine wanted to return. He watches the developing relationship between Catherine and Edgar Linton with helpless anguish. He marks the calendar with cross marks for evenings of Catherine spent with Lintons and with *dots* for the evenings spent with him. Hindley who is jealous of Heathcliff for his father's favour to him degrades him to the level of servants and denies him education after the death of Mr. Earnshaw. When he hears part of Catherine's speech to

Nelly Dean that she would degrade herself by marrying Heathcliff, he leaves the house without hearing about her immense love for him.

The other aspect of Heathcliff's personality is revealed after the marriage of Catherine with Edgar Linton. Walter Allen compares Heathcliff to a river whose "proper channel is dammed, and for Heathcliff the consequence is the destruction of everything lying in his path, energy obstructed is energy perverted." He embarks upon his scheme of revenge solely because of his treatment at the hands of Hindley and the resulting frustration of his passionate affinity with Catherine Earnshaw. He marries Isabella Linton to become the master of Thrushcross Grange. In his own words, "I want the triumph of seeing my descendant fairly lord of their states! My child hiring their children to till their father's lands for wages." As Isabella puts it, he is "not a human being" but "a monster." He is pitiless in his treatment of Isabella and in forcing Linton Heathcliff and Cathy into marriage. He also becomes the master of Wuthering Heights, kills Hindley through drinks, denies education to Hindley's son, Hareton and degrades him to the level of a servant to have his revenge.

Heathcliff wreaks his revenge in order to assuage his hurt feelings. But it is Cathy who understands his position when she says, "Mr. Heathcliff you have nobody to love you; and however miserable you make us, we shall still have the revenge of thinking that your cruelty arises from your greater misery. You are miserable, are you not? Lonely like the devil." His desire to get enjoyment from destruction is gone as soon as he identifies himself with Hareton and Cathy with Catherine in their union against his own cruelty. He realises there is no satisfaction however revengeful he may grow.

The dominating passion of Heathcliff's life is his union with Catherine. This failure leads to revenge. Strange as his life began at Wuthering Heights, he is seen by villagers with the spirit of Catherine after his death.

Wuthering Heights creates a memorable character in

Heathcliff. He is a man. He is a pitiless monster. He is a lonely sufferer. He retains the sympathy of the reader even after becoming a monster. There lies the triumph of Emily Bronte's art.

CHARACTER OF CATHERINE

Catherine is the central figure in Emily Bronte's novel, *Wuthering Heights.* She is one of the most memorable heroines of English literature. She is not a romantic heroine. Like Eustacia Vye or Bathsheba Everdene of Hardy or Flaubert's Emma Bovary, she represents a split personality torn between her warring impulses. She is a tragic figure.

Catherine Earnshaw is the daughter of Mr. Earnshaw, the owner of "Wuthering Heights." She grows up in the company of Heathcliff from her very childhood whom her father had brought from Liverpool as a gypsy child. Her brother, Hindley detests him but she becomes his playmate. She feels for him when after her father's death her brother degrades him to the level of the servant and sends him to work in the field. She does her best to compensate it by teaching him books, giving solace in his troubles and being the sole companion of Heathcliff. But at the same time she develops a relationship with Edgar Linton who represents culture and refinement. Her relationship with Edgar Linton grows stronger. It also brings about a change in the angle of her vision. She can now see that Heathcliff lacks culture. He does not brush his hair and is dirty. She is conscious that her marriage with Heathcliff will "degrade" her and by her marriage with Edgar Linton she will become "the greatest woman in the neighbourhood." The part of her nature which craves civilized social fulfilment is attracted to the agreeable aspects of the life of Lintons. But her pull in two different directions breeds conflict in her personality. She tells Nelly Dean "My love for Linton is like the foliage in the woods; time will change it. I'm well aware as winter changes the trees. My love for Heathcliff resembles the eternal rocks beneath, a source of little visible delight but necessary. Nelly, I am Heathcliff." Though her love for Linton is only superficial and

Heathcliff forms the essential part of the meaning of her existence, her love for the two breeds conflict of impulses in her personality. She is a typical victorian woman who cannot make a bold choice. Her decision to marry Edgar Linton is the tragic error which creates conflict in her personality and finally destroys her.

Catherine is peculiarly innocent in the sense that it had not occurred to her that her marriage with Linton will mean separation from Heathcliff. She is now aware of the tragic implications of her choice. She becomes an angel, exudes sunshine in the house when Heathcliff returns and she is reconciled to God and the universe. But Edgar Linton is not ready to receive him in the drawing room as he belongs to the lower class. Catherine is now sadly aware of her position. Her separation from Heathcliff after his quarrel with Edgar Linton makes her feel that she is wrenched from Wuthering Heights and her all in all, Heathcliff, that with her wrong decision she has been at once transformed into Mrs. Linton, the wife of a stranger. She feels exiled from her own world into a foreign land from where she cannot return. Her love for Linton has proved to be a foliage which has changed with the season. But Heathcliff remains a permanent necessity "like the eternal rocks beneath."

Catherine is a tragic figure. She is herself responsible for her suffering. In betraying Heathcliff she betrays her deepest self on which her capacity for fulfilment depends. There is every reason for Catherine like Macbeth under the compulsion of her circumstances to act against her own interest. Though she identifies herself with Heathcliff, she is different from him in her reactions. Her love for Heathcliff transcends sex. She can be wedded to Edgar Linton and yet continue to associate herself with Heathcliff, on the other hand, Heathcliff is not only tormented by her separation but wreaks revenge upon those who are responsible for it. Catherine is probably able to achieve her fulfilment after death. She is seen walking hand in hand with Heathcliff on the moors.

Catherine is a split personality. The honesty with which Emily Bronte has portrayed her character invests her with a life of her own. No other novelist in English literature portrayed the feminine conflict as Emily Bronte has done in *Wuthering Heights*.

5

A Passage to India by E.M. Forster

In his article, "What I Believe" E.M. Forster declares his belief in personal relationship and "the holiness of the heart's affection." It is the expression of a need for a reliable personal world in the universal milieu of nationalistic, racial and religious madness. In his essay, "The Challenge of Our Time" Forster declares that his books emphasize the value of personal relationship. The novel, *A Passage to India* does the same but at the same time defines the limits beyond which personal relationship cannot go.

The situation of the novel, *A Passage to India* is placed in the pre-independence India. It is not a political novel as Peter Burra claims. Only the background is political where the fissures between the Hindus, the Muslims and the Anglo-Indians or the British are hard facts against which the possibilities of personal relationship are explored. The chapter of "The Mosque" section opens with the discussion of Hamidullah, Mahmood Ali and Aziz as to "whether or no it is possible to be friends with an Englishman." Hamidullah opines that "it is possible in England" but "it is not possible here." In the background of the English-Indian racial relationship reflected in the exclusion of the Indians from the Anglo-Indian club, the unjust treatment of Aziz by the civil surgeon, the general attitude of the English officers towards Indians, a rapport, "a secret under standing of the heart" is established between Aziz and Mrs. Moore who is a new arrival in India and, unlike the English officers, represents a broad liberal and sympathetic attitude towards Indians. The developing personal relationship between Aziz and Fielding is silhouetted against this backdrop. The Bridge Party which is arranged by Ronny Heaslop to bridge the gap between east and west is a total failure on account of the public school morality of the English which leaves the heart undeveloped. The personal party at the residence of Principal Fielding provides a contrast to the official Bridge Party as it is a success. Forster shows through the relationship of Fielding and Aziz how goodwill and spontaneity can bridge the gulf between people of different races. The racial and political barriers are dissolved by the impulsiveness of Aziz and the friendliness of Fielding. Fielding, unlike the Anglo-Indians, had no faith in herd instinct. He believed the world to be "a globe of men who are trying to reach one another and can best do so by the help of goodwill plus culture and intelligence."

The Marabar caves which are "extraordinary" form the extraordinary element in the fabric of the novel. The caves are ancient and primitive, a necessary disruptive force in the fictional world of Forster. Personal relationships developing across the gaps of racial, religious and national barriers are threatened by this chaotic force. In the words of the novelist, "Aziz had challenged the spirit of the Indian earth which tries to keep men in compartments." During the expedition to the caves, Adela Quested levels the charge of attempted rape against Aziz and the division between the English and the Indians reaches the breaking point. Fielding declares his faith that Aziz is innocent, resigns from the Anglo-Indian club and decides not to betray his friend at the cost of his countrymen. It is significant that Mrs. Moore, the symbol of harmony dies on her way to England. Though Adela Quested withdraws the charge against Aziz, Fielding could not join the victory procession. Later his pleadings with Aziz against filing a damage suit against Adela Quested leaves a chink in the relation between Aziz and Fielding. Aziz suspects Fielding's interest in his marriage with Adela Quested and her money. He also stops replying to the letters of Fielding when he is gone to England. He is under the impression that Fielding has married Adela Quested.

In the last section of the novel, "The Temple" Fielding and

Aziz again meet at Mau where Aziz has joined his service under a Hindu Rajah and Fielding comes for inspection of educational institutions. While discussing the cave expedition, Aziz had remarked, "This is nothing to do with English or Indian," it is an expedition of friendship cutting across racial and national loyalties. But when they meet at Mau, both have hardened and the state of politics casts shadows on the relationship of friends, though Aziz's misunderstanding that Fielding has married Adela Quested is cleared, and their friendship is renewed.

Though Forster believes in personal relationship, he does not believe in a magical solution of racial, national or religious madness through personal relationship. The map of India drawn by him in *A Passage to India* is that of fissures and cleavages which are as primitive as the caves. But he seems to suggest even through fissures and cleavages we can ride together like Fielding and Aziz, though not without our horses swerving apart. *A Passage to India* is considered to be a political novel by Peter Burra. It is to limit the value of the novel, only the background of the novel is political, it goes far beyond politics because like all great art, Forster's novel is symbolic.

Justify the title of the novel, *A Passage to India* or *A Passage to India* is more than a passage to India — Discuss

A Passage to India is not about a passage to India but about the universal human condition. E.M. Forster's *A Passage to India* is apparently about the two English ladies, Adela Quested and Mrs. Moore's journey to India in order to see the real India. But the title of the novel is derived from Walt Whitman's poem "*Passage to India.*" It is a poem about more than a passage to India. It is a poem about spiritual exploration:

> Passage to more than India!
> O secret of the earth and sky
>
> ....
>
> Sail forth, steer forth for the deep water only,
> Reckless o soul, exploring, I with thee and thou with me,
> For we are bound where mariner has not yet dared to go
> And we will risk the ship, ourselves and all.

Hence, though the novel portrays the journey of the two English ladies to India as well as Fielding's daring involvement with Indians, it is at the same time the exploration of certain spiritual truths. It presents, in the words of Forster himself, "the twilight of the double vision." This novel of Forster is his masterpiece which is rich in multiple layers of meanings.

Miss Adela Quested's and Mrs. Moore's desire to see real India brings them to the Anglo-Indian club where Indians are not allowed. Mrs. Moore does not remain confined to the club. She dares into the premises of the mosque in the moonlit night where in the light and shade of the mosque, Aziz is consoling himself with the thoughts of the glory of Islam after he was insulted by the behaviour of the English civil surgeon and his wife. When Dr. Aziz and Mrs. Moore meet, Aziz calls her "an oriental" and "a secret understanding of the heart" is established between the two. Mrs. Moore also feels the unity with the earth and the sky, the universe. "In England the moon had seemed dead and alien; here she was caught in the shawl of the night together with earth and all other stars. A sudden sense of unity, of kinship with the heavenly bodies, passed into the old woman and out, like water through a tank, leaving a strange freshness behind." Ronny, the city magistrate arranges a Bridge party to bridge the gap between the east and the west. But it turns out to be a complete failure against the personal party thrown by principal Fielding to Adela Quested, Mrs. Moore and Dr. Aziz at his residence. It is the genuine expression of the holiness of the heart's affection, the warmth of personal relationship and the trip to Marabar Caves is agreed upon.

Apart from the fissures between the Anglo-Indians and the Indians, the possibilities of a rapport through personal relationship that their visit reveals, their visit to the Marabar Caves opens up another deeper vision of realities.

The caves are a symbol of the timeless universe in which there was chaos everywhere. In such a universe of total chaos, there is no place for things such as civilization, order or human life. Everything is reduced to nothing. Mrs. Moore's conceived of the earth as a loving spirit binding man with his fellowmen and also with God. Mrs. Moore has a developed heart and is kind to those whom she meets but what is she in the face of a country in which human beings are but a speck on vast and hostile landscape. The sense of separation between all mankind and all earth which Mrs. Moore experiences at the caves is part of the human condition. The sense of nothingness is so strong that she becomes indifferent to everything, even personal relationship and God and leaves for England. On her journey back to England, the tower of Asirgarh appears, disappears and reappears. This somehow suggests to her the vision of nothingness at the caves is part of the truth and the other part of the truth is that life will go on as usual in spite of everything.

The last part of the novel which presents in great detail the birth celebration of Lord Krishna, combines the wasp and Mrs. Moore in the mind of Godbole and dissolves the misunderstanding between Aziz and Fielding. It also shows the continuity of the spirit of Mrs. Moore in the form of her son, Ralph whom now Aziz calls "oriental." The possibilities of personal relationship re-emerge in the renewed relationship of Aziz and Fielding but they encounter the forces of disorder, the time and space: "But the horses did not want it they swerved apart; the earth did not want it they said in their hundred voice, "No, not yet" and the sky said, "Not there." It is a symbolic novel. It is, as the critics agree, not a novel about India but the human condition.

Comment on the Rhythmic Pattern and Structure of *A Passage to India*

E.M. Forster is a novelist *sui generis.* In his mature novels he weaves a pattern of images and phrases which occur and recur but always with a variety. This repetition plus variation creates an impression or pattern which Forster describes as rhythm in his critical treatise, *The Aspects of the Novel.* This poetic organisation lends a rich meaning or symbolic significance to the novel which goes far beyond the plot, setting or the story. It brings the novel closer to poetry. George Moore's novel, *Esther Waters* comes closer to *A Passage to India* in its technique. But *A Passage to India* is more subtle and emphatic.

In the second chapter of the novel, *A Passage to India*, Dr. Aziz is engaged in discussion with his friends, "whether or not it is possible to be friends with an Englishman." It is followed by the incident in which Dr. Aziz is humiliated by the civil surgeon. Sitting in the mosque with his bruised feelings, Aziz is repeating the poetic line, "the secret understanding of the heart." When Mrs. Moore enters the mosque, soon "the flame that not even beauty can nourish was springing in Aziz" and he declares, "Then you are an oriental." He has learnt that one can be friends with the English woman. In the last chapter of the novel, Aziz repeats the same words, not to Mrs. Moore who is dead, but to her son, Ralph Moore. Aziz asks, "Can you always tell whether a stranger is your friend?" When Ralph says, "yes" Aziz declares, "Then you are an oriental." As in the past, he takes Mrs. Moore to the caves, he takes Ralph Moore out on the river. The words of Aziz in this context suggest the beginning of another cycle.

Ralph is the repetition as well as the prolongation of his mother. The echo that disturbs Adela Quested is not limited to the caves, she is harassed by this sound elsewhere also. It is under this mysteriously benign influence of Mrs. Moore that she feels relaxed. The mention of Mrs. Moore's name as "Esmiss Esmore" at the trial clears her confusion and Aziz is persuaded to waive his claim of damage against Adela Quested. Similarly the image of the wasp appears together with Mrs. Moore's in the first part of the novel and they reappear in the third part of the novel as well. The rhythmical repetition of images and symbols create a poetic effect as T.S. Eliot does through the musical organisation of images in his *Four Quartets*.

The novel consists of three parts, "The Mosque," "The Caves" and "The Temple." Each part has a beautiful prefatory chapter which abounds in symbols and suggestions which interweave different parts of the novel. The first chapter of the novel, "The Mosque" begins and ends with "the extraordinary

Marabar caves." There is also a reference to the temple in the detailed topography of Chandrapore.

In the first part, "The Mosque" Mrs. Moore visits the mosque where she meets Dr. Aziz and a mysterious bond of understanding between them is formed which endures throughout the novel. Aziz repeats the line of poetry, "The secret understanding of the heart" which forms the core of the novel. The party which is arranged by Fielding points in the same direction in spite of the gulfs that divide Hindus, Muslims and the British rulers. At the tea party, Aziz proposes a trip to the caves. Every attempt of Aziz to understand the caves is answered by the brief negatives of Godbole.

In the second part of the novel, "The Caves" Aziz undertakes the promised trip to the Marabar caves. The reference to the caves in "The Mosque" as "extraordinary" is significant as the echo in the caves breaks the ordinary rhythm of life at Chandrapore and introduces the muddle. The caves represent primitive India beyond Muslim or Hindu faith. Aziz, as we are told, is "encountering the Ancient India." In the face of the echo in the caves, Mrs. Moore is disturbed as she is less western, rather oriental. But the behaviour of Adela Quested is "extraordinary." She makes the absurd charge against Aziz. It is comparable to the experience of Helen Schelegel listening to Beethoven in *Howard's End* and Mrs. Moore is like Mrs. Wilcox as a redemptive character. Adela Quested is relieved of the echo when she is in the company of Mrs. Moore. The mention of the name of Mrs. Moore at the trial clears the confusion of Adela Quested. Before the second part ends, Mrs. Moore dies on the sea on the way to England and Cyril Fielding returns to Europe.

In the third part, "The Temple," it is not British India. It is Mau under a Hindu Rajah, where Dr. Aziz acts as a medical officer of the king. Thus the Muslim element is not excluded. Later Cyril Fielding, Ralph and Stella also enter Mau. This part presents the religious ceremony of the Hindu worship where Godbole in his vision for a moment connects the wasp with Mrs. Moore. Aziz tells Ralph that his mother has been his "best friend." The confusion of Aziz about Fielding's marriage with Adela Quested is removed, their ride together is the proof of the revival of their friendship. But in spite of their desire to be friends with each other, the earth and the sky say, "No, not yet, not here."

The novel, thus, began with the question of the possibility of friendship between the Indians and the English and ends with the answer. The structure of *A Passage to India,* has a rhythmic rise and fall that Forster found in *War and Peace.* While the mosque symbolises the values of Islam of unity and brotherhood, the cave suggests primitive darkness and negation resulting in a breakdown of human relationship. The temple signifies harmony and regeneration, the triumph, though qualified, of the secret understanding of the human heart shadowed by the social and political complications.

COMMENT ON THE SYMBOLISM IN *A PASSAGE TO INDIA*

E.M. Forster is an eminent modern English novelist and critic. He has strong belief in personal relationship and his novels carry this message quite artistically. Forster has also paid a good deal of attention to the fictional technique and his novels acquire a new form and colour as a result of the employment of symbols and rhythmic pattern in the novel.

The novel, *A Passage to India* is composed of three major symbols which form the titles of the three sections of the novel, "The Mosque," The Caves" and "The Temple." In the first section of the novel, "The Mosque," Dr. Aziz and Mrs. Moore meet each other in the serene moonlit atmosphere of the mosque. The mosque with its serenity and blend of light and shade emerges as the symbol of harmony. Dr. Aziz and Mrs. Moore, in no time, reach "a secret understanding of the heart." The first section of the novel is composed of a number of variation on the same theme. The personal relationship established between Aziz and Mrs. Moore suggests the possibility of friendship between the races, the Indian and the English. It is immediately followed by the Bridge party where the east and the west meet but only to diverge. No bridge is established between the Indians and the British in the party. Rather the note of disharmony becomes more resonant. The mosque symbol includes the understanding of the heart and the personal relationship between Dr. Aziz and Principal Fielding as well as the romantic understanding of the heart between Adela Quested and Ronny. The mosque thus stands as a symbol of harmony as well as disharmony or divergence.

The image of "The Caves" appears twice on the first page of the novel as "extraordinary" and the mosque section: "the comparatively simple mind of the Mohammedan was encountering the Ancient Night" but it emerges fully as a symbol in "The Caves" section. The caves predate Islam, Christianity and even Hinduism. The Marabar caves represent the void, the nothingness, negation and evil. They are the most ancient aspect of the universe. Mrs. Moore encounters a vision of nothingness in the caves. The echoes of the caves suggest to her that "Pathos, piety, courage — they exist but are identical and so is filth" and "everything exists, nothing has value." She looks into the caves, the heart of darkness and her vision of the oneness of the universe eludes her. Adela Quested too has a nightmarish vision in the caves which releases forces powerful enough to destroy the possibilities of harmony or understanding of the heart "The Mosque" suggested. The caves represent evil as the indestructible aspect of the universe.

The very shape of the caves suggests a void, an emptiness as well as the force of darkness that brings to nothing all the understanding to the heart reached in "The Mosque."

The third major symbol of the novel is "The Temple" which forms the third section of the novel. The temple is situated far away from the caves at Mau. Godbole, the Education Minister of the Hindu State is presiding on the ceremony of Gokul Ashtami, the birth of Krishna, the Lord of the universe in which all the diverse and different elements of the universe are united in an ambience of harmony. Godbole has a vision of Mrs. Moore and the wasp during the celebrations. Mrs. Moore, though dead, is symbolically present in the form of her children, Stella and Ralph and they are recognised by Aziz as such. The misunderstanding between Aziz and Fielding disappears and the friendship is renewed. The temple represents the vision of almost universal harmony. But like the mosque symbol which represents, and underlines, at the same time, the possibilities of understanding between the races, in spite of the musical note of harmony in "The Temple," the novel ends with the scene of the horses of Aziz and Fielding swerving apart.

Forster's novel, *A Passage to India* is symbolic in texture and structure. The map of India drawn by E.M. Forster in *A Passage to India* is that of fissures and cleavages which are as primitive as the caves. But he seems to suggest that even through fissures and cleavages we can ride together like Fielding and Aziz, though not without our horses swerving apart. The novel presents the twilight of the double vision, the tension between affirmation and negation, between positive and negative vision which is the heart of the symbolic novel, *A Passage to India*. The novel operates on the symbolic level like poetry.

CHARACTER OF CYRIL FIELDING

Cyril Fielding is one of the most important characters of the novel, *A Passage to India*. Cyril Fielding is, in many ways, similar to E.M. Forster, the author of the novel. E.M. Forster upholds the liberal, humanist values of tolerance, goodwill, culture, intelligence and holiness of the heart's affection in personal relationship in his article "What I Believe." Cyril Fielding maintains the same liberal values in his day-to-day exchange of life. All these virtues make him an ideal person to prove, that "the world is a globe of men who are trying to reach one another and can best do so by the help of goodwill plus culture and intelligence." Cyril Fielding is the principal of the government college at Chandrapore in the British India which presents a sad spectacle of divisions of race, religion and nationality. Fielding's belief in broad human ethics is the ideal formula to bridge the gaps. Forster takes great pains to show the achievement of Cyril Fielding in bringing about friendship and reconciliation.

Unlike other Anglo-Indians in India, he had no racial feelings because he had matured in a different atmosphere. He was brought up on liberal traditions. He had no faith in herd instincts and was happiest in the give and take of a private conversation. He was not unpatriotic. But he did not fall in with the views of the Anglo-Indian officers who harboured racial prejudice. He had found it pleasant to associate with Indians. The feeling grew that Fielding was a disruptive force. The Anglo-Indian men tolerated him but their wives disliked him because he was not a "Pucca Sahib." Fielding's behaviour towards Aziz is in refreshing contrast to the mindless arrogance shown by the British towards the Indians whom they considered racially inferior. Hence, Fielding's party is a remarkable success in contrast to the Bridge Party arranged by the British officials. The unexpected personal warmth of Fielding towards Aziz releases Aziz's spontaneity and their mutual goodwill results in personal relationship.

Cyril Fielding is a man who has an intense faith in the value of personal relationship. He is a frank atheist but he respects every opinion his friend holds which is the essential basis of his friendship. He is a thorough individualist who does not believe in the fervour of nationalism.

Forster says in his essay, "What I Believe," "If I have to choose between betraying my friend and betraying my country, I shall have the guts to betray my country." Fielding seems to act upon this idea. He has the courage of the conviction to maintain his friendship with Aziz while all Anglo-Indians consider their national duty to oppose Aziz for which at one time he is considered a Japanese spy. He has an instinctive belief against all his countrymen in the innocence of Aziz. When Mcbryde, the police officer talks of some vulgarity in the letters of Aziz, he tells him "I did the same at his age." Though Fielding like Adela Quested does want to be "labelled," he leaves the British club and faces their hatred. Later on when Adela is isolated from Indians as well as the British, he has the courage to risk his intimate friendship with Aziz in order to save her from ruin and desolation. He is superior to Aziz in matters of friendship.

It is the sheer spell of Fielding's persuasion that he succeeds in dissuading him from filing a damage suit against Adela Quested. Cyril Fielding is a good, thoughtful, intelligent fellow on the verge of middle age with a belief in education. He likes his position of an educationist and is a great success with his pupils. He is bound to no particular race or nationality. His fundamental belief lies in teaching the pupil to be individual and to understand other individuals. He prides himself on having conceived an idea rather than a child to carry on his name.

Fielding is essentially a humanist who lays great value on personal loyalty, honesty and freedom as a bulwark against the forces of ignorance, prejudice and hatred. It may be said that he is the member of the aristocracy in which Forster believed, "not an aristocracy based on rank and influence but an aristocracy of the sensitive, considerate and plucky." Though the values of personal relationship, goodwill, tolerance and culture achieve friendship and understanding, the novel ends on an ambivalent note as far as the formula of personal relationship can work in a world divided by race, nationality and religion.

CHARACTER OF MRS. MOORE

Mrs. Moore is a unique creation of E.M. Forster in his novel, *A Passage to India.* She does not conform to Forster's own categorisation of characters into round and flat characters. In the words of Lionel Trilling, she is neither flat nor round but "fragrant" character. Mrs. Moore is less of a real person. She is a disembodied voice. She has not the solidity of a person like Aziz and Fielding. Yet the fragrance of her existence pervades the novel. She is the unique and valuable embodiment of particular values which the world of ill-will, intolerance and conflict badly needs. When, we meet her first in the novel, Aziz is seeking peace in the tranquil atmosphere of light and shade in the moonlit night after his feelings have been injured by the insulting behaviour of the civil surgeon. He notices a dim figure in the shadows. It is no ghost but the figure of a woman who has dared into the mosque to escape the boredom of the English Club. She radiates warmth, kindness, peace and sympathetic understanding around her. Throughout the novel, she remains a mysteriously benign influence spreading the sunshine of kindness, sympathy and understanding. When she meets Aziz, she is impressed by the spontaneous warmth of Aziz. Aziz is also impressed by her intuitive understanding of life for which Aziz calls her "oriental." She has escaped the narrow-mindedness of the Anglo-Indians who consider Indians an inferior race and reflect it in their behaviour towards Indians. She does not represent logic and reason. She has a mysterious power of seeing into things and a power of sensing the divine in the ordinary things of life. When she comes out of the mosque, she experiences a mysterious sense of unity with the universe: "A sudden sense of unity, of kinship with heavenly bodies passed into the old woman and out like water through the tank leaving a strange freshness behind."

Mrs. Moore senses a mysterious unifying love with all the creatures. One night when she is about to retire for the night, she notices a wasp on the peg. She feels an overwhelming sympathy and love for the tiny creature. She is closer to Godbole in the sense that his religious philosophy unites the highest and the lowest in the divine love. She tells her son, Ronny, "God has put us on earth to love our neighbours and show it and He is omnipresent even in India, to see how we are succeeding."

Mrs. Moore is an old woman with her faith in God and His love who has "put us on earth to be pleasant to each other." But something goes wrong during her visit to India. She comes to feel that personal relationship, even marriage does not matter at all. "She felt increasingly that though people are, the relations between them are not important and that in particular too much fuss has been made over marriage. Centuries of carnal embracement, yet man is no nearer to understanding man."

In fact, her hold on life has grown weaker. Her health was failing and she had developed a sympathetic attitude to all the things around herself. She has a sense of nothingness and emptiness. But her experience cannot be explained in terms of bad health only. She has a peculiar psychic experience in the caves. She hears a terrifying echo which seems to suggest to her, "Everything exists, nothing has value." Her vision of nothingness and emptiness is deepened by the echo in the caves and undermines her relations with children and family and her God. She has "the twilight of double vision where the horror of the universe and its smallness are both visible at the same time — a vision in which so many elderly people are involved." After her experience in the cave, the vision of chaos, she loses all interest in life and withdraws into herself. She knows that Aziz is innocent and that her testimony will be useful to him yet she allows herself to be sent away.

Though Mrs. Moore dies during her voyage, her spirit is alive throughout the novel as Esmiss Esmoor. At the trial, the Indians, who think that Mrs. Moore's testimony would have, saved Aziz, chant her name as "Esmiss Esmoor." She appears like a goddess to save Aziz. It is significant that the invocation of her name in the court room clears the confusion in the mind of Adela Quested and she realises that her accusation is wrong. She appears in the mind of Godbole during the religious ceremony towards the close of the novel. The memory of Mrs. Moore and the wasp makes him grasp the vision of the divine reality in which all creation is one. The spirit of Mrs. Moore continues in her son, Ralph, in his intuitive love and wisdom. Aziz also calls him "oriental" and the friendship is renewed. It is her influence that brings about reconciliation and love. Lionel Trilling holds the view on this account that "it is Mrs. Moore indeed, who is the story."

SKETCH THE CHARACTER OF AZIZ

Aziz is the central figure of E.M. Forster's novel, *A Passage to India*. He is a round character if we are permitted to use the critical term coined by Forster himself. He appears much more real and living a person than any one in the novel. He is one of the most memorable characters of E.M. Forster. He is part of the pre-independence scenario of the British-ruled India. He is a Muslim by faith, a doctor by profession and a representative Indian under the British rule. He is so fully drawn that he seems to be as alive as one of our friends in real life.

Aziz is a surgeon in the Government Hospital at Chandrapore. Major Calendor, the civil surgeon holds the view that Aziz is indispensable in serious cases. He loves and uses his knife skilfully. It is his hand, not his mind that is scientific. He relishes the poetry of Urdu and Persian poets like Hafiz, Ghalib, Iqbal and Hali. The choice of his verse reflects the peculiar essence of his personality. The line of Persian poetry that he often repeats to himself contains the phrase "the secret understanding of the heart." This is what he achieves with Mrs. Moore. He is a creature of instincts and impulses. He calls Mrs. Moore "oriental" at the first meeting and remains emotionally attached to her throughout. Mrs. Moore never did anything in his favour but he believed she must have favoured him. He refrains from pressing his suit against Adela Quested under her mysterious influence.

Aziz is remarkable for the spontaneous overflow of powerful feelings at the tea party, where the barriers of formality and distinction between the ruler and the ruled are set aside. He becomes immediately frank with Mrs. Moore in his first meeting and pours out his grievances against the British rulers. At the tea party, he invites Mrs. Moore, Adela Quested and Fielding to his house but later regrets it. He meets Fielding with the same impulsive warmth when he calls on Aziz in his illness. But he feels embarrassed at his untidy room. He shows him the picture of his dead life. Fielding is impressed by the warmth of his emotion and response. But he realises he cannot be carried away by the waves of impulses like Aziz. He also points out to Aziz that his emotions are out of proportions to their objects. Aziz replies to him, "Is emotion a sack of potatoes so much the pound to be measured out?"

Aziz has a romantic sensibility. He does not attend the

Bridge Party because that is the death anniversary of his wife. He suffers from nostalgic melancholy. He keeps the photograph of his dead wife and treats any suggestion of a second marriage with contempt. He seeks solace in the glory of Islam sitting in the crisscross of light and shade in the mosque. He often broods over the transience of beauty and decay of Islam. He is sentimentally attached to the first six Moghul kings especially Alamgeer and Babur. A strong desire for something that is not characterises him.

Aziz overrates hospitality. He is impulsive and responsive. He wrenches his collar stud and offers it to Fielding when he is dressing up for the party. He spends all night at the platform so that he does not miss the train in his trip to the caves. All his decisions and actions are based on emotion rather than reason. He wants to get away from the British India after his acquittal even at the cost of ruining his future. Aziz is volatile by temperament. It is on account of his temperament that his bond of friendship with Fielding comes under a cloud. If he is quick to form emotional bonds, he is quick to distrust as well. He trusts Fielding no doubt as a friend. But at the same time he suspects that Fielding wants to let off Adela Quested because he wants to marry her for her money. Later on he cannot bring himself to reply to the letters of Fielding on account of his suspicion. He has acute sensitiveness to slights imagined or real. This prevents him from responding fully to Fielding's goodwill. Forster comments, "Suspicion in the Oriental is a sort of malignant tumour, a mental malady that makes him self-conscious and unfriendly suddenly; he trusts and mistrusts at the same time in a way the Westerner cannot comprehend. It is his demon as the Westerner's hypocrisy."

The emotional and volatile element introduces a streak of psychological instability and makes him contradictory. He trusts and distrusts. He is kind to the extreme but at the same time he harbours a sense of injury. Though a doctor, he is untidy at home when he is off his duty. Aziz emerges as a convincing Indian with his characteristic vices and virtues. Lionel Trilling remarks, "for good or for bad, he is human." In spite of his spontaneity and warmth when his malignant suspicion about Fielding is removed, the barriers of nationalities, the ruler and the ruled cast a shadow over his personal relationship with Fielding. Forster shows the disruptive forces, the dividing, negative forces that threaten the personal relationship and define its limitations.

6
Tess by Hardy

Tess, a "Pure Woman" is the title of Hardy's novel. In the words of Tonny Tanner, "the purest woman contains the tides of blood" which is associated with sexual passion and death, "[...] if rising of blood is sexual passion and spilling of blood is death." In this way Tess is a "pure woman" with tides of blood as after her rape by Alec she spills blood all through her life which leads to her destruction. Thus the woman in the novel is associated with bleeding or suffering as in Shakespearean tragedy.

The destruction or destiny of Tess is suggested or predicted through the event of Prince, the horse and the symbols of colours "red and white." The colour imagery is very powerful through which the novel communicates its meaning. The "red" colour is stronger and more suggestive symbol than the colour "white" because, it is the colour of blood which is associated with Tess from first to last. It dogs her, disturbs her and finally destroys her. When we observe Tess's life we find that her destiny is nothing more or less than the colour "red." The 'red' colour includes suffering, rape, murder and death of Tess. The combination or contrast of 'white' and 'red' colours is very suggestive. When we see Tess for the first time she is the only girl who, in the company of the girls of 'white' ribbon, wears a 'red' ribbon. Tanner rightly remarks that this contrast of colours suggests "if she is all white at birth, she is to be all red at death."

The "white" colour is the symbol of her virginity which is closely connected with purity as she is frequently referred to as a "white shape." On the night of her rape she is described as a "white muslin figure" and her "beautiful feminine tissue" as "practically blank as snow." But her whiteness or purity is murdered by Alec d'Urberville who stands "like the blood-red-ray in the spectrum of her young life" and after this event she becomes "blank" as the blood of her innocence has been released. On the evening of her rape Tess is first aware of Alec at the dance party when she sees "the red coal of a cigar." This image is a destructive phallic symbol of fiery passion in which Tess is to be burnt. Thus the colour 'red' becomes the symbol of passion as well as of blood and Tess's fate is overwhelmed by this 'red' colour as it is quite obvious that after burning in the 'red-coal of a cigar' she bleeds continuously and it brings to her complete destruction.

The accident of the horse, Prince on the darkened road when "the pointed shaft entered the breast of the unhappy Prince like a sword [...] the hole in his chaste looking scarcely large enough to have let out all that animated him "emerges as the most appropriate symbol of her fate. As we see that after some days she is pierced brutally by Alec on the darkened road from home and from the hole pierced in her body, the blood is bound to run on till the initial violation does finally, "let out all that animated her." But at the same time, the honesty and purity of her character is stressed. She reveals all the truth to her husband in spite of her mother's suggestions. Dorothy van Ghent identifies Tess with the earth which suffers but silently bears. Ghent says that there are a number of women who experience this tragedy but they conceal it or bear silently just like the earth and they lead their life happily, but Tess reveals it and it becomes the cause of her destruction. There is some logic and truth in Ghent's opinion, but it is the purity, honesty and moral conscience of Tess that does not allow her to sweep it under the carpet.

It is Tess's honesty and purity that she informs Angel Clare about her rape before marriage. But chance or fate that mars the happiness in a hostile universe in the Hardyan novel of Wessex presents no exception here. Her letter written to Angel does not reach him on time and she thinks that she has harmonized her impulses perfectly with those of Angel Clare. But there is discrepancy between her thinking and the fact. After marriage when she tells him about her past, he rejects her, because there is discrepancy between the vision of Angel Clare and the actuality of a pure woman like Tess. Angel can conceive of Tess as purely angelic or ideal, "a visionary — any essence of woman [...] merely a soul at large," but Tess is inescapably flesh and blood. She is an actual woman with her body, her sexuality and the experience of rape. Angel is unable to bridge the gap of his ideal vision of a woman and the actual experience of a real woman, Tess. Thus the hole pierced by Alec in her and her bleeding become the symbol of her entire fate.

It is her purity and faithfulness for Angel that she murders Alec when Angel returns while she is aware that it will lead her to death. She is a "pure woman" also in the sense that a woman and suffering are associated closely with each other or it can be said that a woman is made for suffering as the quotation of Shakespeare; "[...] poor wound name! My bosom as a bed/ Shall lodge thee," on the page of the textbook of *Tess d'Urberville* illustrates. Tess suffers all through her life. The suffering of Tess reminds us of Desdemona in Shakespeare's *Othello* who is the most innocent tragic character in the Shakespearean world. The difference between the two is that Desdemona suffers without any reason and Tess suffers for the deed which she has not committed herself.

Tess's failure to claim Angel as her husband, murder of Alec, her hanging and the symbol of 'red' and 'white' which accompany the event bring into prominence their significance. She is a "pure woman" in her body and her character and she bleeds all through her life, spills blood and dies in an indifferent, rather hostile universe. Hardy appears quite modern in his treatment of the theme — the attitude of the society represented by Angel Clare to the chastity of the woman against the indifference to the same in men.

Q. Discuss the poetic expression of the tragic vision in Hardy's novel *Tess d'Urberville.*

Or

Discuss the structure of the novel *Tess.*

Ans. Hardy's *Tess d'Urberville* is a novel *sui-generis* in the sense that tragedy streams out through poetry. The novel is full of the imagery of colours and the sun which plays very important part in the destiny of Tess. The imagery of colours is dominating as the entire novel hinges upon it. In fact the novel is based on the pattern of white and red colours which is often visible in the background of the novel. The structure of "Tess" like that of "Wuthering Heights" is poetic and the essential meanings of the fictional vision are suggested or defined by the images which inform the novel.

When Tess, for the first time, appears in the May dance she is wearing "red ribbon in her hair and was the only one of the white company who would boast of such a pronounced adornment." This pattern of white and red colours is often visible in the background of the novel which is very symbolic. It suggests according to Tonny Tanner, "if Tess is all white at birth she is to be all red at death." But the imagery of colour red is more strong and more suggestive than the white colour as red is the colour of blood which is associated with Tess from beginning to end. It dogs her, disturbs her and finally destroys her. When we see Tess's life from beginning to end we find that her destiny is nothing more or less than the colour red. The red colour includes suffering, rape, murder and finally death.

The white colour is the symbol of her virginity as well. Tess in her youth is referred to as "a white shape" and on the night of her rape, she is described as "white muslin figure" and her "beautiful feminine tissue" is described as "practically blank as snow." What is to happen with this "white shape" is suggested through the historic precedent, "The vale was known in former times as the forest of white hart, from a curious legend of King Henry III's reign, in which the killing by a certain Thomas de Lynd of a beautiful white hart which the king ran down and spared, was made the occasion of a heavy fine." "Against all social injunctions, white harts are brought down" and something like that happens with Tess. In this context we can say that Tess is a "white hart" and Alec is "Thomas de Lynd" who destroyed her life.

The image of the sleeping girl on the darkened road who is awakened by the sudden collision when "the pointed shaft of the cart entered the breast of the unhappy Prince like a sword" and who tries to check the blood putting her hand upon the hole, is highly suggestive. It indicates or indirectly predicts the loss of her virginity as after this event she is brutally pierced by Alec d'Urberville who stands like "a blood red ray in the spectrum of her young life" on the darkened road far from home. Here, Tonny Tanner on this point rightly remarks that "[...] Once the blood of her innocence has been released, she too like the stoical Prince, will stay upright as long as she can until, all blood being out, she will sink down suddenly in a heap compressed in that one imponderable scene we can see her own life." Tanner is absolutely correct, because, we see that after her rape, Tess suffers continuously and after her marriage with Angel whom she loves, her life becomes more complicated. She struggles against her fate as long as possible and when her capacity for struggles ends she murders Alec and embraces death. Thus life ends with the same combination of colours with which the story of her life starts as we see that the landlady who peeps through the key whole reports, "her lips were bleeding from the clench of her teeth upon them." We cannot but agree with Tanner who points out that "it is at once the evidence of the murder and completion of a life which also started with a red patch on a white background, only then it was simply a ribbon and dress."

After the imagery of colours, the sun emerges as the next powerful symbolic imagery. It also performs an important role in the tragedy of Tess. At the dairy, we see that the sun is at its most active position as a course of the fertile surging which animates nature. "Rays from the sunrise drew forth the buds and stretched them into stalks, lifted up sad in noiseless streams, opened petals and sucked out scents in invisible jets and breathing." It is noticeable that the sun in whose profound sensuous atmosphere at dairy, Tess blooms into full female ripeness, becomes hostile to her. When she takes a refuge behind stones after the murder of Alec d'Urberville, the rising sun reveals the policemen closing in and she is arrested.

No doubt in *Tess d'Urberville,* Hardy's tragic vision is expressed in poetic mode as the novel is full of poetic descriptions which comes through the imagery of colours and the sun. The imagery is very important and significant because tragedy rises from it. Hardy's tragic vision through poetic mode runs parallel with Emily Bronte's novel *Wuthering Heights* in which tragedy, just like *Tess d'Urberville,* comes through poetry. The poetic quality of *Tess* also brings affinity with Lawrence's novel *Rainbow* and *The Virgin and the Gipsy* in which the imagery of rainbow and the imagery of flood are dominating and the meanings of the novels are inherent in them. But the difference between *Tess* and *Rainbow* and *The Virgin and the Gipsy* is that the imagery in "Tess" is the vehicle of tragedy while in *Rainbow* the imagery brings promises of new and fresh life and the imagery of flood in *The Virgin and the Gipsy* is the symbol of satisfaction as well as of collapse of the distinction between the sophisticated class of people and the rough-tough Gipsy.

7

To the Lighthouse by Virginia Woolf

Q. 1. Virginia Woolf is an exponent of stream of consciousness novel. Discuss with reference *To the Lighthouse.*

2. *To the Lighthouse* is packed with thought and emotion and integrated with elaborate imagery.

3. *To the Lighthouse* is a poetic novel. Discuss.

4. Discuss the structure of *To the Lighthouse.*

5. "*To the Lighthouse* is the minor fiction at its most triumphant." Discuss.

Virginia Woolf is an exponent of the stream of consciousness novels which project the depth and fluidity of human consciousness. Her outstanding characteristic is "the dazzling technique, a technique akin, in its emotional subtlety and intricate interpretation of moods, to that of Henry James and Proust." D.M. Hoare rightly points out in the introduction of *To the Lighthouse* that her method is "to fix the object and let the mind sway round it and all the associations it brings, with the freedom and suppleness of a gymnast." The novel *To The Lighthouse* is the best illustration of her technique.

To the Lighthouse is the masterpiece of Virginia Woolf. It touches the heights to the point of perfection. It is packed with thought and emotion and integrated with elaborate imagery. The thought and emotion of the character is evoked through the mental poesy and the exterior events lose their hegemony to render and interpret the inner event or experience of the character. The scene in which Mrs. Ramsay weaves the brown stocking, is a case in point. Her knitting of the stocking loses its hegemony to interpret her mental movement which is another pattern of life. When Mrs. Ramsay knits the stocking, her mental flux changes from moment to moment as she thinks about going to the lighthouse, plans for the marriage of Lily and William and many other things. And this absence of exterior events in the novel becomes the major factor for its lack of tragic depth. But it is not a defect, because the novel does not deal with the exterior events. It has no plot as it deals with the mental atmosphere and this is why there is no tragic depth like that of *A Farewell to Arms* and *For whom the Bell Tolls*. The novel *To the Lighthouse* is, infact, an experimental novel. Here, Virginia Woolf experiments with the human experience by projecting human consciousness onto the canvas of fiction with all its multiplicity and complexity of subtle shades. It brings it very close to poetry. Here, we cannot but agree with Leon Edel when he remarks in his book *The Psychological Novel*, "The bright flame-like vividness creates beautiful illuminated surface. There is no tragic depth in them, only the pathos of things lost or outlived."

Mrs. Woolf renders the inner experience of her characters through the brilliantly evocative prose-poetry. The scene in which Mrs. Ramsay after assuring her son about the fine weather of the next day sits in the window and consciousness streams through her mind is described in the highly poetic language:

"[...] but like ghostly roll of drums remorselessly beat the measure of life, made one think of the destruction of the island [...] and warned her whose day had slipped past in one quick doing after another that it was all ephemeral as a rainbow [...] this sound suddenly thundered hollows in her ears." Not only the language in the given passage is rhythmic, but the same kind of rhythm runs through the entire book which is highly significant. It represents the rhythmic movement of the mind of the character.

The novel is conceived and composed on the purely poetic scale. The imagery and the rhythm reflect the nature of the experience on which Mrs. Woolf experiments in this novel. The imagery enacts as symbols. There are three recurrent symbols — window, party and lighthouse which provide "resonance as well as structure." The first part of the novel "window" is various but unified; character is created through "the most economical of means and through all is heard the sound of sea, suggesting the fullness of life and the imminence of death." There are two major symbols in this part. First, the window which is the point of view, the dividing or connecting point and the second, the party. The window divides and connects Lily and Mrs. Ramsay, framing for Lily her portrait and for Mrs. Ramsay the lighthouse, the instrument of her moment of solitary vision. The second symbol, the dinner party reflects Mrs. Ramsay's attempt to bring the whole group of separate individuals together in which she succeeds. It suggests her belief in the globalization of the world. Here dinner symbolism is "projected in terms of three works of art, the perfectly successful *boeuf en daube,* the bowl of fruit beautifully arranged by Rose, and the poem recited whose words and rhythm provide a kind of music to support and universalize the mood visually created."

The lighthouse is the third major symbol. Its symbolism is clear and "Virginia Woolf is no more mystical than E.M. Forster in *Howards End,* where the symbolism of the house performs a similar function and music replaces painting as the source of aesthetic experience." This is why Frank W. Bradbrook remarks that "it is dangerous to discuss *To the Lighthouse* in term of mystical experience." The lighthouse is not flux but stability, not passing time but something permanently fixed above the waste of waters. "The long steady stroke of the lighthouse beam is Mrs. Ramsay's stroke and symbolises the stability and security which her presence imposes on the flux of life." The flashing of the beam is equivalent in life to the movements of the painter's brush, Lily. Mrs. Ramsay and Lily are equally artists. The novel ends with "the long steady stroke of the brush that also completes Lily's picture in the mind of the perfect woman whom she loves." Both in the novel and in the painting, formality and discipline are imposed on the chaos of experience. Here, Virginia Woolf seems to be suggesting that to have something of permanent importance out of one's momentary experience, is the aim of the artists.

Another symbol operative in the structure of the novel is the middle chapter, "Time Passes." It is highly significant. It is "*tour de force*, an answer to a dare." It succeeds as a prose-poem. It shows the effect of time on human possessions—the house gradually decays recording human events in their unimportant relation to the natural process-death. "The death of Mrs. Ramsay, Prue and Andrew is recorded in parenthesis which is like a poetic or ironic mark of punctuation in the long records of time." Here, Virginia Woolf shows a complete mastery in the handling of her subject-time. In most of her novels, time is reduced to a few hours, so that even in *To The Lighthouse*, where a number of years are bridged in the middle passage, "Time Passes." And in this condition it is not wrong to say that "*To the Lighthouse* is the minor fiction at its most triumphant." Like all other stream of consciousness novels the merging of time past and present as Eliot says in "Four Quartets":

"The time past and time future/ What might have been and what has been/ Point to one end, which is always present" is at the very core of the novel.

The end of the novel resembles the conclusion of Jane Austen's *Emma* where the stress is on the wishes, the hopes, the confidence, the predictions of the small band of true friends" just as Mr. Ramsay reaches the end of his journey to the lighthouse and Lily completes the painting inspired by Mrs. Ramsay. The parallel between the completion of the painting and the journey reflects that "art triumphs over life and life triumphs over it."

8

Untouchable by Mulk Raj Anand

Untouchable is the first novel of Mulk Raj Anand. He is a progressive writer for whom the novel takes the form of crusade against the evils of the society. He has his sympathies with the depressed and the underdog. Hence the central character in *Untouchable* is Bakha as Munoo is the central character in *The Coolie*. In his preface to the second edition of *Two Leaves and a Bud*, Anand writes:

> "All these heroes, as the other men and women who had emerged in my novels and short stories, were dear to me because they were the reflection of the real people, I had known during my childhood and youth. As I was only repaying the debt of gratitude I owed them for much of the inspiration they had given me to mature into manhood, when I began to interpret their lives. *They were flesh of my flesh and blood of my blood* and obsessed me with the way in which certain human beings obsess an artist's soul. And I was doing no more than what a writer does when he seeks to interpret the truth for the realities of his life."

Although born in one of the higher castes his father, Lal Chand Anand, served in the Indian Army rising to be a *Subedar* and Mulk Raj Anand as a child had mixed with the children of the sweepers attached to his father's regiment and such associations across caste division had continued during his boyhood and youth. These early playmates and friends became with necessary imaginative idealization and transformation, the heroes of his first novel. Thus the novels of Mulk Raj

Anand present the portrait of living characters. There is a strong realism in his novels. He has an empathetic insight into the heart and mind of his characters. As Munoo in *Coolie,* he sets up the character of Bakha in *Untouchable.* He lets his characters live, act and speak for himself. There is no sentimental portrait, but the portrayal of characters in the real circumstances of life.

Though the characters in Anand's novels conduct themselves as individuals, they are also the members of the class they belong to. Bakha, like Munoo in *Coolie,* is not only the son of Jamadar, Lakha, but also a representative untouchable. Similarly, the novel is peopled by Sohini, the sister of Bakha, Havildar, Charat Singh, Hakim Saheb, Lachman, the washer woman, Gulabo, Gandhiji, the young poet, Iqbalnath Sarshar and playmates of Bakha, the individual representative of several classes of the society. There is no sentimentalisation. Anand employs the technique of contrast to present the various shades of classes and characters which form the warp and woof of the real world. Though Lakha and Bakha; the father and son both belong to the untouchable section of the society, the generation gap is discernible in the contrast of their characters. Lakha, the Jamadar of sweepers and latrine cleaners, *an old man,* represents the generation of untouchables who accepted the discriminating caste system as the law of the society which had to be obeyed. On the other hand, his son, a youth of eighteen belongs to the new generation who has drifted away from the old. Bakha is not an ordinary sweeper but fashionable one who has borrowed trousers and hat from Havildar Charat Singh copying the style of the *Sahibs.* He seethes with anger at his inability to retaliate against the upper caste people who discriminate and heap injustice against the low caste. He tells his father "we are mere dirt because we clean their dirt." There is the portrayal of the hypocrisy of the common people. They beat and abuse Bakha who polluted a high caste man in the market place and Pundit Kalinath with his cry of "Polluted" on his failure to molest Sohini. On the other hand, is Havildar Charat Singh who asks Bakha to light his *hookah* and bring his tea and offers a gift of hockey stick. Then the speeches of Mahatma Gandhi and the poet, Iqbalnath Sarshar are there who try to solve the problem of untouchability. They all suggest a society in a state of transition but without settling down in a particular direction.

Untouchable, like *Coolie* in the words of Edwin Muir is a "character" novel where macrocosm is reflected in the microcosm of Bakha's consciousness. Like Dickens, he has no laborious psychological or ideological preoccupations. His novels seem to emphasize the universal against the particular. If Munoo is all coolies, Bakha is all untouchables. His characters arise out of their particular backgrounds. Their language also fixes them in their social background. For example, Lakha and other untouchables quite naturally flow out in abusive language like "illegally begotten", "rape sister", "rape mother." Anand is a committed writer and his characters in the novel depict the society of their time and rouse our conscience against hypocrisy injustice, cruelty and inhumanity.

CHARACTER OF BAKHA

Bakha is the central figure in Mulk Raj Anand's novel *Untouchable.* The novel focuses on one day in the life of Bakha, suggesting the repetition of such days to the end of his life. The novelist adopts the stream of consciousness technique in the novel so that every incident in the outside world is reflected in the mirror of Bakha's consciousness which is the centre of the novel.

Bakha is the able-bodied son of Lakha, the Jamadar of all the sweepers in the town of Bulandshahr. He himself works in barracks of the British regiment. *He enjoys a sense of superiority before other outcastes.* Though in the novel he is made to represent the untouchable section of the society, he is no ordinary scavenger, who is rude, uncouth and unclean." Bakha has great fascination for the English ways of living. He puts on the discarded English dress, boots, puttees, overcoat, jacket and buys Red-Lamp cigarettes. He also has a desire to speak "tishmish, tishmish" that the Sahibs speak. Though he is compelled to live a life of scavenger outside the boundary of the town in his dirty and dingy area and home, *he has a strong impulse to escape his sordid reality and forge out an identity on the imaginative plane.*

But the events in the outside world break his dream and remind that he is "mere dirt" because he clears their dirt. From this angle his craze for fashion is comic and pathetic at the same time.

Bakha is a representative of the oppressed untouchable caste. We have sympathy for his suffering as he meets with unjust treatment at the hands of the upper caste. But at the same time we realize that he is also different from his caste-men. He is neat and clean. He is fashionable. He is a champion of games specially hockey. He is uneducated. But he has a strong desire to receive education. He cannot seek admission in a school because untouchables are not admitted there so he pays one anna per lesson to two upper caste boys to teach him. *A strong desire to rise from his low position characterises Bakha while it is found absent in boys who have no handicaps.*

Bakha belongs to the new generation of the untouchable. He is different from his father, Lakha who considered his suffering as untouchable as his *lot* which could not be altered. Lakha could not conceive of retaliation against the upper caste. But whenever Bakha suffered, he was seized with the impulse to retaliate against cruelty and injustice. He considers upper caste as his 'superiors' like his father. Though he never carries out his retaliation, it is the only idea that gives him immediate mental satisfaction. Physically, he is superior to his oppressors who slapped him and abused him. He could easily push them away but he could not break the centuries old system which compelled him to passive suffering. *So in the highest moment of this strength, the slave in him asserted itself and he lapsed back wild with torture biting his lips ruminating his grievances.* Thus, he is a split personality and there is a conflict between his two selves — the slavish and the revengeful. The one thwarts the other. Thus there is the interplay of contradictory traits in his character.

It is for his suffering that he is attracted to Mahatma Gandhi and Christ. The fact that Sahibs and Mohammedans treat him like a human being but only the upper caste Hindus have contempt for him rankles in his mind. Otherwise he responds positively to acts of generosity. He forgets his humiliation when he is given a cup of tea by Havildar Charat Singh. His servility is the badge of his character. When he is given a new hockey stick by Havildar, he is not so much happy but proud of a gift from the upper caste men. He feels extremely miserable when he is snubbed even for his act of love and sympathy for the upper caste child or slapped by a man for touching him.

Bakha represents a part of the social history of India. He is a victim of social superstition of untouchability. He feels strongly against inhuman injustice meted out to him. But the protest of the individual is ineffective against the strength of the false morality of the established society. Hence, Bakha is presented as a feeble person who is unable to translate his resentment into action.

UNTOUCHABLE AS A PIECE OF PROPAGANDA

"I do not deny that art may be affirmed to serve ends beyond itself, but art is not required to be aware if these ends, and indeed performs its function whatever that may be, according to various theories of value better by indifference to them" says T.S. Eliot in his article, "The Function of Criticism," while dealing with the difference between criticism and creation. When the artist is conscious of the ends his art is going to serve, the art is likely to promote the ends by exaggerating, overstating or overemphasizing the problem — and turn into a piece of propaganda. We can examine Mulk Raj Anand's novel *Untouchable* in the light of the foregoing criteria.

Mulk Raj Anand does not believe in art for art's sake. He is a committed artist. He believes in purposive art. He is committed to the task of highlighting the plight of the downtrodden in his novels *Untouchable* and *The Coolie*. James Joyce's novel *Ulysses* presents one day in the life of hero.

Anand presents one day in the life of Bakha who belongs to the outcaste of sweepers and latrine cleaners. The day breaks and the life for Bakha, the son of Lakha begins in Bulandshahr. It suggests that the life of Bakha is just the repetition of the experience that he goes through in a day.

Anand's portrayal of the society in *Untouchable* is a realistic picture of the Hindu society in the pre-independence era. Anand had the first hand knowledge of the life of the untouchable. He knew some of them as his playmates in childhood as sweepers were attached to the regiment where his father was employed. His portrayal of the untouchables in the Indian society has a ring of authenticity. This is perhaps why E.M. Forster remarks "*Untouchable* could have been written by an Indian who observed from the outside. No European, however, sympathetic, could have created the character of Bakha, because he would not have known enough about his troubles. And no untouchable could have written the book because he would have been involved in indignation and self-pity." Anand objectively creates the character of Bakha and places him amid the realistic circumstances of life in the Hindu society with an empathetic insight into the soul of his character with all his humiliation and torment. The novel presents a chain of events and their impression on the mind of Bakha. The pollution episode in the market place, the molestation of Sohini at the temple and the like are created with complete detachment. There is no exaggeration, distortion or moralising. In the words of Saros Cawosjee "What immediately strikes the reader is the gentle and balanced writing." The picture of exploitation and subhuman treatment of the untouchable outcaste is completed with the molestation of Sohini by Pundit Kalinath.

The writer does not sacrifice truth and realism in the cause of enlistment of sympathy for the suffering of his hero. He presents the Hindu society in a state of transition. The multiple face of truth forms the fabric of the novel while the pollution episode in the market place and Sohini's molestation underline the indignity, humiliation and inhuman subjugation of a section of humanity in the hypocritical Hindu society. The figure of

Havildar Charat Singh stands out for undiscriminating acceptance of all humanity. He is uncontaminated by caste prejudice and asks Bakha to take pieces of coal from the kitchen for his hubble-bubble and pour tea in Bakha's pan. There is no sentimentality or idealization of the hero. There is balance and propriety in the attitude of the writer. But the artistic restraint seems to falter in the last part of the novel. Too much space has been devoted to the Bakha-Hutchinsen episode, the long speech of the poet, Iqbal Nath Sarshar with the predilection for the machine as the solution of the problem and the appearance of Mahatma Gandhi on the scene. The artistic reticence breaks down to accommodate the propagation of a particular point of view for the solution. The committed writer is in evidence in *Untouchable* more than in *The Coolie* and seems to take on the form of propaganda as the writer is conscious of the ends his art is going to serve.

Discuss *Untouchable* as a realistic piece of fiction

Mulk Raj Anand is a realist. While the writers wrote about the upper class or middle class life, none of them cared to produce realistic or naturalistic fiction after the manner of a Balzac or a Zola. It was Mulk Raj Anand who was associated with the progressive writers' movement of the thirties and turned his fictional focus on the plight of the untouchable in the figure of Bakha, a sweeper and latrine cleaner as he deals with the life of the coolie in *Coolie.*

Anand's novel, *Untouchable* is a realistic piece of fiction. Its selection of the subject-matter is one day in the life of a sweeper and latrine-cleaner, Bakha is itself realistic. It suggests the life of Bakha to be a repetition of similar days one after another. *Untouchable* presents the realities of the life of the untouchable without any glorification. Bakha, the anti-hero of *Untouchable* belongs to the outcaste colony of Bulandshahr which is situated outside the city where the high-caste Hindus live. It is a colony of mudwalled cottages inhabited by scavengers, leather workers, the washermen, the barbers etc. Bakha also lives with his father, brother and sister in a small-roomed, dark and dingy cottage: "The absence of a drainage system, and, through the rains of various seasons, made of the quarter a marsh which gave out the most offensive smell. The ugliness, the squalor and the misery which lay within it an uncongenial place to live in."

It is almost a photographic depiction of the outcaste colony with its "lane soiled by the dirt and filth of the public latrines situated about it, the odour of the hides and skins of dead carcasses left to dry on its banks." Prof. Nagrajan rightly points out that "Anand sees life in the raw and exposes it mercilessly, flesh, wounds, blood and all [...] shedding sentimentalism and writes with a touch of scorn of social and economic inequalities."

Mulk Raj Anand, like Arundhati Roy, exposes the inhumanity of the caste system of untouchability and religious hypocrisy. While Arundhati Roy depicts the Christian society in India, Mulk Raj Anand depicts the Hindu society in pre-Independence India. Bakha, the central figure of the novel is the eighteen-year old son of Lakha, the Jamadar of the sweepers. There is great naturalistic and realistic accuracy. Bakha is shown as cleaning three rows of latrines in the cantonment. There is a photographic fidelity about the picture that convinces us at once, though it also overwhelms us by its cumulative ferocity and force of detail. K.R.S. Iyengar compares Anand with Dickens in his task of effectively exposing certain social evils. Anand evokes powerfully the pity of being a member of the untouchable caste in the world of the high-caste Hindus. Born unclean, Bakha pollutes a high-caste man with his touch. As a result, he stands surrounded by a crowd which is "without a shadow of pity for his remorse" and "stands unmoved without heeding his apologies. The crowd takes a sort of sadistic delight in watching him cower under the abuses and curses of its spokesman." Bakha is slapped and his "much treasured jalebies are scattered in the dust." The fault of Bakha is that he had forgotten the duty of announcing his arrival and "was moving like a Lat Saheb" for which he is cut to size. Untouchability emerges in this scene as a means of domination of the highest Hindus over the lower caste. It is a means of forcing them to a life of indignity. The other significant realistic account of the society in the novel focuses on untouchability in connection with Sohini, the sister of Bakha. Pundit Kalinath who asks Sohini to sweep the courtyard is not polluted by Sohini's touch when he molests her. He gets polluted only when she refuses to yield to his lust. Here Anand throws light on the hypocrisy in the practice of untouchability. Untouchables are touchable for the gratification of lust but otherwise remain untouchable. Bakha's angry reaction is recorded in these words, "we are dirt because we clean their dirts."

Mulk Raj Anand's characterisation is also realistic. He does not divide his characters in black and white. He does not idealise his central character, Bakha, though he is different from ordinary scavengers with his craze for fashion. If Pundit Kalinath represents the hypocrisy of the high-caste Hindus, Havildar Charat Singh is far above caste prejudices and gifts Bakha a hockey stick and asks him to light his tobacco. He inspires respect for himself in the heart of Bakha. Mahatma Gandhi and the poet, Iqbalnath Sarshar oppose untouchability. Lakha, the father of Bakha does not react against untouchability like Bakha. He accepts it fully remembering the kindness of Hakim Sahebs and others. Thus the difference between Bakha and Lakha reflects the generation gap.

Not only Anand creates realistic scenes and characters, he allocates language to his characters according to their standing in life. The low-caste people, uneducated as they are, speak a language packed with abuses and swearwords. Mulk Raj Anand translates them directly into English, for example "rape-sister", "rape-mother", "son of a pig", "illegally begotten" etc. Thus life in the lower stratum of the society with its naturalistic details are present. In the words of C.D. Narsimhiah "we should learn not to be shocked by these swear-words which abound in Anand's novel and must abound if they are to reflect life faithfully." The other words which portray the peculiar Indian ethos are "accha", "salam", "huzoor" etc. They build up the Indian atmosphere realistically. We note realism in the subject-matter, its presentation, atmosphere, characterization and language.

9

Macbeth by Shakespeare

Shakespearian tragic heroes are not like the heroes of the Restoration or heroic tragedy where there is all admiration for the hero. In the Shakespearian tragic world, the heroes are not all white nor the villains, all black. Nor the attitude of the dramatist is to allow his audience to reduce its attitude to simple approval and disapproval. Shakespearian tragedy, from this point of view, has affinities with Greek tragedy. Greek tragedy envisages a moral order. Justice had to be maintained by the punishment of the protagonist. But the protagonist was linked to the audience by the closest ties of sympathy. The protagonist had therefore to be so developed as to appear to the audience both the hero and the criminal. Greek tragedy called for the dramatist and the audience to sympathise with and yet concur in the destruction of the heroes. Similarly, in the Shakespearian tragedy, the specific conflict exists on a deeper level than the struggle of the protagonist with other characters or fate. A conflict is set up in the mind of the reader or audience himself — a conflict between the impulse to condemn the protagonist as he breaks the moral laws in which the audience believes and the impulse to sympathise with him in his struggle.

Our attitude to Macbeth is also complex as he is the most mature product of Shakespeare's imagination. Though he has the qualities of a villain, he is the hero of the play as Shylock in *The Merchant of Venice* is a villain towards whom readers feel a little sympathetic. We condemn Macbeth when he breaks the moral laws to realize his ambition and sympathise with him in his struggle. He becomes the symbol of mankind with his strength and weaknesses.

Macbeth is the kinsman and a general of king Duncan of Scotland. He is "the worthiest cousin and "Bellona's bridegroom" as he is able to put down the rebellion against the king. He is faithful, loyal, noble, brave and dutiful. He is made the Thane of Glamis and Thane of Cawdor by the king. He buys golden opinion from others and wears new honours with their newest gloss.

Macbeth is ambitious and witches have fired his ambition with the prophecies of the future. The witches are gone but he is absorbed in his imagination of the future. Macbeth has just put down the uprising against the king and the murder of the king is the only way to secure the golden future for himself. In this way, he can become the king of Scotland. He does not want to break the image he has just created of himself. He is in conflict with the circumstances and himself. He is propelled by the witches and Lady Macbeth towards something he does not want to proceed to. This conflict in Macbeth is a prolonged one and commands our sympathy. Macbeth experiences the qualms of conscience in breaking the triple trust of the subject kinsman and host. He considers the possible consequences of his act and shrinks from it. He has no desire to proceed further in this business. His consideration of the moral implication of this act also takes away his power to act. His mind becomes the seat of conflicting impulses for and against murder.

Left to himself, Macbeth cannot act. He moves like a pendulum between the two points of his desire. Lady Macbeth is conscious of the fact that Macbeth is too full of the milk of human kindness to catch the nearest way to success. She takes care to remove this obstacle in the way. With her iron will she drives Macbeth to the realisation of his half-hearted desire. When his mind is set for murder, he sees blood stained dagger in the air. The impact of the act of murder on Macbeth is immediate. While Lady Macbeth remains quite undisturbed, he loses his balance of mind. He suddenly becomes conscious of the magnitude of his crime to see his blood-stained hand.

He hears a voice that Macbeth has murdered sleep and that Macbeth will sleep no more. When he gets Banquo murdered, he is haunted by the ghost of Banquo in the banquet scene. For Macbeth who is a military general and who has killed numberless soldiers in the battlefield, the murder of a sleeping old man like Duncan is an unnerving experience. After the murder of Banquo, for sometimes, he loses his balance of mind. Macbeth cannot bring himself to commit the immoral act. But subsequent murders show that Macbeth has steeled his breast against tender feelings. It is the result of Macbeth's habituation to crime.

Macbeth is psychologically a weak character. He needed the support of Lady Macbeth at the time of his first murder. When he becomes king of Scotland, he needs assurances of the future security from the witches and then hangs on to the last shred of hope. As every tomorrow turns into today, his hopes are dashed to pieces. Thus he is a disillusioned person. He considered kingship the ornament of life. But he fails to get from kingship what he had expected. He loses his peace of mind and honour. He realises that the witches have deceived him by keeping the word of promise to his ears and breaking it to his hopes. His future is foreknown but he does not give up the unequal fight against fate. Thus he establishes the dignity of man in his struggle like Oedipus. At this point, he wins our sympathy.

Macbeth is a murderer. But before the immoral act of murder he is trapped in a moral conflict and after the act he loses the balance of his mind for some time. He is trammelled up in the sound and fury of the consequences of his act. In his fears and hopes during his struggle as well as his conflicts he remains human. More than king Lear, Othello or Hamlet, Macbeth becomes the symbol of mankind as the conflict between morality and immorality and consequent psychological impact on his psyche is much more heightened in Macbeth than in any other Shakespearian tragedy. Macbeth is rooted in the tradition of the morality plays where the central character in the play is Everyman.

COMMENT ON THE USE OF THE SUPERNATURAL IN *MACBETH*

The supernatural is part of the framework of the Shakespearian tragedy, *Macbeth*. Shakespeare uses the supernatural devices to indicate the course of future events in *Julius Caesar* and *Antony and Cleopatra* also. But in no other tragedy the supernatural powers are so prominent as in *Macbeth*. The supernatural powers are the superhuman powers which appear in the plays to suggest the predetermined patterns of events in the human life. The pattern is not of our making. Yet Shakespeare allows a limited free will in this tragic picture of the universe. Only in the major tragedies, Shakespeare preserves the precarious balance of fate and free will.

The play, *Macbeth* opens with the scene of the weird sisters where they decide amid thunder and lightning to meet Macbeth upon the heath. The weird sisters are not subjective or symbolic as the Eumenides in Aeschylus. Not only once or twice they appear in the play, the spell they weave goes beyond the fourth act. The way they seem to be involved with the events suggests the picture of a world where man is subject to cosmic forces. It is argued that the weird sisters do not plant the seed of evil in Macbeth and that they have no power over the innocent and that love and hatred are human response. It is a fact that they do not plant the seed of evil in Macbeth but they certainly fertilize it by holding out hopes in the future. The mind of Macbeth registers a deeper influence of the prophecies as the witches have announced in the first scene their intention to meet Macbeth and to influence him. Banquo is not their target, so he exhibits complete freedom from their spell.

Three is a magical number and magically the three witches know all about the past, the present and the future. Nature seems subordinated to their influence. The immediate fulfilment of their prophecy that Glamis will be Cawdor lends credibility to other prophecies which they make. They play both the role of temptation and retribution. The foreknowledge of each step in the action puts the witches in a different category from other tragedies of Shakespeare. It seems to imply that it is not the diseased will of Macbeth that leads to the disturbance of the order rather it is the fortune that infects the individual and frame of things. The impression of predestination is strongly built up. The supernatural is not only a tempting agent, it is also a source of retribution. "There are irony and nemesis in the appearance of the murdered Banquo at the feast to which he had been invited, as a ghost, and in the vision of Kings headed by Malcolm and terminated by the descendants of Banquo, who smiles upon me and points at them as his." There is retribution in the voice that cries "sleep no more", "Macbeth hath murdered sleep", "Glamis hath murdered sleep" and in the sleepwalking scene where the suppressed images of horror unfold themselves in the mind of Lady Macbeth.

Night which is invoked both by Macbeth and Lady Macbeth wraps them round. The murder takes place at night and nature is in upheaval. The raven is hoarse that croaks the fatal entrance of Duncan, horses of Duncan eat each other. Strong winds blow, owls shriek. Lamentings are heard in the air. Strange screams of death and accents terrible rend the air. They are all the shadows of the coming event determined by the supernatural forces which shape the fate of men. Fall of monarchs or murder of kings is always attended with supernatural portents in Shakespeare. It builds the impression that Macbeth and Lady Macbeth are tangled in the net which is not of their own making.

But this is the only one side of the picture. The equilibrium of the major Shakespearian tragedy rests on the tension of fate and free will. In Greek tragedy, for example, in *Oedipus*, the pattern of events is foreordained. Only the character is free in his thoughts and feelings to react to it. In the Shakespearian tragedy action is not separable from thoughts and passions. Rather it directly issues from them. That is why Macbeth and Lady Macbeth in spite of the prophecy do not give the impression of an automation. The whole action of the play revolves round the ambition of Macbeth to become king. He is passionately drawn to the idea of murdering king Duncan and yet his reasoning — that Duncan has been so noble and clear in his office, he is his guest, relative and king, that he can do all that may become a man — takes away the impulse to act. Yet he is urged on by the persuasions of Lady Macbeth. Thus Macbeth and Lady Macbeth are so convincingly drawn as human beings, as in actuality, it appears always that freedom of choice exists even though it be that the overall pattern is not of their own making. He is not responsible for the pattern of events but for the initiation of the evil chain or release of evil forces latent in a situation. The witches tempt. Lady Macbeth persuades. But Macbeth acts himself. If we feel that his sin is decreed, we also feel that temptation could be resisted. The force of ambition that drives him to action seems to be the force of fate. Having once initiated an action, he is trammelled up in its consequences. The more he dives in his crime, the more he loses his humanity and the course of action seems set for him. The damnation that Macbeth meets is his own earning. Therefore, it will not be wrong to conclude that Shakespeare has drawn Macbeth and Lady Macbeth in such a way that there is only one line of conduct possible for them in the particular situation in which they find themselves. For them it is the doom-in-character rather than the doom on the house brought about by the supernatural agencies. Shakespeare is able to preserve this equilibrium of fate and free choice in his major tragedies. In his romance a providence safeguards the character from the ultimate harm.

CONSIDER LADY MACBETH AS THE FOURTH WITCH

The first scene of Macbeth introduces three witches. They greet Macbeth with the future prophecies and kindle the royal hope in Macbeth. Macbeth is lost in the thoughts of the future and wants Banquo's comments on the witches' prophecies. In the opinion of Banquo, they are "the instruments of darkness." They give Macbeth the knowledge of the future and make him restless to jump to the life to come. They kindle the dormant ambition in him and tempt him to the path of evil. It is the temptation of kingship, the knowledge of the future that stirs Macbeth's imagination to catch the nearest way to success.

Without this knowledge of the future, Macbeth could not have thought of acting at all. It is the temptation of the witches which impels him on. Yet he lacks the will to translate the idea into a reality. Left to himself, Macbeth would not have acted. Lady Macbeth is the fourth witch in so far as she tempts to the act of murder. She acts as the spur and pushes him on to action. She perceives that Macbeth is "too full of the milk of human kindness to catch the nearest way" and decides to chastise him with "the valour of her tongue." The phrase, "the valour of the tongue" is significant. "Valour" is the quality which can be associated not with Lady Macbeth but only with her tongue. It is quite in keeping with the nature of things that she boasts that she would have dashed the brain of the child that sucks if she had sworn as Macbeth. It is the example of the valour of her tongue.

Challenging the manliness of Macbeth she herself decides to do the deed. She comes back to report "Had he not resembled my father as he slept, I had done it." Though Lady Macbeth pushes Macbeth to the act of murder and completes the action initiated by the three witches, her nature is essentially feminine. The sight of the sleeping old king awakens in her filial compassion for the parent. It is "the valour of her tongue" that makes the impression of her being a pure agent of evil like the witches. But an objective assessment of Lady Macbeth reverses the judgment. She strains her real self to "unsex" her so that she can put on temporarily the role of the fourth witch. It is always to be kept in mind that this "unsexing" of Lady Macbeth is exhibited only on the plane of words and not on the plane, of action. There is a wide gap between Lady Macbeth and her valour of tongue.

Macbeth is one of the most sensitive and imaginative characters of Shakespeare but Lady Macbeth is equally unimaginative. Macbeth foresees the consequences of his action but she could not think of its implications in the future. Macbeth thought "all great Neptune's ocean will not wash this blood/ clean from my hand." She had said that "a little water clears us of the deed." She could not see the blood that she washed clean from the hand would stick to her soul. She is unable to sleep by night. She rises from her bed every night and re-enacts the entire scene of murder. She bears in her mind the torturing memories of her past that will not let her sleep. She could not free herself from the smell of blood: "All the perfumes of Arabia will not sweeten this little hand," that she had thought would be cleared with a little water. Lady Macbeth had unsexed herself temporarily in order to realise the ambition of her husband. But for it she had to pay dearly with the peace of her mind. Macbeth and Lady Macbeth were partners in crime. But they had drifted apart and Lady Macbeth was forced to live alone with the weight of guilt on her mind. It leads to her pitiable death. Her life is the tale of an unimaginative soul. She is not the fourth witch but a tragic feminine character who could not look into the seeds of her action and so she had to reap the tragic harvest of its consequences. She took upon herself a task for her husband which proved too heavy for her. Her personality broke down under the strain and she met a tragic end.

CHARACTER OF MACBETH

Macbeth is the most mature product of Shakespeare's imagination. He is a complex character. Though he has the qualities of a villain, he is the hero of the play. He is a murderer yet we have sympathy for him. Our attitude to him is also complex. We condemn him when he breaks the moral laws to realize his ambition and sympathise with him in his struggles. He becomes the symbol of mankind with his strength and weakness.

Macbeth is a general and kinsman of King Duncan of Scotland. He is "the worthiest cousin" and Bellona's bridegroom as he is able to put down the rebellion against the kingdom. He is entitled thane of Glamis and thane of Cawdor by the King. He is faithful, loyal, noble and dutiful. Naturally he buys golden opinion from others and wears new honours with their newest gloss.

Macbeth is ambitious and his dormant ambition is stirred

up by the prophecy of the three witches. He is highly sensitive. The witches are gone but they have activated his mental process and he is completely lost in his imagination of the future. Macbeth is the man who has just put down the uprising against King Duncan. The murder of the king is an idea from which his conscience revolts. He does not want to break the image he has created for himself. He experiences qualms of conscience in breaking the triple trust of the subject, kinsman and host. He considers the possible consequences of his act and shrinks from it. He has no desire to proceed further in this business. His consideration of the moral implications of this act also takes away his power to act. His mind is very tense. It becomes the seat of conflicting impulses for and against murder.

Left to himself, Macbeth cannot act. He moves like a pendulum between the two points of his desire. Lady Macbeth is conscious that Macbeth is "too full of the milk of human kindness" to catch the nearest way to success. She takes care of him so that he does not stop midway. With her iron will, she pushes Macbeth to the realization of his half-hearted desire.

Macbeth is one of the most sensitive and imaginative characters ever created by Shakespeare. His mind is teeming with images. He has a very strong power for vivid imagination and a seismographic sensitivity to register the slightest vibration. When his mind is set for murder he sees blood-stained dagger in the air with its hilt towards him. He can foresee the consequence of his murder. The impact of the act of murder on Macbeth is also immediate. While Lady Macbeth apparently remains quite undisturbed, he loses his balance of mind. He suddenly becomes conscious of the magnitude of his crime to see his blood-stained hand. He hears a voice that Macbeth has murdered sleep, and that Macbeth will sleep no more.

The first murder by Macbeth has been an uphill task for Macbeth. But he is later so habituated to crime that he needs no elaborate preparation in planning the murder of Banquo. Later murders show that he is slowly hardened in crime. It is the progress of Macbeth in crime who was "too full of the milk of human kindness." On the other hand, Lady Macbeth who was quite quiet now betrays a deep sense of guilt, breaks down under the strain and dies.

Macbeth and Lady Macbeth had started as partners in crime. But they drift apart as both are imprisoned in the loneliness of their mind. While she suffers as the scenes of murder enact themselves in her mind, Macbeth is trammelled up in the sound and fury of the consequences of his act. He has no time to even grieve for her, when she dies.

Macbeth is the king of Scotland. But he is not at peace. He seeks the help of the witches to have a sense of security. He becomes doubly sure of his safety to think that no woman born man can do him any harm. Macbeth is psychologically a weak character. He needs help from Lady Macbeth at the time of murder. After that he loses his nerves. When he becomes king of Scotland he needs assurances of the future from the witches and then he hangs on to the last shred of hope. Every tomorrow turns into today, his hopes are shattered and in the end he is a disillusioned man.

Macbeth loses under the impression of gaining. He considered kingship the ornament of life but when he becomes king, he feels he has failed to achieve what he had expected from it. He loses his humanity, his peace of mind, loyalty, honour and instead gets mouth-honour and curses not loud but deep. Macbeth sees the witches in the true light in the end, when he realizes that the juggling fiends have deceived him by keeping the word of promise to his ears and breaking it to his hopes. Life is emptied of significance for him. He is lonely but he clings to life at the time of losing it. His future is foreknown. But he does not give up the unequal fight against fate. Thus he establishes the dignity of man in his struggle like Oedipus. At this point, he wins our sympathy and admiration. Macbeth remains the most interesting, sensitive, imaginative and complete character of Shakespeare.

"Macbeth is the tragedy of ambition" — comment.

Or

Macbeth defines a particular kind of evil that results from the lust of power — Discuss.

Macbeth is the tragedy of ambition. It presents an evil which is defined against the background of positive values which are one with life. Against this background, Macbeth's evil appears unnatural and hostile to the order and peace of nature. The very first scene points to the disorder in nature as thunder is disjoined from lightning. The disorder in nature reflects the disorder in the moral order of man where the fog prevails in the air and it is not possible to distinguish clearly fair from foul and foul from fair. The theme of the reversal values, the conflict between appearance and reality and its unnaturalness is introduced powerfully by the first scene. The play only translates it into full poetic and dramatic terms.

The witches who are "the instruments of darkness" provide the necessary fire for the flaring-up of Macbeth's ambition. He does not wait for the time when fate will crown him king. He jumps to "the life to come." The speech of Lady Macbeth echoes the same note:

> Great Glamis! Worthy Cawdor
> Greater than both, by the all hail hereafter!
> The letters have transported me beyond
> This ignorant present and I feel now
> The future in the instant. (Act I, scene V)

Instead of moving naturally from the present to the future, jumping beyond the present and holding "the future in the instant" suggests the idea of the overreacher. Francis Furgusson underlines the same theme in his essay on *Macbeth* where he insists on the image of "outrunning the pauser, reason" in the speech of Macbeth:

> "The expedition of my violent love
> Outran the pauser, reason."

It describes the action of the play. The murder of Duncan is also an act of violation of reason as there is every reason against the murder. As it is an act against reason, it is an evil that implies disorder and chaos in the broader and deeper sense. As such it introduces disorder at all levels. It is the violation of the natural time as Macbeth wrests the future into the present. It is the violation of the humanity of Macbeth as Lady Macbeth had feared the human nature of Macbeth which is "too full of the milk of human kindness." It is the violation of the bond between the king and the subject, the guest and the host, the bond between one relative and another. Macbeth is sharply sensitive and imaginative as he is fully aware of the horror of the deed he is going to commit "We but teach/ Bloody instructions which being taught, return to plague the inventor." The unnaturalness of Macbeth's evil is defined and judged against the background of human nature. The essential characteristic of that nature — its capacity for intimate dependence on relationship is powerfully evoked.

> The service and loyalty I owe
> In doing it plays itself your highness part
> Is to receive our duties and our duties
> Are to your throne and children, children and servant.
> Which do but what they should by doing every thing.
> Safe toward your love and honour.

The ties that bind one to another form the recurrent reference of background against which Macbeth's evil is judged. The words "duty", "host", "guest", "state", "throne", "kinsmen", "thanes", "subject", "children" frequently recur in the play and references to the condition of positive human living in words like "concord", "peace", "unity", "services", "loyalty" are equally frequent in the play. Macbeth had wanted to trammel up the consequences, to disjoin action from the consequence. The consequences of the unnatural deeds are natural. The remark of the doctor of Lady Macbeth that "unnatural deeds do breed unnatural troubles" is relevant here.

The greatest irony of Macbeth is that under the illusion of gaining, he has lost. His commerce with phantoms has brought him to the point when we can say, that his life is emptied of significance. "Nothing is but what is not" is the text of Macbeth.

Macbeth had knifed the bond of relationship. He must face loneliness in consequence.

I have lived long enough, my way of life
Is fallen to the sere, the yellow leaf
And that which should accompany old age
As honour, I love, obedience, troops of friends
I must not look to have, but in their stead
Curses, not loud but deep, mouth-honour.

"Mouth-honour" ironically echoes the suggestions of Lady Macbeth, "Look like the innocent flower but be the serpent under it." Macbeth has violated the natural order of time, so the beat of time has become meaningless for him and life becomes a tale told by an idiot. The play ends as the natural heir to the throne, Malcolm has been restored and illusions have been dispelled. Life has renewed itself as before. The speech of Macbeth when he has reached the last point of disillusionment makes a judgment on the values exemplified by the life of Macbeth himself.

And be these juggling fiends no more believed
That palter with us in a double sense
That keep the word of promise to our ears and break
To our hopes.

Macbeth is the tragedy of ambition. The ambition of Macbeth is defined as unnatural evil that violates natural bonds and values. As a consequence, the life of Macbeth becomes "a tale told by an idiot," full of sound and furry signifying nothing. It is the tragic harvest that Macbeth reaps after he has sown the seed of ambition.

Bring out the significance of the opening scene in *Macbeth*

Shakespeare is one of the greatest poets and dramatists of the English language. His tragedies are well-constructed. There is a beginning, a middle and an end. There is an organic growth in his play. Therefore, the first scene in a Shakespearian tragedy assumes great significance. The first scene of a Shakespearian tragedy strikes the keynote of the play. It is pregnant with symbolic suggestiveness. The subsequent scenes fully work out the implications in terms of events and actions and images. The opening scene of *Macbeth* is no exception. It is a scene of only thirteen lines. But it sums up the tragedy of *Macbeth* as well as its atmosphere.

This scene, begins with thunder and lightning. Three witches appear on the scene. This scene introduces us to the supernatural agents who play a significant role in the tragedy. The witches plan to meet Macbeth. Tragedy is set in motion when the meeting takes place. Thus, the impression of predestination is built up strongly. It suggests supernatural supervision over the human drama. The entire scene is symbolic and prophetic and moves on line by line to its dramatic close.

The first witch puts the question "When shall three we meet again/ In thunder, lightning or in rain?" The question is loaded with symbolic connotations. Thunder and lightning are not separate from each other in nature. But in this particular question natural elements disintegrate. Thunder is separate from lightning. It suggests an unnatural disturbance in the world of nature. Nature in the Shakespearian tragedy always reflects the human world. The disintegration of the natural elements reflects the tragic world of Macbeth. The tragedy of Macbeth involves the break-up of natural relations. The reply to the second question refers to "hurlyburly" and "battle". The disturbance in the rhythm of nature is connected with the hurlyburly in the human world. Before three witches disappear in the air they speak together:

> Fair is foul and foul is fair
> Hover through the fog and filthy air.

These words precisely define the nature of "hurlyburly" in the human world. The first line states the tragic process of the fair Macbeth turning into the foul. It suggests reversal and confusion of moral values in the sound and fury of Macbeth's tragedy. It also implies a conflict of moral values. The second line symbolically presents the atmosphere in which *Macbeth* is enveloped. The air is described as "filthy" and full of "fog." The vision in the foggy air must be blurred. It accounts for the conflict of appearance and reality as well as confusion of moral values.

If we apply the symbols to the world of *Macbeth*, the implications reveal themselves. Macbeth is the kinsman, subject and the host of king Duncan. His role in all the three capacities is reversed. Macbeth has a clear vision of right and wrong, service, duty and loyalty. But it is befogged by the thoughts of the murder. Though Macbeth appears to be kinsman, subject and the host of king Duncan, he plays none of these roles. The relation between the appearance and the reality is broken. Duncan is murdered by Macbeth who is referred to by Duncan as "valiant cousin" and "worthy gentleman." Lady Macbeth's instruction to Macbeth is to "look like the innocent flower/ But be the serpent under it."

In this way, the first scene of *Macbeth* is the microcosm of the tragedy. It sums up the tragic process as well as the atmosphere of the tragedy. It is pregnant with symbolic suggestiveness which are worked out in terms of events and images throughout the tragedy.

10

Othello by Shakespeare

Othello is the tragedy that hinges on the handkerchief. It is the view of Thomas Rymer. *Othello,* unlike other tragedies of Shakespeare is a domestic tragedy. The range of tragedy is not as wide as that of *King Lear, Macbeth* and *Hamlet.* It operates within the narrow range of the domestic life. It is a tragedy that strikes the personal life of Othello and Desdemona and its effect does not flow beyond the narrow range to the world outside, to the entire kingdom of Venice. The tragedy of *Hamlet, King Lear* or *Macbeth* is a personal tragedy also no doubt, but it involves a larger world, the state of Scotland, Denmark or France. The disorder or anarchy is introduced into the harmonious rhythm of the life of Othello and Desdemona only unlike *Hamlet, King Lear* or *Macbeth.*

The three important counters of the tragedy are Othello, Desdemona and Iago. With the opening of the play, we are aware of the adventurous marriage of Desdemona with Othello. Othello is a black, middle-aged Moor and Desdemona, a white, Venetian beauty. Desdemona had heard her father listening to the romantic tale of his adventurous life of war, imprisonment and strange escapes. As her attention was divided between, listening and domestic duties, she requests Othello to pour out once more the strange adventures of his life for her. She is charmed by such an adventurous life "I saw Othello's visage in his mind." Against the traditions of her family, race and country, she achieves a clandestine marriage with Othello which she is not shy to defend. She cannot wait while Othello is sent to Cyprus to defend against the possible attack of Turks.

She boldly seeks the permission of the Duke to accompany him there. When Iago observes Othello and Desdemona in Cyprus, he is irked by the music of their harmonious relationship which he decides to turn into discord.

Iago's cynicism, as Coleridge points out, is nothing but "the motive hunting of a motiveless malignity." He cannot believe in and stands to oppose the beauty of human values of love and fidelity represented by Othello and Desdemona and of dutifulness that Cassio stands for. The calculation of Iago for the success of his plan is based on his concept of the incongruous marriage of a middle-aged black Moor with a young white Venetian beauty. The middle-aged black Moor is Othello and the young, white Venetian beauty is Desdemona. Iago smells the seeds of infidelity in such a relationship and engrafts his imagination on to the mind of Othello. Othello begins to see things with his jaundiced eyes. This is why F.R. Leavis holds that Iago is not outside but inside Othello's mind — just a dramatic mechanism to precipitate the tragedy. But viewed in the perspective of Othello's character, Iago is more than a mechanism. Othello is a Moor employed in the service of the Venetian state. He is in the noble profession of a soldier who has a royal lineage, and who is proud of his splendid military prowess and career. He commands and relishes a language as majestically picturesque as his own background. His military prowess which he is proud of and which is so valuable in the battlefield turns into a demerit in his domestic or conjugal field. Othello, as a fine soldier, is a man of action rather than a man of thought. It is for being a soldier from top to toe that instead of pausing and scrutinising the facts he responds to Iago's suggestion like a robot and moves forward in his revenge like the currents of the Pontic sea. The handkerchief upon which the entire tragedy hinges supplies the ocular proof that Othello demands from Iago. The grip of Iago on Othello's mind, as critics have noted, is reflected in the animal imagery and the broken syntax of his language which now supersedes the former confident majestic march of his language.

The military background of Othello as well as his equally emotional commitment to the goddess of love and chastity, Desdemona is responsible for the tragedy of "Othello". Iago cannot believe in the continuance of the kind of incongruous relationship (as love is the lust of the blood only) in which Othello and Desdemona stand. While Iago transfers his imagination on to the mind of Othello, Desdemona cannot believe that Othello is made of "such base stuff as jealousy." Hence she takes no precaution and the handkerchief, the token of their mutual love, which is procured by Iago provides the ocular proof of infidelity. The handkerchief can form the ocular proof, for the kind of character as Othello is, with his military background, his life of action rather than of thought. It is not for nothing that Shakespeare stresses repeatedly the pride of Othello in his military skill which accords well with his credulity and swift speed of judgment and action. Like the end of all great tragedies when Desdemona is done to death, the faces of "honest Iago" and "devilish Desdemona" are revealed by the confession of Emilia, the wife of Iago, regarding handkerchief and the noble Moor at the time of his suicide asks to set down in records the tale of a person "who loved too well but not wisely."

CHARACTER OF IAGO

Shakespeare excels in the study of human nature. Keats admires Shakespeare for his negative capability, his ability to create an Imogen and an Iago at the same time. Through his creation of Iago, he has added to his study of human villainy. Iago is a villain and a class in himself.

Iago has puzzled critics, especially the main motive of Iago behind his machinations. F.R. Leavis holds that Iago is not a real, convincing character but a necessary dramatic mechanism to precipitate the tragedy in a dramatic action. But Iago is a real, convincing human character whose villainy is defined by Coleridge as "the motive-hunting of a motiveless malignity."

Iago is a person of twenty-eight years only. Yet he is devilish and cynical. Motive hunting for his motiveless malignity is present throughout the play. He tells Roderigo that he hates Othello because he never considered his claim to promotion. Later he says that he wants to take his vengeance on Othello because of Othello's liaison with his wife, Emilia. This is why A.C. Bradley says that "Iago did not clearly understand what was moving his desire, though he tried to give himself reasons for his action; even those that had some reality made but a small part of the motive force." Iago is, in fact, an egotist. He says that Cassio blocks his promotion, but he speaks the truth when he says that Cassio "hath a daily beauty in his life that makes me ugly." Herein lies the basic reason for Iago's hostility towards Cassio. When Cassio has so much "daily beauty in his life" to make Iago appear ugly, Othello and Desdemona have much more daily beauty to arouse the jealousy of Iago.

Dowden calls Iago "an absolute infidel." He does not mean that Iago is an atheist. He is an infidel in the sense that he does not believe in human values, beauty and morality in life. He believes reputation is an idle and most false imposition. He considers love as the lust of the blood. His crass sensibility cannot accept the finer things of life and values that impart a touch of beauty to human life.

Iago is a consummate villain. He has great intellectual powers. It is on account of his intellectual supremacy that he succeeds in achieving his negative aim. In the words of Herford, "The basis of his character is a union of absolute egoism with prodigious intellectual force." His intellect is diabolic. He is armed with the understanding of the weakness of Othello's character. He is sure that Othello will be led by the nose as the asses are, and he succeeds in his plan. Yet the prodigious diabolic intellect of Iago fails to foresee the reaction of his wife to his own plot. Iago is a great actor. It is for this capacity that he can present the honest image of himself to others. Iago is repeatedly addressed as "honest Iago" by Othello. It is on account of Iago's failure to understand the nature of his wife that he is unmasked in the last scene.

Time and again Iago has been compared with Shakespeare's

Richard III and Edmund of *King Lear*. But Edmund has a moment of compunction. Richards III has a dream of remorse. But Iago is never touched by remorse or qualms of conscience. Iago at one time says "I am nothing if not critical." By the term "critical" he means "satirical" or "cynical." His misogyny and misanthropy are the expression of his cynicism. Iago is the embodiment of evil. He reminds of Milton's Satan who says "Evil be thou my good." Othello says "I look down towards his feet but that's a fable. If thou be'est a devil, I cannot kill thee." Maud Bodkin in her book *Archetypal Patterns of Poetry* defines devil, "our tendency to represent in personal form the forces within and without us which threaten our supreme values" and feels convinced that Iago fully answers this description. The word "devil" occurs again and again in the play to suggest the devilish nature of Iago. Satan was envious of God because of his superiority. He hated Adam and Eve because of their sanctity. Iago is hostile to Othello and Desdemona because they represent the virtues and moral beauty that he himself denies. Adam and Eve lose their paradise. Othello and Desdemona lose their own on account of Iago.

IMAGERY IN *OTHELLO*

Shakespearian criticism was enriched by the imagist movement in English poetry. Imagery was the staple vehicle for poetic communication in the poetry of the Imagists. Quite naturally and logically works of art were approached through their images. Hence critical attention was directed to the imagery in the Shakespearian tragedies and *Othello* is no exception.

The poetic meaning of *Othello* like other Shakespearian tragedies depends on its imagery. It determines the general atmosphere and setting of the play. Several references to the sea and ships remind us of the background of Venice, the Mediterranean and Cyprus. As *Hamlet* emphasizes the images of physical corruption, *Macbeth*, sickness, *Othello* lays stress on the images of disgust which manifests itself through ferocious animals and insects. The images in *Hamlet, Macbeth* and *King Lear* take us far beyond the particular agonies of *Hamlet* or

Macbeth. But the images in *Othello* are closely attached to the particular characters and are not charged with universal significance.

Robert Heilman emphasizes the imagery of magic and witchcraft. When Brabantio is informed of the elopement and marriage of Desdemona, he tells Othello: "Damned thou art, thou hast enchanted her." He complains that Desdemona has been bound in "chains of magic." Brabantio complains to the Duke:

> She is all used, stol'n from me and corrupted
> By spells, and medicines bought of mountebanks;
> For nature so preposterously to err.
> Being not deficient, blind or lame of sense
> Sans witchcraft could not.

In his reply, Othello refers to the "drugs and charms" of love by which he "won" his daughter. Magic, superstition and "devil" figure prominently in *Othello*. It is also the magic of Iago's devilry that blinds Othello to the reality of Desdemona. Towards the end Othello refers to Iago as a devil and imagines his soul seized by fiends.

But Caroline Spurgeon is of the opinion that "the main image in Othello is that of animals in action, preying upon one another, mischievous, lascivious, cruel or suffering and through these, the general sense of pain and unpleasantness is much increased and kept constantly before us." There are recurrent images of flies, dogs, asses, a spider catching a fly, wolves, goats, monkeys and wild cats in the play. Othello refers to toads in a cistern, summer flies, ominous raven, crocodile tears, goats and monkeys. Lodovico refers to Iago as a viper. In *King Lear* there are references to animals which are ferocious *e.g.*, tiger, wolf, serpent, boar and sea monster which have grandeur and dignity. But in *Othello* the animals are low creatures like insects, flies and reptiles which have no grandeur. They symbolise sensual passion and disgust.

The other images significant in *Othello* is that of sea. Iago refers to himself as "belee'd and calmed" and also speaks of "chidden billows," "wind-shaked surge." Cassio speaks of guttered rocks, furious sea, determined to destroy the ship of Desdemona. The sea imagery also becomes powerful when Othello expresses his joy at the reunion with Desdemona.

> O My soul's joy
> If after every tempest come such calms
> May the winds blow till they have waken'd death.

He refers to the terrible nature of his revenge and compares his firm determination to "the icy current and compulsive course." Caroline Spurgeon refers to the image of smell. Iago refers to the marriage of Othello and Desdemona as something unnatural:

> "Oh! One may smell in such a will most rank.
> Foul disproportion, thoughts unnatural."

Othello compares his beloved to a lovely weed:

> O thou weed
> Who art so lovely fair and smell'st so sweet
> That the sense aches at thee, wouldst thou ne'er been born?

He also refers to Desdemona's sin so horrible as "Heaven stops the nose at it."

It cannot be denied that these images have their place in *Othello* but the images of preying, ensnaring, catching in a net are frequent in the play and hammer continuously on the theme of the play. Iago speaks about Cassio "with as little as web as this will I ensnare as great a fly as Cassio." Iago repeatedly harps upon this imagery while speaking of others: "My medicine work! Thus credulous foods are caught" and

> So will I turn her virtue into pitch
> And out of her goodness make the net
> That shall enmesh them all.

Thus the images in Othello weave a pattern which adds to the suggestive power of dramatic poetry in *Othello* as in other tragedies of Shakespeare.

CHARACTER OF DESDEMONA

Desdemona is the heroine of the Shakespearian tragedy, *Othello*. She is a unique product of Shakespeare's imagination. In the words of G. Wilson Knight, she is "at once divine and warmly human." The hallmark of her personality is soft gentleness which cannot only resent but cannot resist. Dr. Johnson has also emphasised it as the main streak of her personality.

Desdemona is full of feminine charm. Cassio describes her as "the most exquisite lady and another name for perfection." Othello, whose sense of beauty is never blurred, waxes eloquent even on the point of killing her. Desdemona's skin, he describes as "whiter" than snow and as smooth as "monumental alabaster." She is compared to a lovely rose. She is the cunning's pattern of excelling nature.

Before meeting with Othello, Desdemona is a modest and shy girl. She is described by her father as "a maiden never bold" of spirit so still and quiet that her motion/ Blushed at herself." But love brings about a change in her. She has the strength of Cordelia when she says, "My noble father, I do perceive here a divided duty." Desdemona exhibits this change as she puts her case both to her father and the senate with strong sense, courage and plain-speaking. She refutes the charge that Othello applied any form of magic to influence her. She defends her choice of Othello by saying that — "I saw Othello's visage in his mind."

Desdemona was attracted to Othello for his personal qualities. She transcended the limitations of the senses in her response to him. There is something spiritual about her love. She is full of the milk of human kindness. She is moved to pity when Othello tells the story of his adventures and sufferings. The sympathetic bond formed at this stage later turns into love. She is romantic by temperament. Othello appeals to her imagination. In spite of the remarkable incompatibility in age, colour and race she falls madly in love with him. She defies her father and leaves her hearth and home for the sake of her love.

Desdemona is perfectly innocent. She holds a very high opinion of the Moor that he is "made of no such baseness as jealous creatures are." But what she fails to understand is that he can be worked into a jealous frame of mind. She is so unsuspecting that she confides in Iago in her days of crisis. She does not suspect what is the cause of Othello's anger when he calls her "whore" and slaps her. She only tells Othello she does not deserve it.

Her only fault is the fineness of spirit or excess of gentleness. She goes out of the way to help a man in distress. She tells Cassio:

> If I do vow friendship, I'll perform it
> To the last article.

It is her tender solicitude for Cassio that brings about her tragedy. She is too mild. She suffers passively but does not react. When she comes to know Othello means to put her to death, she only requests to be allowed some time for prayer which is not granted. There is a fundamental difference between Desdemona and Emilia. Emilia knows when to obey and when to disobey her husband. But Desdemona only knows how to obey but does not know when to disobey the husband.

If Othello is an egoist, Desdemona has merged herself completely in her love. She actually practices what she says to her husband, "whatever you be, I am obedient." This is a peculiarly romantic quality of Desdemona. When Othello strikes her in Lodovico's presence, she does not even record her protest. She only says "I will not stay to offend you." She is stiffled. To Emilia's question "Who has done it?" She replies "Nobody, myself, farewell, commend me to my lord." She remains the supreme paragon of romantic love. Even in her death throes, she does not utter a single word against Othello who once appealed to her imagination. Iago has made a discord of Othello music, but completely failed to make a discord of Desdemona's love. The more harsh and cruel Othello grows to her, the more she sticks to him. Love is her religion and she becomes a martyr to the cause of her love.

CHARACTER AND DESTINY IN *OTHELLO*

It is quite common in Shakespeare criticism to say that a Shakespearian tragedy is different from a Greek tragedy. In Greek tragedy, the fate of the protagonist is predetermined by superhuman powers. But in Shakespearian tragedy, the tragic hero is a man of noble character and important position who is ruined by someone flaw of his own character. In other words, character is destiny in a Shakespearian tragedy. But it is not an exaggeration of the importance of character in Shakespearian tragedy. As Herford points out, "The tragedy of Shakespeare is the ruin and death of a man of extraordinary greatness and intensity by the concurrence of an outward, usually hostile situation with some weakness or blindness rooted in his own character and often it is derived from the noblest and his most splendid traits." Allardyce Nicoll stresses the same point, when he says that "the conception of tragedy involved, over and above character, the suggestion of fatal forces operating on action of mankind placing these men of power, nobility, strength and courage in just those situations with which they were incapable of dealing." We cannot but agree with Nicoll that both character and destiny are important in Shakespearian tragedy. But opinion is sharply divided in the case of Othello. Coleridge and A.C. Bradley are of the view that Othello the moor is a noble hero who is ruined by the superior diabolic intellect of Iago. F.R. Leavis, a modern critic holds that Iago's power in the temptation scene is that he represents something that is in Othello, the husband of Desdemona and thus the essential traitor is within the gates." In his opinion, Iago is only a necessary mechanism to precipitate the tragedy in a dramatic action. He holds that *Othello* is not Iago's plot in action. He argues that the promptness with which Othello responds to Iago's suggestion confirms that Iago represents something that is in Othello, and thus tragedy is inherent in Desdemona — Othello relationship. Iago believes in the incongruity of the marriage between the black moor and the white Venetian woman, Desdemona. He succeeds in transplanting this idea and the consequent suspicion in the mind of Othello on account of his credulity. It is the tragic flaw in the character of Othello. Though Othello is not "naturally jealous," he becomes "easily jealous" due to this weakness. Othello's credulity is not the evidence of the fact that Iago is just the reflection of his mind. His free and open nature which "thinks men honest that but seem to be so" and that he is a man of action who lacks the capacity for introspection precipitates his tragedy.

Iago is not a necessary mechanism to precipitate the tragedy in a dramatic action but a convincing character. The tragedy of Othello provides a fertile ground. Othello demands the ocular proof of Desdemona's infidelity which is secured by Iago in terms of the handkerchief. Iago cannot be compared to the witches in *Macbeth*. The witches stir up the ambition in Macbeth but they do not personally participate in the action. But as the witches cannot be separated from the drama of Macbeth, Iago cannot be separated from the tragedy of Othello. Without the intrigue of Iago, Othello cannot be caught in the net of tragedy.

The diabolic intellect of Iago cannot be disputed nor the credulity of Othello. But the diabolic intellect of Iago cannot be effective in the absence of Othello's credulity. It leads him to reap the harvest of tragedy. The storm scene in the play is highly significant. It demonstrates that Othello, the man of action is well-equipped to stem the storm in the outside world. But the stuff he is made of cannot deal effectively with the new kind of storm in the domestic life.

OTHELLO — DOMESTIC TRAGEDY

William Shakespeare is the author of four great tragedies *King Lear, Hamlet, Macbeth* and *Othello,* no Shakespearian tragedy but *Othello* is described as "domestic tragedy." In *King Lear, Hamlet* and *Macbeth,* the personal tragedy of the hero becomes a tragedy on the national scale. The hero is the person of the highest rank and position and on his fate depends the fate of the country or the nation. In *King Lear* King Lear is the hero. In *Hamlet,* the hero is the Prince of Denmark and in *Macbeth* the hero is the King of Scotland. But Othello does not hold the highest rank or position in Venice. The person of the highest rank and order is the Duke of Venice who is in no way involved with the tragedy of *Othello*. The state of Venice in *Othello*, unlike France in *King Lear*, Denmark in *Hamlet* and Scotland in *Macbeth*, remains undisturbed by the turmoil in the personal life of Othello and Desdemona.

Othello is a domestic tragedy in the sense that the world in which tragedy operates is very small. The geographical area of the play is also limited. Except for a few scenes in Venice, the scene of action is Cyprus. Venice is completely forgotten after Act II Scene II. The last three Acts make us concentrate on a purely, personal world created by Iago and Othello. We are locked physically and symbolically into the claustrophobic bedroom tomb of the doomed pair.

Othello's narrowing mental path also contributes to the sense of contraction. The breadth of Othello's character and the scope of his imagination shrink to a single obsession which usurps the government of his whole being. Moreover, this state is arrived at not by voluntary action but by a robot-like response to Iago's suggestion. Othello, according to Helen Gardner, has made his attempt to found the social bond of marriage on passionate love. It is a great adventure of the spirit but it brings with it the possibility of an agony that those who seek for so much unity in their experience do not risk. Iago torpedoes the musical harmony of Othello's life by creating at first suspicion and then complete belief in the infidelity of Desdemona. The tragic catastrophe is the result of Othello's credulity as well as the diabolic intellect of Iago.

The geographical narrowing of focus is reinforced by the absence of the allusive widening of scope normally present in Shakespearian tragedy. There is no metaphorical creation of a surrounding universe. There is no choral comment to give a context to the lover's fate such as we find in *Romeo and Juliet* no vast world history that affects and is affected by the doings of an Egyptian Queen and one of the pillars of Rome as in

Antony and Cleopatra. There is no rich pattern of reference to another world like that provided by the witches in *Macbeth* or the ghost in *Hamlet,* "Julius Caesar" or "Richard III" or by the easy conjuring of elemental forces in *King Lear.* Despite the Turkish invasion and the Venetian origin of the action, there is no vital connection between private decision and public event such as made by Fortinbras's presence in *Hamlet.* Othello has not the power of dilating the imagination by vague suggestions of huge universal powers working in the world of individual fate and passion.

It is also the ending of the play that separates it most strikingly from the other tragedies. In the first place, there is no emphatic re-establishment of public order such as Malcolm's prognostication of a healthier Scotland after Macbeth's death or the powerful entrance of Fortinbras as Hamlet's heir or even the gesture of picking the pieces of Albane and Edgar after Lear's purgatory. The tragic catastrophe of Othello does not affect any one Venetian or Cypriot. All we hear in Gratiano's arrangements, for Desdemona's estate with Cassio's lip-service remark. "For he was great of heart" standing for the final panegyric that other tragic heroes receive. The real emphasis is on the punishment of the villain. There is no effort to understand the nature of the catastrophe, no attempt to visualise the hero's end. *Othello* is a domestic tragedy as the scale on which it operates is very small in comparison with other tragedies of Shakespeare.

11

Dr. Faustus by Marlowe

Christopher Marlowe, the most important predecessor of William Shakespeare left behind his finest achievement in the form of the poetic drama, *The Tragical History of Dr. Faustus.* More than any other dramatist of the time, Marlowe's *Dr. Faustus* is the finest flowering of the Renaissance spirit. The character of the tragic protagonist, Dr. Faustus, embodies in himself the prominent traits of the Renaissance milieu. The first chorus of *Dr. Faustus* defines the lines on which the play is to develop:

So soon he profits in divinity,
The fruitful plot of scholarism graced
That shortly he was graced with doctor's name
Excelling all whose sweet delight disputes
In heavenly matters of Theology,
Till swollen with cunning of self-conceit,
His waxen wings did mount above his reach
And, melting, heavens conspired his overthrow
For falling to a devilish exercise
And glutted now with learning's golden gifts
He surfeits upon cursed necromancy.

The first chorus places emphasis on the massive intellectual background of Faustus in "glutted", with learning's golden gifts", "surfeits upon cursed necromancy" and "graced with doctor's name" etc. The driving force is the intellectual curiosity. Faustus's appetite for sensations and will to power are necessary accessories to it. The satisfaction of the intellectual curiosity leads him to bartering away his soul with the devil. The bartering is conscious and damnation, a choice.

There is no chief but only Belzebub
To whom Faustus doth dedicate himself
The word, "damnation" terrifies him not
For he confounds hell in Elysium.

Faustus's choice offers a contrast with Macbeth. While Macbeth is left with no choice, Faustus makes a conscious bartering of his soul. Macbeth is unconsciously playing into the web. He cannot cut out a course for himself. With the murder of Duncan, the action is dissipated and he is trammelled up in the coils of the tragic consequences of his action. The tragic implications spring from the utter helplessness of man. Faustus works out his own destiny according to his wishes. He is in full control of the action. As a result, the tragic inevitability is lost. In the beginning of *Dr. Faustus* is inherent its end. Faustus understands the implications of his choice. He has not to look into the seeds of time like Macbeth, to know the future, it is already known to him.

The development of the tragedy, is linear only in the beginning which is followed by the episodic progression of the play. The interaction between the linear and the episodic produces monotony in the repetitive magic sequence. Faustus enjoys the sound and fury of the magic, whereas Macbeth is trapped in the sound and fury of the consequences. The tragic tension in *Macbeth* acquires greater intensity as it moves on. In *Dr. Faustus* the dramatic tension is relaxed in the middle scenes which in contrast with the brisk pace and speed of the beginning offer a deceptive relief to Faustus, because there is an intended tragic intensity to be secured in the final scenes. The key is not sustained and the poetry becomes spasmodic. The speeches in the middle scenes in spite of their dramatic relevance do not compare with the intense poetic ones of the beginning and the final scenes. It is just a commonplace of criticism that tragedy is built upon a contrast between illusion and reality as well as a contrast projected in the character of the protagonist or a division or dichotomy in the inner and outer world. The magical achievement of Dr. Faustus together with the desire to rule over the world does not allow the contrast to be violent. The foreknowledge of damnation and the elected choice for it do not do what the compelling dramatic situation in *Macbeth* does. The tragic contrast is implied in his desire to leap over the shoal of time and to trammel up the consequences. Even in *Hamlet*, the contrast between the experience of an action and the lethargic meditative bent of the character provides unexpected moments in drama. Considered from this point of view, the foreknowledge of damnation and the elected choice for it do not allow the audience to be surprised even to be intimidated as the word "terror" implies as an element of catharsis.

The entire course of the tragedy runs as manipulated by Faustus himself. There is a certain sense of surprise under the pressure of the situation, an organic growth in *Macbeth* where fair is foul and foul is fair. There is a contrast in the contrasted moments of life but *Dr. Faustus* lacks the creative suddenness, the organic growth. The final speech of Dr. Faustus has the support of the entire text behind it. For nature asserts and intellectual defeat is accepted by the character. Tragic implications spring from the inescapable human frailty. Thus the structure of *Dr. Faustus* is built up neither on the linear nor on the episodic or circular lines. There is the interaction of the two which is suited to the drama of the legendary figure of Dr. Faustus.

WRITE A NOTE ON THE POETRY OF *DR. FAUSTUS*

The poetry of *Dr. Faustus* cannot be considered in isolation from other constituents of the drama, the character and the situation. Poetry must spring from the nature and quality of the situation and character elected for dramatic exploitation. And with the fluctuating intensity of the action poetry would be matter-of-fact and eloquent.

Marlowe's tragedies depict the fall of the protagonist due to his inordinate passion for attaining dizzy heights of glory, power, knowledge and wealth. For the kind of stuff, the rhymed verse of Chaucer was inadequate. The blank verse invented by Surrey in his translation of Virgil's Aenied and by Thomas

Norton and Sackville in *Gorbuduc* which was according to Swinburne more "blank" than "verse" could hardly be the vehicle of the passionate intensity of Marlowe's plays. Hence Marlowe set out to create a suitable verse for his tragedy. Therefore Marlowe's blank verse is not stop-end but run-on blank verse and capable of great eloquence.

In *Dr. Faustus* poetry is much more integrated to the action than in *Tamburlaine. Tamburlaine* is full of magnificent patches of poetry but in no way supports and develops the action and the character. As Faustus is the only dominant character in *Dr. Faustus,* the allocation of fine poetry among several characters is out of the question. Faustus's fascination for magic finds expression in magnificent poetry.

O what a world of profit and delight,
Of power, of honour, of omnipotence,
Is promised to the studious artizan!
All things that move between the quiet poles
Shall be at my command: emperors and kings.
Are but obeyed in their several provinces,
Nor can they raise the wind or rend the clouds,
But his dominion that exceeds in this,
Stretcheth so far as doth the mind of man,
A sound magician is a mighty god.

The rhythms communicate the high-vaulting ambition of Dr. Faustus. The majestic movement of the verse has the echoes of Spenser as the musical potentialities of the language have been exploited. Faustus made a deliberate choice of his course of action to satisfy his intellectual curiosity. He is on the verge of embarking on it, full of the sensations of the realization of possible impossibilities and the poetry is the vehicle for them. But the poetry is not well-sustained. Unlike Macbeth Faustus is not trammelled up in the consequences of his own action. He enjoys the sound and fury of magic. Naturally, the middle scenes do not move forward with mounting intensity towards the denouement. The tension is relaxed and the poetry in the middle scenes is not at par with the scenes in *Macbeth* as the sound and fury of the action dies out into its quiet realization.

Towards the close, the poetry of *Dr. Faustus* gets charged with passion as the tormenting apprehension of the approaching damnation strikes Faustus and all the intellectual vanity collapses suddenly:

> Ah Faustus
> Now hast thou but one bare hour to live
> And then thou must be damned perpetually
> Standstill, you ever moving spheres of heaven
> That time may cease and midnight never come
> Fair Nature's eye, rise, rise again and make
> Perpetual day; or let this hour be but
> A year, a month, a week, a natural day
> That Faustus may repent and save his soul
> O *lent, lent currite, noctis equi*
> The stars move still, time runs, the clock will strike
> The devil will come and Faustus must be damned.

The passage exhibits a degree of rhythmic flexibility and variety. Faustus is horrified at the thought that he is moving towards the end. First, there are long vowels, the movement of the verse is slow. But the last two lines contain maximum number of short, quick vowels especially "i" ("still", "time", "will", "strike" and "devil"). As a result, the pace of the verse is quickened and the successive sense-breaks as also the frequent internal rhymes sounding like the striking of the clock at each hour register the time — obsessed consciousness of Dr. Faustus.

The poetry of *Dr. Faustus* issues from and supports the character and action. It is spasmodic only because the situation of the play does not permit it to be otherwise. The poetry of *Dr. Faustus* is not a pretty decoration to look at but a medium to look through. The speech of Dr. Faustus foreshadows the speech of Edward II in the final scenes. But it is for the superior quality of the poetry that *Edward II* is not comparable to *Dr. Faustus,* though it is a better constructed play.

Consider the theme of temptation in *Dr. Faustus*

Or

***Dr. Faustus* is more a morality play than a regular play. Discuss**

Or

Consider *Dr. Faustus* as a Renaissance play or tragedy.

Christopher Marlowe's *Dr. Faustus* is a tragic play that has been considered from time to time from various angles. It is sometimes said that the theme of *Dr. Faustus* is one of temptation and the suggestion has also been put forward that *Dr. Faustus* is more a morality than a regular play. Similarly, it is often proclaimed that *Dr. Faustus* is a typical Renaissance tragic play. We have to consider all these critical statements in-depth in order to bring out the real nature of *Dr. Faustus* as a tragic play.

Marlowe borrowed the real material of this play from the German book entitled *Faustbuch.* In fact the legend pertaining to the life and history of Dr. Faustus was very popular in Europe during Marlowe's time. In his play, Marlowe describes Faustus as the son of poor parents living at Rhodes in Germany who attained a fair degree of scholarship at Wittenburg and who eventually settled there as the Doctor of Divinity. As we go through Marlowe's play, we find that Faustus enjoys great respect among the scholars. However, in spite of his all learning, he spurns divinity, law, medicine and rhetoric and decides to take to black magic or necromancy for the sake of honour, power and authority. It is only natural that in a short span of time, he becomes what Marlowe calls him "a conjurer's laureate." Furthermore, Faustus enters into a contract with the lord of the devils, according to the terms and conditions of which he surrenders his soul to Lucifer in lieu of Mephistophilis's unstinted service to him for a period of twenty-four years. It is also agreed upon between Faustus and Lucifer that on the expiry of the stipulated period the Lord of the Hell would be completely free to do whatever he decides to minister to his body and soul. This agreement is signed by Faustus in his own blood. It is with this agreement that the action in the tragedy of *Dr. Faustus* begins.

Faustus does, indeed, seem to get power-drunk with the help of Lucifer and Mephistophilis. He travels through space, moves round the earth, visits Paris, Venice, Naples, Padua and Rome, plays pranks upon the Pope and cardinals, assaults the Priors, conjures up the spirit of Alexander and his paramour and brings the famous ancient Greek beauty, Helen almost back to life. The miracles that Faustus performs do constitute an outstanding testimony to his magical skill and power. It may be contended at this point that the word, "tempt" or "temptation" does occur three or four times in this particular play. Secondly, the occasional appearances of good Angel and evil Angel do seem to make us believe that in spite of good Angel's persuasions and warnings, Faustus is lured and tempted away by the evil Angel's insinuations. Thirdly, the appearance of the Seven Deadly sins in the play seems almost to reinforce the thesis that the theme of *Dr. Faustus* is one of temptation. Fourthly, as we go through Marlowe's play, we find the forces of good to be in continual combat with the forces of evil in this tragedy and this is precisely why such terms as "God," "Scriptures," "the Saviour Christ", "the Trinity", "the Joys of Heaven", "holy saints", "salvation" are juxtaposed against "blasphemy", "damnation", "devils", "pride" and "insolence", "Lucifer", "Mephistophilis", "Belzebub" and "eternal death." Lastly, it does seem that the theme of temptation is the theme of *Dr. Faustus*, because even though we find Faustus being pulled all the time in the two opposed directions of Christ and Satan, finally, it is the Devil that prevails over him. It is for this reason that he utilises the services of Mephistophilis and as the period of contract expires, Lucifer takes his soul to hell for eternal damnation. A number of critics tell us that these are the very elements which we find in morality plays that Marlowe had been influenced by the morality plays, while writing *Dr. Faustus* and that because the theme of temptation does operate through this play, it should be regarded more as a morality play rather than a regular play.

On a close and careful scrutiny of *Dr. Faustus*, however, we find that *Dr. Faustus* is a Renaissance tragedy and not a morality play. Faustus is a character who impresses us by virtue of his individualism, his confidence, his impatience with earthly limitations, his spirit of revolt and his love of beauty and learning. As a typical Renaissance hero, Faustus seems to be obsessed with a spirit of enquiry and the first question that he puts to Mephistophilis reveals he is tempted not so much by a love of power, as by a spirit of curiosity. The truth is that Faustus abjures God and religion in search of superhuman knowledge. This is exactly what we find in Goethe. Goethe's Faustus is committed to the task of moving from the finite to the infinite. It is an altogether different matter that Marlowe's Faustus meets his doom in his quest for knowledge and even moves over to Lucifer's camp for the sake of curiosity.

Marlowe's *Dr. Faustus* is not a morality play. Its theme is not that of temptation but that of a quest for knowledge and as such it is a typical Renaissance tragedy.

12

EDWARD II BY MARLOWE

Edward II, like other heroes of Marlowe, is dominated by a single passion. Tamburlaine has limitless desire for power. Dr. Faustus has insatiable lust for magical knowledge. Their boundless passions lend them a grandeur of stature and a gigantic height to their personality. Edward II's passion for his favourite Gaveston is also boundless. But the way Edward II indulges in his passion, instead of imparting him grandeur, lends him a touch of indignity.

Edward II lacks the noble character of the tragic hero, though he is a man of high position. Gaveston, his favourite proved an evil genius in his life. Gaveston had been his playfellow in his childhood and he had taken to him very favourably. His father, Edward I had correctly foreseen the evil influence Gaveston might exert on the future King of England. This is why he had banished him from England. But as soon as his father died and Edward II came to throne, he called him back and gave him the highest place of honour in the kingdom. This naturally excited the jealousy of the barons who could never tolerate an upstart, an undeserving fellow claiming so much of king's confidence and love for no satisfactory reason. For Gaveston was capable of rendering no tangible service to the country except dancing attendance on the king and keeping him in an indulgent mood. Thus the conflict between the king and the barons over Gaveston became inevitable and proved ruinous not only to the king but to others around him.

It is true, as some of the barons say, at the time of compromise, there is nothing wrong in having favourites.

Many ancient kings and nobles had them in the past. Even Hercules and Alexander the great had their favourites. But love for the favourites should not be allowed to go beyond normal limits. The undue and inordinate fondness for the favourite was a tragic trait in Edward II's character. Favourites should be concerned with the private life of the kings and nobles. They should not be allowed to interfere with the duties of a king, a husband or a father. Edward II failed miserably because he allowed his favourite to override his nobles, his lords and influence his career as a king. He himself admits on the eve of his death:

"O Gaveston, it is for thee that I am wronged."

Edward II presents the irony of kingship. He does not rule as much as he is ruled by others. It is so because he does not put on the dignity of his position. He is arbitrary from the very beginning of his rule. He fails to take his barons into his confidence but keeps them at arm's length by showing undue preference for his favourite, Gaveston. He has no far sight. He is unable to anticipate things correctly. Probably he never bothers about the future. He is satisfied with the present only. He has to pay dearly for this. He is always conscious of the dignity that is attached to the crown. But he never realises the duties and responsibilities that a king should necessarily have. He gets unduly incensed with the petty lapses on the part of his lords whereas he allows himself to commit errors one after another. As a result, he earned more ridicule than respect from his courtiers. He never realises that a king is far above the rest in dignity and goes out of the way to avenge petty faults. He never cares as much for his position as for Gaveston.

Even if Queen Isabella develops illicit love for Mortimer, King Edward II is to be blamed. There are reasons to believe that Isabella would have been constant to her husband, if Gaveston had not come in between them. The King's excessive fondness for his minion and indifference towards the queen is mainly responsible for her infidelity. Edward II undergoes a change of fortune. His end is inglorious. He attached no value to his kingship but he clings to it at the time of parting with his crown. His end excites pity. He does not command the sympathy of the reader. He lacks the nobility and dignity associated with a tragic hero. He is not a tragic but a pathetic character.

"Marlowe reached the summit of his art in Edward II." Comment

Or

"Edward II" is the best constructed play. Comment.

In his play, *Edward II,* Christopher Marlowe turned from romantic tragedy of *Tamburlaine, The Jew of Malta,* and *Dr. Faustus* to history of the type which Shakespeare has given in *Richard II,* a drama of more sustained power. The most convincing proof of the dramatist's genius is conveyed in the transformation of a chronicle into a tragedy. *Edward II* is considered to be the best constructed play of Marlowe. The praise of *Edward II* has probably been extravagant.

Edward II is the first historical play of the stricter type and because there is more characterization and episode in it than in his earlier plays, it is singled out as Marlowe's best dramatic effort. Every play based on intimate history has an advantage. The fine, "restraint" for which *Edward II* is admired is partly due to the fact that unlike *Richard II* with which it is compared, it chooses a more extended period of history and quite naturally there is greater scope for condensation.

Marlowe's earlier plays are, no doubt, dominated by the commanding figure of the hero which overshadows and dwarfs the other characters. *Tamburlaine* moves round the centre of the heroic personality of *Tamburlaine.* He is a man invested with remorseless power. He has the gigantic hugeness of figure with a soaring passion for infinite power. The second play of Marlowe, *Dr. Faustus* maintains the same key. It is also centred round the heroic personality of Dr. Faustus. *The Jew of Malta,* the third play explores the tragic possibilities of lust for wealth. One can very well detect variation upon the same theme. The characters of these plays do not present the contest of wills in terms of different characters.

Edward II is an achievement different from Marlowe's previous plays. The hero of the play, king *Edward II* is not a towering personality who can brook no resistance. He has to submit before the will of others. It is, thus, clear that the will of the individual either of king *Edward II* or of younger Mortimer is not predominant in the play as in the case of Marlowe's previous plays. *Edward II* shows the conflict of the opposite forces.

The tragedy of *Edward II* is the tragedy of human weakness. Only in this play, Marlowe comes down to earth and knows the earthly limitations. In *Tamburlaine,* "a god is not so glorious as a king" but in *Edward II,* Marlowe sets out deliberately to destroy his earlier idea of kingship. Edward's career seems to be an ironical retort to Tamburlaine's exultant cry, "Is it not brave to be a king?"

Characterisation in Marlowe's tragedy is largely an affair of the protagonist. Minor characters receive no attention in the play. They are mere sketches without any sustained and consistent delineation. Only in *Edward II,* the antagonist receives much attention in the form of Mortimer. From the viewpoint of characterisation, the play is perfectly balanced. Not only Edward II, but Mortimer, Queen Isabella, Kent and Leicester retain their individuality.

From the viewpoint of plot and construction, *Edward II* stands on a level very different from any of Marlowe's previous plays. Instead of being a collection of unconnected episodes as *Tamburlaine* or *Dr. Faustus, Edward II* is not the imperfect fulfilment of a great design. There is a beginning, a middle and an end. But the much admired condensation goes against the dramatic interest and denies the dramatist the opportunity of fuller characterisation. Moreover, the characters do not secure or even excite any finer sympathy or more serious interest than attends upon the mere successive events or the mere display of emotion rather animal than spiritual in their expression of rage or tenderness.

The final scene of the king's deposition is moving but not

more than the final scene of *Dr. Faustus.* In passion and word music, the play never surpasses the earlier plays. The shackles of chronicle keep it from the imaginative range of *Tamburlaine* or *Dr. Faustus* or from the reach of great tragedy. But as an effort to interpret history on the stage, it is the first of any account and best in the genre. But it does not represent Marlowe's summit of art. *Dr. Faustus,* though not without its defects, is certainly more appealing as tragedy than *Edward II.*

CHARACTER OF GAVESTON

Gaveston is not only the creation of Marlowe in "Edward II" but also a historical figure. He was the son of a knight, Sir Arnold Gaveston. He was brought up as a foster brother and playmate of Edward II. He was banished from the kingdom by Edward I for the evil influence he exerted on Prince Edward II. But he was recalled to the court immediately after Edward I's death because the new king, Edward II needed his company badly. He proved an evil genius in Edward II's life and practically his undoing as the king himself admits on the eve of his death.

Gaveston knew king Edward II's weaknesses and follies. He exploited them fully to his selfish ends and became the hottest favourite of Edward II in no time. The king lavished his attention and favours on him rather unnaturally leading to the neglect of his wife, Isabella, who loved him dearly.

Gaveston basked rather foolishly in the affections of the king. He did not have the mental power to see the consequences of the unnatural intimacy between him and the king and its effect on the barons and the people. He became foolishly proud of his position in the court and began to relish it by bold and saucy behaviour with powerful barons. He did not confine himself to the private life of the king. He began to interfere with the official and domestic duties of the king. He rather usurped the attention of the king to the neglect of his wife and kingdom.

Gaveston had, no doubt, charms of manners and personality. But he was devoid of intellectual powers. He had not a single admirable quality so that he could not create a single friend besides the king. Everybody in the court was disgusted with his insolent and overbearing attitude. He had only the ability of diverting the king from his duties both — political and private by providing low kinds of pleasure. The barons and the people therefore demanded his banishment from the kingdom. He had started acting on the king as an intoxicating drink. He could not be persuaded to part with him on any condition. This led to the civil war in the country.

Gaveston was the bone of contention between the king and the queen and the king and the barons. He knew how to bask in the sunshine of the king's favour. But he did not know how to put out the fire he had ignited. He was as ambitious as Mortimer. But he did not have even half of the resourcefulness, tact, organising ability and diplomatic shrewdness of Mortimer. He lacked self-restraint and did not know how to conceal his feelings. Therefore, he was unable to look after his own interests.

Whatever charm or magnetism Gaveston wielded on the king, he could attract neither love nor regard from the audience. He is placed far below Mortimer in our esteem who is condemned as a wicked person. He is completely without any admirable quality. He is wiped off easily from the memory of the audience. Probably he deserved the fate he got for the ruin he brought upon the realm of Edward II. He only stirs pity in us for the affection he bore towards the king till the last breath of his life.

Examine *Edward II* as a chronicle play

Or

Examine *Edward II* as a tragedy.

Edward II is a chronicle play as the title *The Troublesome Reign and Lamentable Death of Edward II, the King of England: with the Magical fall of Mortimer* suggests. But the running title, *The Tragedy of Edward the Second* represents the play better, for it is Edward rather than Mortimer who holds the central position.

Marlowe has based his play on Holinshed's *Chronicle of England*. He takes liberties with the chronicler's record. He throws away much material connected with the wars with Scotland, and Ireland and France, between barons and barons and many trivial details that the chronicle recorded. The ecclesiastics in Marlowe's play are opposed to the king but in the chronicle they were vacillating from one side to another. With his art of selection, condensation and adaptation, Marlowe shows an awareness of dramatic skill for which there was little dramatic precedence in his own earlier plays and none at all in the English historical plays he had before him.

Edward II is the only play of Marlowe which is not dominated by a single character. The balance of one character with another is part of the essential scheme of the play as Marlowe, for the first time, makes a study, not of strength but of weakness. Edward of the chronicle is a weak king. "Weakness does not act but is acted upon and if at all it acts, its actions are frustrated." Marlowe is, thus, compelled by the nature of his theme to distribute interest over a number of characters. Edward does not act. Those who are opposed to him act upon him. There is a similarity between Edward II and Shakespeare's Richard II. Both have fundamental weakness in their characters. There is change in both the characters. But the change in them is not so much as in our feelings to them. Their passing from the cruel, selfishness of power to the suffering and helplessness of powerlessness accounts for the change in our feelings.

The speech of Edward II presents the image of the sea overwhelming the land which is a symbol of chaos:

> I have my wish, in that I joy thy sight;
> And sooner shall the sea overwhelm my land.
> Than bear the ship that shall transport thee hence.

It proves prophetic as the turning point of Edward's fortune comes with the death of Gaveston. The beginning of his end is accelerated with the escape of Mortimer to France where the queen and the young Edward have already been sent. There is certainly change rather than development in the character of Isabella and Mortimer to which critics have objected. It is to be noted that *Edward II* is not a naturalistic play. The change in their characters is just to add pity and terror to Edward's end and to bring about the swing from contempt of Edward when he is abusing his power to pity for Edward when he falls from his high position. Mortimer is not a bit different from the proud and self-serving lords but as soon as Edward is defeated and power comes to his hands, he turns into a Machiavelli and Isabella into a she-Machiavelli. Mortimer is related with the idea that he makes the fortune's wheel turn as he pleases. When his end is in sight, he acquiesces in the decree of fate.

Marlowe makes no mistake in departing from chronicles which make no mention of an intrigue between Isabella and Mortimer before Edward's murder. It is mentioned by Gaveston and Edward II in the early scenes. But it has the effect of lighting up Edward's own vicious passion for Gaveston. In her speech after the king's accusation we find the first hint of affection for Mortimer. Her pretensions of concern for the king's fortunes and her secret liaison with Mortimer adds to the pity of Edward.

Marlowe leaves out little details of the humiliation and murder of Edward as recorded in the chronicle. There is cruelty in the last scenes which is not found in Shakespeare's *Richard II*. Richard II is brought face to face with his accusers and he indulges himself in scenes which turn him to a playboy and a poet. He takes affectionate farewell from his queen. Isabella is completely different from her image in the chronicle. It adds to the pity and horror of Edward that he is never brought face to face with his tormentors. The fear of cruelty preys upon his consciousness in prison. He is full of concern for himself and his son. The chronicle presents a penitent Edward. But in the play, on the contrary, he exclaims, "How have I transgressed/unless it be with too much clemency." The murder of Edward by Lightborn who takes pride in his art of killing a man adds to the horror and pity. In a short scene that follows Edward III takes control and Mortimer and Isabella meet their doom.

Marlowe's heroes, except in *Dido* and *Massacre at Paris*, are men of humble origin. *Edward II* is his full study of kingship rather of the irony of kingship. Though history is not fully assimilated to drama in Act II and III, Marlowe with his dramatic gifts has shaped out of the chronicle of a disagreeable reign a historical tragedy.

Though we pity Edward II for his loss of power and suffering, he does not win our admiration as a *Hamlet* or *Macbeth*. Macbeth puts up his fight against the mighty fate and asserts the dignity of man. As dignity cannot be associated with Edward II for lack of admirable traits in his character, the tragic hero presents only the spectacle of suffering for which we pity him.

Write a note on the Grand Style of Milton

Or

Milton exhibits a feeling for words rather than a capacity to feel through words. Comment.

T.S. Eliot, the iconoclast who had to find his way through the past tradition to the natural idiom and rhythms of modern poetry, for the first time, became conscious of the fact that Milton's grand style was irrelevant to a modern poet in the contemporary situation. F.R. Leavis observes that "Milton exhibits a feeling for words rather than a feeling through words." His poetry lacks the rich sensuous quality associated with English poetry. Eliot attributed the absence of visual imagery in the poetry of Milton to his blindness. According to him, his poetry is too musical. The auditory imagination is exploited at the cost of visual imagination. Milton was interested in music which he inherited from his father. He played his words like notes in music. The mellifluous music of his poetry was devoid of speech rhythm and visual imagination.

As Milton was a scholar of Greek and Latin, foreign words and syntax flowed into Milton's verse at the cost of the native words and phrases and modes of syntax. Milton's poetry is replete with classical references, proper nouns, Latinised phrases and syntax. Nouns do not follow adjectives in the manner of English syntax in the poetry of Milton. Rather nouns are followed by adjectives in the Latin manner sacrificing the natural English idiom and rhythm. Keats tried to imitate Milton in his *Hyperion* but he gave up the attempt in despair. He remarked, "Milton corrupted the English language." Like Eliot, he too was conscious that Milton was a remote, majestic star in the firmament to which the natural English poet could not relate himself as he belonged to a different contemporary world of his own. In *The Paradise Lost,* we do not come across a stanza in the conventional or accepted sense of the term. A stanza in this epic poem is generally a paragraph which is technically known as period and which runs from one full stop to another. This paragraph unit is so expansive that it provides the poet with the ample opportunity for exploiting the musical potentialities of words, phrases or lines used therein. It certainly goes to Milton's credit as a poet that he could invent this kind of verse unit in order to allow full and satisfying play to his taste for music.

The kind of diction that we find in *The Paradise Lost* is patently Latinized. This is so because Milton, while writing this poem, thought more about the European tradition of epic writing than about the British tradition. The words used in *The Paradise Lost* are generally inflated, pompous and rather are inspiring. Milton's orientation in this regard is first and last rhetorical. Shakespeare also at times makes use of pompous expressions but he does so chiefly for the sake of novelty and new coinages. Milton had, perhaps, no such taste for novelty which is associated with Donne and Hopkins. Milton makes use of difficult words or expressions such as "Adamantine", "combustion", "Eupyreal" and "suppliant", partly because of his oppressive erudition and partly because of his intention of imparting heroic grandeur to his poem.

T.S. Eliot, who criticised Milton, in his second essay restores Milton to his high pedestal, though he does not refute what he had already remarked about Milton in his previous essay. Eliot concedes the fact that Milton was concerned with the superhuman world in his epic. His visual imagination was not at work in *The Paradise Lost.* Nor it was needed as it was not possible for Milton to describe heaven and hell quite vividly as they stand completely outside his realm of experience. Obviously Milton needed a kind of verse, a different instrument of medium from the one relevant to a poet in his contemporary situation. Milton's grand style is "a many splendoured pleasure dome" for those who can enjoy its majesty and eloquence, nevertheless would sound artificial or unnatural in our contemporary situation as far as the expression of natural human feeling is concerned.

Milton's grand style is well-suited to the epical drama of God, Adam, Eve and Satan and angels. It serves its purposes best in *The Paradise Lost* and probably exhausts the possibilities of the English languages in that particular sphere. It is really grand and majestic though it is irrelevant to a poet in a contemporary situation where symphony has been replaced by cacophony. Hence in spite of being quite majestic, Milton's grand style stands apart from the natural English verse. The verse of Shakespeare, Donne, Pope and Hopkins is the memorable record of natural human emotion and feelings in their natural rhythm. It is a mirror that reflects the rich variety and complexity of the human feelings and emotions which blends the particular and the universal, the temporal and the timeless. The majesty of the grand style of Milton is *The Paradise Lost* stands at high pedestal with all its beauty and magnificence for removed from the rhythm of the common human life.

13

Twelfth Night by Shakespeare

The structure of *Twelfth Night* is loose and rambling. It is not a closely knit structure in the sense that there is no causality in the sequence of events. One event does not lead inevitably to another. The world of *Twelfth Night* is governed by chance and fortune. It is by chance that Viola survives the shipwreck. The same is true of Sebastian. They happen to be identical twins. It is also just by chance that Antonio comes to rescue Cesario in the duel under the impression of Sebastian, and Andrew Aguecheek strikes Sebastian under the impression of Cesario. All this can be attributed to chance. Finally, the reappearance of Sebastian in the presence of Viola which resolves the tangle of the play is a good turn of fortune. The random sequence of events which follow no logical or causal scheme is a basic feature of romance or Shakespearian comedy. But in *Twelfth Night* it is related with the theme of mutability, impermanence and instability of life.

The words "perchance", "fate" and "fortune" are reiterated frequently in the play to suggest the capricious nature of life. In the second scene of the play after the shipwreck, Viola expresses the hope of her brother's survival, "Perchance he is not drowned." The captain of the ship reminds her that "It is perchance that you yourself were saved" to which Viola replies "and so perchance he may be." "Chance" dominates the conversation as well as the play. Similar references to time, fate or fortune punctuate the play. After her first meeting with Cesario Olivia says "Fate show thy force [...] what is decreed, must be and be this so." When Viola realises her difficulties on account of her disguise where she cannot express her love for Orsino and bring Olivia back to her senses, she trusts to time to "untangle" too hard a knot for me to untie. Time really does so. Malvolio talks to himself "'Tis but fortune, all is fortune." When the wind of fortune is carried to its extreme and Olivia, a complete stranger, showers her affection on Sebastian, he is compelled to think:

> "That this may be some error, but no madness
> Yet doth this accident and flood of fortune
> So far exceed all instance, all discourse
> That I am ready to distrust mine eyes
> And wrangle with reason that persuades me
> To any other trust but that I am mad."

Twelfth Night like other Shakespearian comedies is a love story and love is part of the design that reflects waywardness, impermanence and instability. Nothing is fixed or stable in Illyria and the lover's mind is the microcosm of the universe that the play presents. In the very first scene of the play Orsino wishes the music to be played on as it is the food of love and soon asks to stop it. In scene IV, Act II Orsins admires the constancy of men in love and after sometimes talks of their inconstancy in comparison with women. The instability and transience is further reinforced in the Duke's reference to women's beauty. "For women are as roses, whose fair flower/ Being once displayed doth fall that very hour."

Olivia presents a similar fickleness of mood and mind. It seems the caprice of fortune in the play is related to the caprice of lovers. Olivia who vows not to see the face of any lover of seven years falls violently in love with Cesario at first sight. As Orsino's self is a fabrication of his fancy of a lover, Olivia's self is also a fabrication of her fancy, while her true self has potentiality for intense love of the senses. Thus in the shifting, fluid world of Illyria art and nature keep on shifting. As Orsino loves art rather than nature, Olivia also loves art (Cesario) rather than nature (Viola). It is the good turn of her fortune that the art turns into nature while retaining the facade of art as Viola's identical twin, Sebastian appears on the scene. Malvolio is encouraged to cast off thy humble sloughs and appear fresh as he dresses up in yellow garters and puts on ridiculous airs to win his mistress, Olivia. He is the antithesis of Viola who dresses as a boy to become a servant. In his disguise like Viola's in hers, he is manifesting the true nature of his secret desires and ambitions. Feste is disguised as Sir Topas to cast out the devil in him. *Twelfth Night* appears to be the translation in human terms of the philosophy of Pythagoras as it is exposed in a song of Ovid's "Transformations":

> "All things do change, but nothing sure doth perish
> The soul is aye the self-same thing it was and yet
> It fleeteth into sundry shapes.
> In all the world, there is not that standeth at a stay
> Things ebb and flow and every shape is made to pass away."

The song reflects the macrocosm of *Twelfth Night.* But at the end of the play the characters transcend mutability as the wall that separates art and nature collapses in order to pave the way for characters to attain wholeness, harmony and perfection which are expressed in the harmony of the union of Olivia and Sebastian, Viola and Orsino and Maria and Sir Toby Belch.

CHARACTER OF MALVOLIO

Malvolio is a product of Shakespeare's comic imagination. But he is a Jonsonian character as he is a humour character. He is dominated by a ruling passion. He is not an artificial character. He is quite convincing as a human being. Shakespeare explores the comic possibilities of a particular humour in the character of Malvolio. In fact *The Twelfth Night* bears a close resemblance to Ben Jonson's "Every Man in His Humour."

Malvolio is the steward in the house of countess Olivia. He is grave, diligent and honest in the discharge of his duties. Olivia turns to him in difficulties. She holds a good opinion of him and it is the ample testimony of his merit. But he suffers from a peculiar flaw which turns him into a comic character.

Olivia precisely defines this quality when she says, "You are sick of self-love, Malvolio."

Self-love is the ruling passion of Malvolio's life. His entire character reflects this passion. He has a very high opinion of himself. He is particular about his dress. He prides himself on his 'branched, velvet gown.' He entertains the illusion about his complexion that anybody who chances to look at him must love him. He thinks that Maria admires him and pays him exalted respect for his complexion.

Malvolio considers himself superior to others in wit, manners and decency also. He is too full of self-conceit and vanity. Naturally he is inclined to fault-finding. Anything that falls outside his narrow range of sympathies is wrong. He is himself sober to the point of absurdity. Any mark of joviality and merry-making is "disorders" for him. He takes Sir Toby, Sir Andrew, and Maria to task for this. He considers himself the sole authority of manners and decency.

Malvolio is completely devoid of the sense of humour. His sobriety is a kind of disease for him. He loves to enjoy the place of authority and position. He loses no opportunity to impose his authority on others. He dreams of "calling his officers" when he becomes count Malvolio. He derives special satisfaction in delivering Olivia's reprimand to Sir Toby and Maria. He is over-virtuous. It is just an excuse for making others realize his authority. He has no sympathy with others. He is incapable of loving any one. His relations with his fellow servants can be well inferred from the remark of Maria that if he goes mad and is confined, "the house will be quieter". He is a malicious spirit. He is always ready to judge and condemn others. He is mentally so dull that he cannot relish a joke. The clown's wit he fails to appreciate.

It is Maria who reads Malvolio's character thoroughly and perceives the defects hidden from others. In her letter she plays upon his weakness. Malvolio, the victim of vanity and self-deception is caught in the trap laid by Maria. His imagination is stirred up by her letter. He toys with the dream of becoming count Malvolio. He joyfully conceives the picture of his future with his branched velvet gown, "calling his officers". He has the desire of putting Sir Toby in his right place. He tends to forget his position that he is no more than a steward. The idea that Olivia will prefer him to Duke Orsino does not sound absurd to him. He is fully sure of Olivia's feelings. He is confirmed in his belief by observing that such instances of marrying below rank do occur. Therefore Malvolio appears before Olivia in yellow stockings and with his legs cross-gartered. He has to suffer for his vanity as he is confined to a dark room. He suffers more than he deserves. We feel sympathy for him. But his confinement fails to break him. His letter to Olivia is a clear proof of it. It is further confirmed by the way he accuses Olivia for doing him 'notorious wrong'.

Some critics have compared him to Shylock for being an unpleasant character who is nevertheless human and excites sympathy. But there is a world of difference between the two characters. Shylock is a real villain whereas Malvolio is only a nuisance. Moreover, we lose sympathy for him when we knew that Malvolio was behind the arrest of Antonio.

The use of masks in *Twelfth Night*

The usual theme in Shakespearian comedies is love and its fulfilment. The fulfilment of love is generally delayed by an older generation of parents or rulers. The hindrance is later removed and love achieves its fulfilment. This pattern is followed by *A Midsummer Night's Dream* and *As you like it.*

Twelfth Night does not follow this pattern. The older generation is completely absent, the ruler here is a love-sick Duke, Orsino. Olivia is herself the ruler of the household. Viola is fatherless and motherless. The senior generation in the play consists of only jokers, jesters and gulls. The barriers that confront Hermia and Lysander, Rosalind and Orlando do not stand in the way of the fulfilment of the lovers. The play assumes that whether we do or do not know, living implies playing a role. Sometimes we know the roles we play. Sometimes we play the roles without knowing and become comic in our behaviour. Playing a role also implies that we are not ourselves or we do not know ourselves. The barrier in *Twelfth Night* is provided by the lack self-knowledge or on account of the masks the characters have put on.

When the play opens, we find that Orsino and Olivia have accepted the aristocratic and literary idea of the romantic lover and the grief-stricken lady. They are comic characters because they do not know their real selves and playing a role which masks their true identity. Orsino indulges in the peculiar moodiness and fickleness of a romantic lover. In the opening scene he wishes the music to be played on as music is "the food of love". He, then, orders the musician to stop. In the absence of the actual experience of love, there is excessive imagination of being in love. It is commonly accepted that Orsino is not in love with person but in love with the idea of love.

Olivia is another character in the dance of masks that *Twelfth Night* presents. She is a countess who has lost her brother. She has vowed to mourn for the brother for seven years and avoid all mirth and jollity. She has taken up the romantically glamorous role of a grief-stricken lady. But soon we are aware that she has imposed on herself a role which stands in antithetical relationship to her real self. That Olivia really wants to love becomes evident as soon as Cesario turns up before her.

She becomes comic for us as she falls in love with the male exterior of Cesario. The way she falls in love with Cesario at first compels us to revise our opinion of Olivia and recognise the new energy of passion with which she is possessed.

Viola, like Rosalind, disguises herself as a man. But unlike Rosalind, her disguise creates complications for her. She serves as foil to Olivia. Like Olivia she has lost her brother. But her situation does not allow the luxury of grief. She in the form of Cesario dutifully plays the role of messenger of love to Olivia. Viola never lets us forget the gap between Viola and Cesario. It is for self-preservation that she puts on a disguise. But she trusts to time for untangling the complications created by her disguise.

Sebastian is the reality of Cesario. The comedy arises from the fact he insists on his identity in the face of the unanimous public opposition. He is faced with the problem in a world because he is unmasked in a world where mask is the norm. He refers to the response of Olivia to himself as a dream and wishes it to continue.

Malvolio and Andrew Aguecheek do not belong to aristocracy. They are ruled by their mistaken notions of the role of an upper-class gentleman.

Both Malvolio and Andrew Aguecheek are not so much in love with Olivia as a victim of self-love. Aguecheek is befooled by Sir Toby who holds up a painted mirror before him in which he finds himself a worthy suitor for Olivia. Another victim of self-love is Malvolio who is proud of his image as it is reflected in the letter shrewdly written by Maria. Like Aguecheek, he also fails to see the comic gap between himself and his ideal role and the gap between his ideal and the social reality. Feste is the only character in the business of masking who is a professional. He does it for a living. He unlike others does not make the mistake of confusing his personality with his mask. As his age is growing it is becoming difficult for him to retain his mask.

Viola differs with Orison and Olivia, because she can see things with absolute clarity, she rejects artificial masks of love. But she is not rational to the point rejecting the blind, irrational passion of love. She directly admits her irrational love for Orsino and rationally accepts her inability to cope with the situation!

> O Time, thou must untangle this, not I;
> It is too hard a knot for me to untie.

The miracle she waits for occurs in terms of the appearance of her identical twin, Sebastian. The confusions are removed. Olivia had married Sebastian under the impression of Cesario. Cesario turns into Viola. The frayed temper of Orsino turns into the acceptability of Viola as his wife. *Twelfth Night*, the title of the play is connected with the occasion of the festivity on the *Twelfth Night* of Christmas. The sub-title of the play is "what you will". It is the dance of masking on the festive occasion when every one puts on the mask he wills. The play ends with the unmasking of realities and identities. The song of Feste at the end of the play suggests the nature of the play. "Our play is done/ And we will strive to please you every day."

CHARACTER OF VIOLA

Viola is the central figure in the romantic comedy of Shakespeare, *The Twelfth Night.* She belongs to the class of Shakespearian heroines who are disguised as a young man. She has to disguise herself because she has been separated from her brother by shipwreck as Rosalind in "As you like it" is forced by circumstances to disguise herself as a young man in the forest of Arden [...]. Portia in *The Merchant of Venice* plays the lawyer to save her husband's friend. The disguise in the case of Viola is sometimes a help and sometimes, a hindrance.

Like the heroines of Shakespeare's romantic comedies, Viola is charming and graceful. She is extremely beautiful in her disguise as a young man. When she faces Olivia, Olivia almost forgets her speech and falls in love with her at first sight. But Duke Orsino marks the feminine features in the beauty of her lip and voice.

Viola has imagination and a power of quick decision. When she is left on the coast of Illyria after shipwreck and learns from the captain about Orsino and Olivia, she quickly conceives the plan of disguise. She has tact and good sense to carry out her plan. This is the secret of her growing favour with the Duke and his employment of Viola in his service of pleading his love to Olivia. She exhibits her tact and intelligence in securing access to Olivia. All other messengers had failed to achieve it. She rejects all pleas from Malvolio and finds entrance into the house.

Viola is loyal, faithful and dutiful. In spite of the fact that she bears secret love for Orsino, she does her best to plead his case with Olivia. It is another matter that Olivia falls in love with her on account of her disguise. She is true to Olivia also. She does not disclose Olivia's deception to *Malvolio* regarding the ring and maintains her dignity.

Viola puts on her male identity but she bears the heart of a woman. It reveals itself especially on the eve of a duel with Sir Andrew Aguecheek. She is completely nervous and in a mood to return into the house. She clearly confesses to herself her inadequacy to meet such situations in life. She is on the point of disclosing her identity, "A little thing would make me tell them/ How much I lack of a man." But the situation is averted by the timely appearance of Antonio.

Viola is the most outstanding character of the play. Her personality contrasts with Olivia, who has also lost her brother. Her response to the death of the brother distinguishes her from Olivia. While Olivia is sentimental, Viola is practical. Though Viola grieves for her brother's death she realizes that she has to go on living in this business world. On the other hand, Olivia makes a theatrical show of her grief. Viola is different from Olivia and Orsino in matters of love also. Orsino is fickle and fanciful in love feeding his fancy with music. Olivia is impetuous in her passion and throws all norms of decency to the winds. Viola remains restrained and modest. Her love is quiet and constant. She reveals her feelings for the Duke indirectly through her tale of a sister who "never told her love but let concealment like a worm in the bud feed on her damask cheek". She adopts this beautiful style to express her deep love and her suffering on account of concealment. Her disguise is the obstacle in her way. She is puzzled at this riddle of the situation and trusts time to unravel this tangle.

Viola, like Rosalind and Portia is one of the disguised heroines of Shakespearian comedy. But she is different from them. Rosalind is possessed of a high spirit that carries her through her difficulties. Portia is endowed with an indomitable strength of mind. But in spite of her male disguise, Viola remains completely feminine to herself and the reader. She is always sweetly conscious of her femininity and never forgets that she is playing a part.

TWELFTH NIGHT AS A ROMANTIC COMEDY

Shakespeare and Ben Jonson are exponents of diverse kinds of comedy. Ben Jonson's comedies are comedies of humour which satirize deviations from the norm. On the other hand, Shakespearian comedies are romantic comedies. They are not satiric but humorous and lead us into the realm of imagination and romances. They are poetic and creative, an embodiment of Shakespeare's romantic imagination. *Twelfth Night* provides us with a perfect example of romantic comedy.

Twelfth Night is a romantic comedy. It is a combination of romance and comedy. Shakespeare uses the usual material of romance, the shipwreck, twins, disguises, exile and a magical resolution of the whole tangle. The play begins with a shipwreck like *The Tempest* where the twins, Viola and Sebastian are separated. Viola hopes that his brother has survived the shipwreck and she enters the service of the Duke Orsino disguised as a boy.

As usual in Shakespeare's romantic comedies, love is one of the central themes of *Twelfth Night*. At the opening of the play, Orsino and Olivia have accepted the idea of the romantic lover and the grief-stricken lady. They are comic characters because they do not know themselves and are playing a role which is only their mask. Orsino indulges in the peculiar moodiness or fickleness of a romantic lover. In the opening speech he wishes the music to be played on as music is the food of love, then he demands the musician to stop the music. In place of the actual experience of love, there is only excessive imagination of being in love. It accounts for such fickleness. Orsino is not in love with a person but in love with love.

Olivia is another figure in this romantic drama. At first, she is an impressive grief-stricken lady who after the death of her dear brother has abandoned all mirth of life. But soon we discover that her rejection of Orsino's love is only a mask and that she lacks self-knowledge and really desires to love. Her suppression of her real nature takes a peculiar comic revenge. At first sight, she falls passionately in love with a male exterior with an aggressiveness which makes Orsino look feminine. Olivia changes from the character who has put on a socially attractive mask to one who cannot see through the mask which society has imposed on Viola. Though Olivia's love for Viola seems ridiculous for Viola's being a woman with a male exterior, it forces us to revise our view of Olivia completely and recognise the new energy of passion with which she is possessed.

Viola resembles Rosalind of "As you like it". Like Rosalind, she disguises herself as a man but her disguise creates complications for her. She serves as a foil to Olivia. Viola has also lost a brother. But her situation does not allow her the luxury of grief. She is deeply in love with Orsino but she most dutifully takes the message of Orsino's love to Olivia. Olivia falls in love with her male exterior at first sight and creates a romantic complication. Viola's love for Orsino is not affected or sentimental but healthy.

Malvolio and Andrew Aguecheek are ruled by their mistaken notions of the role of an upper class gentleman. Malvolio as well as Sir Andrew is not so much in love with Olivia as a victim of self-love. In the case of Aguecheek, Sir Toby befools him by holding up a painted mirror to him in which he finds himself a worthy suitor for Olivia. Another victim of self-love is Malvolio who is proud of his image as it is reflected in the shrewdly written letter of Maria in Olivia's hand.

Viola cuts through all masks and disguise with absolute clarity. She admits her irrationality of her passion for Orsino. She has no illusions. She needs a mask. She is in the form of Cesario, an imitation Sebastian which creates confusion. "What we will" at this stage is the arrival of Sebastian. The confrontation of the two identical images, Viola and Sebastian brings the plot to a close as it provides for discarding all masks and disguises revealing all the errors and follies. All the lovers thus unmask to reveal or realise their true identities.

Twelfth Night is a romantic comedy. At the heart of the play is love and the play has a peculiar romantic charm. Love in the play comprises of a variety of subtle shades. Like other romantic comedies there are twins, disguised identities and an almost wonderfully magical resolution of the plot.

14

"Lycidas" by Milton

Milton's "Lycidas" is a pastoral elegy on the premature and accidental death of his fellow, poet, Edward King who was drowned in the Irish sea. It is a pastoral elegy. The very name "Lycidas" which is used as a pseudonym for Edward King occurs in the pastoral elegies of the classical poets. This along with the other paraphernalia of the pastoral elegy like invocation of the Muse, pastoral imagery, train of mourners and universal lament confirm the impression of a pastoral elegy. This is the surface of the poem. But there is a strong, personal undercurrent throughout. Edward King's death provides Milton with an occasion to struggle with his own personal problem. "Lycidas" is thus, comparable to Shelley's "Adonais" which formally deals with Keats's death but actually the poet is preoccupied with his own personal problem.

If we understand the true nature of the poem, the digressions in the poem will fall exactly in place. The poem tends to be personal from the very beginning. "Lycidas is dead ere his prime" and Milton comes to shatter the leaves of his poetry "before the mellowing year". The immaturity of Milton as a poet compels him to introduce his personal note at the outset:

> "So may some gentle Muse
> With lucky words favour my destined urn,
> And bid fair peace be to my sable shroud"

The poem tends to focus not on Lycidas or Edward King but on the pastoral background which Milton shares with Lycidas. Here their dedication to their pastoral trade signifies their dedication to the art of poetry.

For we nursed upon the self-same hill,
Fed the same flocks by fountain, shade, and rill,
Together, both, ere the high lawns appeared
Under the opening eyelids of the morn
We drove afield, and both together heard.

The poetic paragraph is replete with repeated references to their shared past in terms of such words and phrases as "we", "self-same", "together", "both", "our" and their frequent repetitions. Milton finds his own shadow with the image of Lycidas all along and thus his death brings to his mind some personal questions which he tries to answer through this poem.

Milton had before him the lofty ideal of the classical poet and he was leading a life of dedication for this ideal. With the sudden and premature death of a fellow poet who was also dedicated poet, the question about the use of self-denying labour crops up in his mind when fate can split the thin thread of life any time:

> "Alas! what boots it with uncessant care to tend the homely, slighted shepherd's trade/ And strictly meditate the thankless Muse?"

The question and the reply of Phoebus that fame is not the plant that grows on the mortal soil and that the real reward is set apart for such labour in the heaven do not form digression from the central concern of the poem. Lycidas is dead. But Milton is another Lycidas who is alive and needs the answer to this question. The possible, premature death hangs like a shadow in the mind of Milton from the very beginning. This is the central question of the poem. Therefore, it is not a digression.

What we call digression concerns the speech of the pilot of the Galilean Lake (St. Peter) in the poem which is directed against the corrupt clergymen who do not tend their flock, and scramble for the feast. In fact, the speech of St. Peter digresses from the central concern of the poem. But since Edward was also ordained to be a priest, St. Peter mourns the loss to the church in the death of Lycidas. Though really a digression, it has some relevance also. It reflects the personal struggle of Milton against the corrupt practices of the clergymen. "Lycidas" is, of course, a personal poem where Milton is less concerned with the sorrow for the dead than trying to resolve his own personal conflict through the poem. The two, so-called digressions reflect the personal nature of the poem which professes to be a pastoral elegy.

Q. "Lycidas" is a moving poem. Discuss.

Ans. "Lycidas" is a pastoral elegy written at the death of one of Milton's friends, Edward King, a young scholar who was drowned in the Irish Sea. At this time, Milton was a relatively young man and engaged in his pursuit of literary fame. The poem is a perfect pastoral elegy with its pastoral background and imagery, the invocation to the muse, the classical allusions, the universal lament, procession of mourners and the final reconciliation.

The poem moves us at times especially where Milton laments the change that has taken place with the death of Edward King:

> But, O the heavy change, now thou art gone,
> Now than art gone and never must return.

There is certainly a deep sense of loss registered in the plangent rhythm of the lines. The voice of grief breaks out in the form of the immediacy of utterance. There is pressure of feelings behind the words and rhythm in the lines where the poet requests the dolphins to carry the dead body of Edward King to the shore:

> Look homeward, angel, now, and melt with ruth
> And ye dolphins, waft the hapless youth.

There is pathos in the rise and fall of the rhythm and the phrase "hapless youth" particularly evokes pity for the drowned.

But "Lycidas" is not a poem of four lines. It consists of one hundred ninety-four lines. The cumulative impression that the poem leaves on the mind of the reader is summed up in the remark of T.S. Eliot "If we think that an elegy requires the justification of unfeigned and cordial regret we find the poem frigid." Dr. Johnson has also remarked that "it is not to be considered as the effusion of real passion; for passion runs not after remote allusions and obscure opinions [...] where there is leisure for fiction there is little grief." Thus the critics largely agree on the point that "Lycidas" is devoid of genuine grief for Edward King.

Critics have ignored the fact that "Lycidas" cannot be a cry of personal grief as Tennyson's "In Memoriam" or Wordsworth's "A Slumber Did My Spirit Seal." They communicate the intensity of genuine grief because they are rooted in close relationship. Milton had not intimate personal relationship with Edward King whose premature death is the occasion of the poem. Milton verges on the personal apprehension of death rather than on the communication of suffering as the result of a friend's death. As in Shelley's "Adonais" and Arnold's "Thyrsis", Milton turns Edward King into a mediumistic character to exploit his own feelings. Hence the proposition of the poem is one and the communication of the poem is another. W.M. Tillyard rightly points out that critics have failed to distinguish between the nominal subject of the poem and the real subject of the poem between what it profess to be and what it is about.

"Lycidas" is also conceived and composed in a different mood and temper from that of "In Memoriam" of "A Slumber Did My Spirit Seal." It has formal affinities with Shelley's "Adonais" and Arnold's "Thyrsis" as it belongs to the pastoral tradition. Critics have ignored the limitations that the pastoral tradition imposed on Milton's poem. Poetry is the spontaneous over-flow of powerful feelings which when recollected in tranquility acquires a form. As a result of the pre-elected form, Milton had to work within the limitations of the pastoral form. The forging out of a form under the stress of powerful feelings was out of the question. Milton was compelled to exploit the classical allusions. The swarming classical allusions which demand strained and informed attention impede and obstruct the singular flow of emotion and thus impair the emotional impact of the poem. Our attention is deflected from Edward King to the allusions which impart a breadth rather than depth to the poem. It is not out of place to mention that the pastoral shepherd has got an identity beyond Milton and so Milton's grief expressed through the shepherd cannot be as personal and direct as in non-pastoral elegies, for example "In Memoriam or Lucy poems."

"Lycidas" moves us as a pastoral elegy does. It is not a condensed and direct expression of sorrow as it has a pastoral form. The reasons for the absence of an intense emotional grief in the poem is partly personal and partly formal.

THE STRUCTURE OF LYCIDAS

John Milton was a poet as well as an organist. He had a highly developed sense of the music of words. Therefore, music plays a prominent role in his poetic compositions and "Lycidas" is no exception. Milton had a perfect sense of form. It is evident from the structure of "Lycidas".

"Lycidas" is not written in stanza form. It consists of laisses of varied length, variously rhymed, with unrhymed verses and trimeters here and there. Each laisse is the reflection of a mood of the poet. The poem is, thus, a musical organisation of successive emotional moods. It moves in successive waves of emotion and with each outbreak, the poet returns to the pastoral ground. E.M.W. Tillyard points out that the poem has the plot-obliquity. He means the same thing as he refers to the various sections of the poem to suggest the plot-obliquity.

The first two sections of the poem which deal with the premature death of the promising poet, Lycidas or Edward King form the moving background of the poem where the occasion for the poem is fully stated:

> For Lycidas is dead, dead ere his prime
> Young Lycidas and hath not left his peer.

Milton expresses the apprehension of his own premature death, the possibility of sharing a fate on the ground of sharing a common background of life.

The central question which agitates the mind of the poet bursts out in the third section of the poem. The poet asks what study and self-discipline avail if one should die before they bear fruit:

> Alas! what boots it with uncessant care
> To tend the homely slighted shepherd's trade
> And strictly meditate the thankless muse?
> Were it not better done as other use
> To sport with Amaryllis in the shade
> Or with the tangle of Naera's hair?

It gives the impression of a monologue. But as soon as the voice of the speaker ends, the voice of Phoebus is audible who points out that the true reward lies not in this worldly fame but in heaven.

The climax is reached in the speech of St. Peter where the thought of the young poet's death makes him turn wrathfully on the corrupt clergy whom death has spared but judgment will not spare. The bitter criticism of the clergy is made by St. Peter as he mourns the loss of the church in the death of Lycidas.

The fourth section strikes a note of calm and joy after the fury has burst out. The conflict is resolved as the speaker has found his solace in the thought that in place of this worldly fame Lycidas or Edward King has been rewarded with eternal fame in heaven. Then the speaker of the poem is identified as the "uncouth swain". He decides to take up again his pastoral trade which he had suspended on account of the death of Lycidas.

The structure of the poem is complex. The poem begins with the personal pronoun "I" suggesting that the speaker of the poem is Milton himself. But by the time the poem ends, Milton has distanced himself completely from the speaking persona in the poem who is identified as an "uncouth swain". Thus apart from the musical structure of the poem, the poem takes on the form of the dramatic narrative also in which the dominant voice is the voice of the "uncouth swain". But it gives way to other voices in the poem also. The voice of the "uncouth swain" is interrupted from time to time by the voice of Phoebus, the Herald of the sea, Hippotades, the pilot of the Galilean lake. The poem ends with the resolve of the uncouth swain to stop his lament and take up anew his pastoral trade which he had suspended on account of his friend's death. It, thus, lends a dramatic narrative touch to the poem. The poem is a collocation of the poet's moods which are reflected in each laisse of the poem. The tone in the poem goes on modulating and finally acquires a dramatic form.

"LYCIDAS" AS A PASTORAL ELEGY

John Milton's "Lycidas" is a pastoral elegy. The pastoral elegy is different from the elegy where the grief of the poet finds a direct, natural expression as in *The Lucy* Poems of Wordsworth and "In Memoriam" of Tennyson; The impression of intense, personal loss is very strong in these poems. But in the pastoral elegy, there is no direct expression of feeling. The poet has to mould his feelings in keeping with the conventions of the pastoral elegy. Milton's choice of the pastoral form imposes its limitation on his elegy, "Lycidas."

As a pastoral elegy "Lycidas" belongs to the tradition of Shelley's "Adonais" and Arnold's "Thyrsis". The very name, "Lycidas" a pseudonym for Edward King occurs as the name of a shepherd in classical elegies. This along with the other paraphernalia of the pastoral elegy like the invocation of the Muse, pastoral background, train of mourners, universal lament, classical allusions and reconciliation confirm the impression of a pastoral elegy.

"Lycidas" is not a cry of personal grief as Tennyson's "In Memoriam" or Wordsworth's "A Slumber did My Spirit Seal" is because Milton did not have intimate personal relationship with Edward King whose premature death provides Milton with the occasion for the composition of "Lycidas". Edward King was not a close friend of Milton as Hallam was of Tennyson. "Lycidas," is thus, not a lament for the loss of a friend. Edward King stands as a symbol of the dedicated poet-priest. His premature death with its context of unfulfilled promise raises some doubt in the mind of Milton with which he struggles in this poem:

> Alas! what boots it with uncessant care
> To tend the homely, slighted shepherd's trade
> And strictly meditate the thankless Muse?

Milton questions the meaning of dedication to the Muse of poetry and living a life of renunciation and labour when blind fate can slit the thread of life before the achievement of fame. Milton's lament is not so much for Edward King as for the premature death of a dedicated poet-priest. Milton identifies himself with this poet-priest because at the time of the composition of Lycidas, Milton was "shattering the leaves" of his poetic talent before "the mellowing year". The critics, who fail to distinguish between the nominal and the real subject of the poem, what the poem professes to be and what it is, are inclined to make derogatory criticism of "Lycidas".

The pastoral form imposes its limitation on Milton. He is compelled to exploit classical allusions in the poem. The classical allusions demand strained and informed attention and impair the cumulative effect of the poem. They impede and interrupt the singular flow of emotion. Eliot is not wrong when he says, "If we think that an elegy requires the justification of unfeigned and cordial regret, we may find, the poem 'frigid'". The poem is, in fact, not meant to register the sense of loss but to focus on the issues raised by the premature death of a promising poet-priest. The choice of the pastoral form where there is no direct, immediate and spontaneous expression of personal grief was probably dictated by the personal need of Milton. The subject of the poem is neither Edward King nor Milton himself but the premature death of a promising poet-priest. Hence the poem does not concentrate on the communication of suffering as a result of a friend's death rather than on the issues raised by the death of Edward King, the poet-priest.

15

The Paradise Lost by Milton

Sketch the character of Satan.

Or

"Milton is of the devil's party" Comment.

Or

"Milton justifies the ways of God to men". Discuss.

John Milton's *The Paradise Lost* like Homer's *Odyssey,* Virgil's *Aenied* and Spenser's *The Fairy Queen* is a great English epic. But the difference between these epics and Milton's *The Paradise Lost* is that they have aroused little controversy while Milton's *The Paradise Lost* has kicked off controversies about one of the main figures of the epic. Milton, like Shakespeare, is a rich and complex artist. As the images of Shakespeare find a different reflection in the criticism of every age, the image of Satan in *The Paradise Lost* found varying interpretations from age to age. Milton had his declared intention in *The Paradise Lost* to justify the ways of God to men. But with the changing interpretations of *The Paradise Lost.* Satan was seen to be a projection of Milton himself and Milton was found of the Devil's party.

To say like Blake in the nineteenth century or W.M. Tillyard in the twentieth century that Milton is the hero himself or Milton is of the Devil's party is to suggest a discrepancy between Milton's declared intention and his achievement, between the conscious and the unconscious purposes of Milton's achievement. *The Paradise Lost* is the poetic document of Christian faith in the providence of God and the differing and different interpretations of the epic are rooted in the brilliant projection of Satan in the first two books of *The Paradise Lost.* Satan is seen as a mighty, terrible and immortal being infinitely superior to man in dignity of his nature as well as the dreadful powers he retains still about him. He is invested with the heroic qualities of character. This admirable figure of Satan is confined to the first two books of *The Paradise Lost.* Viewed in the entirety of the epical scheme, the heroic qualities of Satan are not to be imitated or admired. As B. Rajan points out with Milton's contemporaries the response was predominantly one of fear. The effect, as Addison said of Satan's portrayal was "to raise and terrify our imagination". The vision served to remind the reader that it was only by God's grace that they could hope to overcome the enormous forces against which they were contending.

Milton was trying to explain the introduction of sin into the heaven. Satan is the image of pride or self love. Christ is the image of abnegation in self-love. The poem presents a contest and conflict between these two states of being with the temptations which provoke men and women in that state of injured merit. Milton's *The Paradise Lost* can be understood fully with reference to his passionate vision of divine order and the reign of disorder in their souls, in nature and history with the sin of Adam and Eve at the instigation of Satan. If in the first two books of *The Paradise Lost* the image of Satan acquires impressive brilliance, it is not on account of Milton's sympathy with the rebel. Milton gave the rebel his due. His empathetic insight into the mind of the Devil which is the *sine qua non* of artistic creation imparts the false glory to the character of Satan. It is not true to say that Milton projected himself into the figure of Satan. Satan is not Milton's self-portrait nor Milton is of the Devil's party and his unconscious sympathy is not with the Devil. Milton's *The Paradise Lost* cannot be looked upon only as an exercise in Christian Theology but a magnificent artistic creation.

Milton's critics have overlooked a very important fact while jumping to their conclusion that the presentation of the heroic qualities of Satan is continually accompanied by explicit or implicit condemnation. The poet not only uses derogatory names, but also suggests the accompanying condemnation by the overtone of imagery. Words like "Memphis", "Alcari" and "Sultan" were associated not with splendour but tyranny. Fallen angels are likened to a plague of locusts and a barbarian invasion. It is not Milton who failed in his declared purpose behind the creation of *The Paradise Lost*, it is his critics who read themselves into the image of Satan as a rebel hero. Milton has made sufficiently clear the consequences of pride which is associated with the figure of the Devil. The character of Satan is a complex character. A number of contradictory qualities are mixed up by poetic alchemy into a complex whole. This is why his character arouses complex human emotion and response in the reader.

16

Rape of the Lock by Pope

Heroic poems are like the *Odyssey, The Aenied* and *The Paradise Lost* dealing with man in his exalted aspects. The action is weighty, their personages are dignified and style elevated. Mock-epic or heroic poems imitate this style and by applying it to situations that are not at all exalted create a comic effect. Thus a mock-heroic poem always involves a contrariness between the form and the content. *The Rape of the Lock* is the masterpiece in this manner because it provides a parallel to a complete epic poem. *Dunciad* and *Mac Flecknoe* are the hollow imitations of the heroic ritual of the epic. But *The Rape of the Lock* provides a perfectly rounded parallel to the epic.

The very title of the poem contains the essential form in which the poem develops. "Rape" is a word pregnant with connotations of high moral significance which is juxtaposed with "lock" which deflates the sense of gravity with its bathos. Pope announces at the very outset: "slight is the subject but not so the praise." The juxtaposition of the serious with the ludicrous, the magnificent with the trivial, this contrast constitutes the very form of the poem.

The poem begins with the scene of the sleeping Belinda who receives a dream message from the gods through her guardian sylph, Ariel. Ariel informs her that she "is the distinguished care of thousand bright inhabitants of the air" and warns her against the impending danger." It recalls the visitation of angels in Milton's *The Paradise Lost.* The use of the machinery of the sylphs is in keeping with the mock-heroic vein in which the poem is conceived and composed. It enhances the mock-heroic effect by the involvement of the celestial beings in the human affairs. It lends the impression of universal significance to the happenings and we share the concerns of the sylphs and wait with them the dreaded event:

> With beating hearts the dire events they wait
> Anxious and trembling for the birth of fate

Thus the use of machinery accentuates the gravity and seriousness of the anticipated event. But when the action takes place, its triviality is thrown in sharp contrast with the charged atmosphere which is built by Ariel's distribution of duties among sylphs, "the light militia of the lower sky" to meet the situation. The climax of the action comes which is elaborately prepared for and anxiously anticipated. But the action — cutting off a lock of hair from Belinda's hair is insignificant. Yet Pope knows the art of making the small into the great, the trivial into the magnificent. Such a trivial action is dressed in the vocabulary packed with the association of grandeur : "fatal engine", "fate urged the shears", "sacred hair", "forever" imparting the impression of something grand and formidable. The mock-heroic vein is maintained all through the poem. In the passage describing the effect of the clipping of the lock of Belinda, husbands and lapdogs are equated:

> Not louder shrieks to pitying Heaven are cast
> When husbands or when lapdogs breathe their last
>
> or
>
> Not fierce Othello in so loud a strain
> Roared for the handkerchief that caused the pain.

The juxtaposition of husbands with lapdogs and the allusion to Othello are examples of the blend of the levity and seriousness in the poem.

Pope is out to make his poem perfect from whatever angle it is seen. The journey to the cave of spleen by Umbriel runs parallel to the journey to the underworld in classical epic. *The Rape of the Lock* probably would not have been complete imitation of an epic poem without battles. Boileau's *Le Lutrin* had mimicked a Homerick battle by means of books, Garth's

Dispensary by means of urinals and brass-weights. Pope has his battles with fans and snuff. But the parody is twice intensified by having also a battle in the form of the game of ombre. The preparation of Belinda for the day has too the echoes of the arming of the epical hero:

Her files of pins extend their shining rows
The fair each moment rises in her charms.

There is an allusion to the military preparation in "files of pins" extending their shining rows like columns of soldiers lined up in polished armour. Belinda's various items of armour are listed: "puffs; powders, patches, bibles, billet-doux." Alliteration gives precision to the catalogue and adds force to the telling juxtaposition, of "Bibles" and "billet–doux". As one by one she puts on her "arms" she becomes a more redoubtable protagonist for the epical contest with the Baron. Finally her beauty is "awful" and her eyes flash with "keener lightnings". The poem finally ends with the moral: "Beauties in vain their pretty eyes may roll/ Charms strike the sight but merit twins the soul." Clarissa's speech is almost word-for-word adaptation of Sarpedon's speech to Glaucus from Illiad. It has no effect on Belinda. Therefore gods intervene and settle the dispute by the apotheosis of the lock.

The Rape of the Lock is a perfect parallel to an epic poem with its machinery, arming of the protagonist, the journey to the underworld, the battles, the moral and the divine intervention. But the epic grandeur and magnificence is used in order to set forth the experience which is the opposite of the magnificent and exalted.

Write a note on the use of machinery in *The Rape of the Lock*

The machinery signifies that part of a poem in which the deities, angels or demons are made to act. This machinery is generally an essential part of an epic. Alexander Pope as he models his poetry on the heroic examples employs machinery in his poem, *The Rape of the Lock.* Originally the poem was written in two cantos only. Later it was enriched with the machinery of sylphs and extended into five cantos. The sylphs were inserted into the most appropriate places so that nowhere in the text of the poem the patchwork is discernible.

The epic poet, took the machinery from the religion of the country as Milton took it from the Bible. On the other hand, lay the examples of Homer and Virgil who used Roman and Greek gods in their poems. Alexander Pope employed neither Christian machinery nor the classical one. He based his machines on the Rosicrucian doctrine of spirits available in *Le comte de Gabalis* by Abbe Villars. According to this doctrine, the four elements inhabited by spirits are called sylphs, gnomes, nymphs and salamanders. The sylphs inhabit the airs, the gnomes, the earth, the nymphs, water and salamanders inhabit fire. Pope modifies his source to suit his purposes. He explains the existence of these spirits in keeping with the tone of the poem. The fiery termagants are transformed into salamanders, the soft yielding women into nymphs. The graver prude takes the shape of gnomes and the light coquettes acquire the form of sylphs. They help to establish the parallel between the poem and epic traditions with the consequent ludicrous effect.

The very title of poem *The Rape of the Lock* contains the form that develops through the poem. "Rape" is a word pregnant with high moral significance which is juxtaposed with "lock" which deflates the sense of gravity with its bathos. Pope declares at the very outset, "Slight is the subject but not so the praise." The juxtaposition of the serious with the ludicrous, the magnificent with the trivial — this contrast constitutes the very form of the poem. The machinery of the sylphs is part of the mock-heroic framework of the poem as it puts the trivial material of the poem on the epic scale. The consequent tension between the form and the content creates a comic effect.

The machinery in the classical epic is employed to project the magnitude of the events which are supervised, controlled and are the concerns of the gods. A parallel between the classical epic and *The Rape of the Lock* is evident in the very first canto. The poem begins with the guardian sylph appearing in Belinda's dream. It recalls the somber epic visitation of angels or dream messages from gods:

Her guardian sylph prolonged the balmy rest
'Twas he had summon'd to her silent bed
The morning dream that hovered her head.

The guardian sylph fully explains to Belinda the nature of the existence of the four types of spirits as also how sylphs, coquettes turned spirits, are behind the mysterious flirtish behaviour of the virgins. These sylphs guard the purity of the melting maids by "shifting in time the moving toyship of their heart." Belinda, the fairest of mortals, is "the distinguished care of thousand bright inhabitants of the air". She holds this status because she is fair and chaste and only such coquettes deserve this position:

Know further yet whoever fair and chaste
Rejects mankind, is by some sylph embraced.

Finally the guardian sylph discloses his identity as Ariel and warns Belinda of the impending danger:

In the clear mirror of thy ruling star
I saw, alas! some dread event impend
Ere to the main the morning sun descend;
But heaven reveals not what, or how or where.
Warn'd by the sylph, oh pious maid, beware,
This to disclose is all thy guardian can
Beware of all, but most beware of man.

It creates a high level of expectation of some serious event striking Belinda. So the classical machinery, "The light machinery of the lower sky" has moved into action to send her the message through a dream. Belinda becomes oblivious of the warning in dream:

Wounds, charms and ardours were no sooner read
But all the vision vanished from thy head.

Now the impending danger becomes doubly sure and we watch the progress of events with anxious care. It is in the fitness of things that Canto II unfolds the brilliant action of the poem. Belinda sails on the Thames and under the command of the Ariel numberless sylphs are immediately distributed their duties as the nature of the danger remains unrevealed.

Therefore, the spirits keep their watch everywhere and all the time. Under the threat of punishment for neglect of duty, the spirits take their places and dread the event:

> With beating hearts the dire event they wait
> Anxious and trembling for the birth of fate.

The dreaded event takes place in spite of the care of spirits as Belinda's chastity of thought is violated because the earthly lover lurks at her heart and so the aerial guard is withdrawn from her.

As the sylphs retire, the gnomes take their charge. The chief gnome, Umbriel dives into the cave of spleen and from there brings bagfuls of sobs, sighs and tears. At once she is stricken with grief at the removal of a lock of hair from her head.

The use of machinery in *The Rape of the Lock* as in the classical epics serves to accentuate the seriousness and gravity of the action. It is the external surface of the poem. As the action (cutting off a lock of hair) unfolds itself, its triviality is thrown in sharp contrast. The juxtaposition of the magnificent and the trivial is meant to secure a mock-heroic effect.

ALEXANDER POPE

Alexander Pope (1681-1744) is the greatest figure in the eighteenth century poetry. He is the true successor of Dryden and the best representative of his age. On the advice of Walsh, he set out to be a correct poet which meant a closer approach to the Ancients. Hence Pope's "Pastorals" have nothing of the Wordsworthian touch in them. His scenery and shepherds are taken from his classical models.

Pope's poetry can be divided into two main groups. The first group consists of poems like *The Pastorals* of feeling, imagination and harmony. The second group consists of poems in which satirical, witty and didactic elements are paramount. Joseph Wharton considers Pope a great wit but not a great poet. He recognizes that he wrote poems which are works of imagination. These include *Windsor Forest, The Rape of the*

Lock, Translations from Homes, Eloisa to Abelard, Elegy to the Memory of an unfortunate Lady and *The Temple of Fame.* The best of those poems are *Eloisa to Abelard* and *The Rape of the Lock.* The first has a poetic and dramatic value. There is an eloquent rendering of the ebb and flow of passion and the conflict between human love and religious devotion.

The Rape of the Lock is the masterpiece of Pope. The occasion of the poem was slight. Lord Petre, a fop at the court had clipped a lock of hair from the luxuriant hair of Arabella Fermor. The relation between the two houses were strained on this account. Pope used this incident for the composition of his masterpiece, *The Rape of the Lock.* It is a mock-heroic poem which reminds of, as it contrasts with, the serious epic of Homer, Virgil and Milton. *Instead of the gods* of the epics, Pope introduced the gnomes, spirits, sylphs and salamanders. But the pre-dominant interest of the poet is the brilliant picture of the fashionable life of the time. It is the greatest poem of its kind.

The form of Pope's satire is enjoyable. It is not inspired by any larger view of human nature, its vices and weaknesses as the satire of Swift and Juvenal. The element of personal animosity animates his satire. Hence one must be familiar with the social history of the time in order to understand fully "Moral Essays," "The Dunciad" and "Imitations of Horace".

Pope devoted the middle period of his life to the translation of "Illiad" and "Odyssey." During this period, he composed his "Essay on Man." There is nothing original in Pope's doctrines. They are the doctrines of the Neo-classicists but they are expressed with memorable point and felicity. Pope took from his friend Bolingbroke the Philosophy that is well in the best of all possible ways. "The Essay" is a series of either common-place or disputable propositions. His poetry can be described well in his own terms as "what oft was felt but never so well expressed". The eloquence is so flowing as in "The Essay on Criticism". Pope's wordings are so felicitious that common places acquire a new attractiveness. The phrases from Pope have passed into common proverbs and became so much part of it that people use it without knowing that they came from Pope.

"The Dunciad" which started as a controversy regarding Shakespeare later turned out to be a condemnation of dullness in general and of the literary men of his age who had aroused Pope's anger by their criticism of Pope's genius. It was very popular in its time but it is only of topical interest until we come to chaos. "The Epistle to Dr. Arbuthnot," a shorter poem will probably interest the modern reader more than "The Dunciad". The satiric portraits of Sporus, Addison or Lord Harvey are master strokes of his satiric art.

Pope is at his best in his satires. The satirical element is predominant in *Essays on Criticism, The Rape of the Lock* and *The Essay on Man.* The follies of poets and critics, the follies and foibles of woman and of mankind are the themes of these works. Horace was his chief model. Temperamentally both were different. He has given finished expression to the wisdom of common sense, the wit and satire of a keen observer of the foibles and follies of men and women in a condensed felicitous language whereby its balanced rhythm heightens the pointedness of the aphorism, epigram or impassioned declamation. Pope was a perfect artist. But he lacked the profundity of vision. His satires are occasional, personal and prejudiced.

17

Epistle to Dr. Arbuthnot by Pope

The heroic couplet was the main channel through which all English literary imagination flowed during the eighteenth century. The history of literary movements is not the history of artificial imposition but the result of a series of circumstances. The heroic couplet of the eighteenth century is not a deliberate artificial medium but the natural one. The blank verse became loose in the hands of the Jacobeans and the prosaic looseness set in. The iambic beat was maintained in Shakespeare with great freedom, variety and remarkable precision but later on the freedom of the Jacobeans degenerated into license. The basic iambic beat was lost and the blank verse became indistinguishable from prose. There was reaction against this looseness towards greater prosodic control. The greater use of the heroic couplet was the reaction against formlessness.

Dryden is the master of the heroic couplet. The heroic couplet acquired smoothness from him. But it was Pope who perfected the medium. After Pope there was no possibility of any subtlety. In a typical Popean couplet, balance and antithesis, neatness and felicity of expression are the chief characteristics. The heroic couplet gives Pope the remarkable vision, power and prosodic control for the achievement of greater satiric effectiveness.

Pope exhibits a very wide range of rhythmic effects. Strictly confined within the limits of the heroic couplet, he achieves the effects of blank verse, soliloquy and dialogue and renders it a powerful satiric medium. Consequently, the emotional range of Pope's poetry is very wide. He responded to different kinds of things with remarkable variety. The perfection and variety in his poetry derive from the perfect adjustment of style to feeling in such widely different poems as *The Rape of the Lock, The Dunciad, Eloisa to Abelard* and *The Epistle to Dr. Arbuthnot.* Pope is set apart from other poets not so much for the quality of his vision but for the skill with words, images metaphors, rhythm and rhymes: "True wit is Nature to advantage dressed/ What oft was felt never so well expressed." Pope's poetry was to illustrate a sustained felicity of style and sweetness of versification to the point of perfection in well-balanced couplets with none of the lapses in which the poetry of Dryden abounds.

Pope's poetry offers a wide spectrum of excitement and variety. The tone is superbly adjusted to the theme. Though the medium is, by and large, the heroic couplet, he achieves a sense of variety by the superb manipulation of rhythm. Dryden achieved variety by the means of triplets. Pope achieved variety by the manipulation of internal resources. He changes the places of pause. The change in the place of pause gives a sense of variety in the movement. Edith Sitwell remarks "Pope is capable of infinite variation. Far from being mechanical, the heroic couplet remains a natural medium of expression. While the structure remains the same, the texture varies in Pope." The rhythm is adjusted to the movement of the feeling. The heroic couplet reaches its high water mark with the poetry of Pope. Each word strikes our ears with a confident solidity. The rhythm of the line helps isolate the word for contemplation.

Donne's couplets are not closed like Pope's and the rhymes do not call attention to themselves as Pope's do. For while Pope uses rhyme words to point and sharpen his lines, Donne makes his rhymes unobtrusive so they provide an artful counterpoint to the seemingly artless flow of narrative and reflection. The words in Pope seem to stand apart from one another like the parts of a machine in "an exploded diagram," each word possessing its own special weight of meaning and value. The other style of Pope where he is capable of achieving the effect of blank verse within the limits of the heroic couplet is present here: "Shut, shut the door, poor John, fatigued I said/ Tie up the knocker, say I am sick I am dead/ The dog star rages! Nay, it is past a doubt/ All Bedlam or Parnassus is let out." The whole mood of exasperation is dramatised. The movement of the rhythm is controlled to suggest the mood of disgust. The repetition of the word "shut" gives the sense of urgency to avoid poetasters. The adjectives "sick" and "dead" combine to emphasize disgust. The rhymes do not sound like rhymes as metrical emphases coincide with the fall of emphasis in common speech as in Donne's poetry. It reads like a soliloquy in an Elizabethan tragedy. Words are dropped in place and properly stressed. The rhythm of the dialogue is also produced at times in the poem and we are not aware of the medium at all. The transition of mood makes for the dramatic appeal of the poem.

Byron appreciated Pope. Though the poets of the nineteenth century give him no regard, Pope wrote with the ease of speech, rhythm, the ease and flow associated with the blank verse. As Pope exhibited a wide spectrum of rhythmic effects through his poetry, he exhausted the possibilities of the heroic couplet in his age.

Discuss *An Epistle to Dr. Arbuthnot* as a satire.

Or

Comment on the portrait of Atticus and Sporus.

Or

"Pope is a man of peace goaded into satire" Comment.

Or

***"The Epistle to Dr. Arbuthnot* is a blend of satire and biography" Discuss.**

An Epistle to Dr. Arbuthnot is a rich and complex poem. Pope had "no thought of publishing it, till it pleased some persons of Rank and Fortune to attack in a very extraordinary manner, not only my writings but my person, morals and family." The "persons of Rank and Fortune" who prompted this poem of self-justification and defence were Lord Hervey and Lady Wortley Montague who joined in an attack on Pope entitled *Verses Addressed to the Imitator of Horace.* In *The Epistle to Dr. Arbuthnot,* Pope presents himself as a man of peace goaded into satire by the intolerable behaviour of fools and Knaves. Unlike *The Rape of The Lock,* it is a purely personal poem arising from the background of his personal circumstances but it is the art of Pope which has transformed it into a thing of timeless beauty.

The poem is full of the portraits of the real persons who figured in the personal life of the poet. The portrait of Atticus is modelled on Joseph Addison. Pope starts by giving a fair tribute to Addison's talent in a forthright and frank manner. He exhibits open-mindedness in his reference to Addison's "genius", "fame" and "talent" and "art". He does not condemn him directly. There is indirection and irony. The restraint renders the satire more effective. Addison's ability "to write, converse and live" is qualified by "ease" which gives a sense of refined affluence. But Addison's faults are the faults of Addison, the man. The faults in so great a man make them appear worse by setting the example of the corruption of the best:

> Should such a man, too fond to rule alone
> Bear, like the Turk, no Brother near the throne
> View him with scornful, yet with jealous eyes
> And hate for Arts that caus'd himself to rise,
> Damn with praise, assent with civil lear,
> And without sneering teach the rest to sneer
> Willing to wound, and yet afraid to strike
> Just hint a fault and hesitate dislike.

The portrait of Atticus consists of one single sentence with multiple clauses. Couplet after couplet turns Atticus into the perfect image of hypocrisy and the balance of antithesis reflects the duplicity of the character of Atticus. There is a supreme control of personal fury in the portrait of Atticus. It is the example of sustained and subtle organistation. Lytton Strachey compares Pope to "a monkey on a upstairs window ladling out boiled oil upon such passersby whom the wretch had a grudge against". But here his malice does not get the better of his art. He gives the devil his due as there is an attitude of fair concession. There is almost Drydenian mellowness and maturity. The personal animosity is transmuted into detached irony. Addison's portrayal is an excellent account of his cool and controlled manner but the effect is devastating. Atticus's dishonest dealing serves as a striking contrast to the honesty of the poet who deals fairly with his fellow poets.

There is great variety in the satiric models of Pope. The same cannot be said about Dryden's satire. The portrait of Sporus offers a sharp contrast with the polite urban tone of Pope in the portrait of Atticus:

Let Sporus tremble — what? That thing of silk
Sporus, that mere white curd of Ass's milk.

Here Arbuthnot is supposed to interrupt but his advice is rejected. There is surely an outrageous outburst of personal feelings. There is a note of intimate *tete-a-tete* and complete rejection of politeness:

Yet let me flap the Bug with gilded wings
The painted child of Dirt that stinks and stings.

But the anger is transmitted into art. The outburst of rage is subdued into the play of sensuous imagery of "gilded wings" and "painted child". To Arbuthnot, Sporus is "a thing of silk"; "a white curd of Ass's milk", "a butterfly" but to Pope he is "a gilded bug that stinks and stings" or "a fawning spaniel", "a hunter" taught to cringe from killing, then an ugly toad like Satan "close at the ear of Eve" and finally a snake. Like Dryden though the style is witty, unlike Dryden's verse it is also capable of carrying a degree of sensuousness. There is an esthetic beauty in the images, "painted child", "shallow streams run dimpling", "cherub's face" and "gilded wings" which contribute to the total effect of repugnance. In the portrait of Sporus the poet works by suggestion rather than by statement:

Eve's Tempter thus the Rabbins have exprest,
A cherub's face, a Reptile all the rest.

Beauty that shocks you, parts that none will trust
Wit that can creep and pride that licks the dust.

It is subtle, compressed and allusive. It makes demands on the mental and emotional alertness. It is by the use of the original sin as a point of reference that the poet controls the emotional and intellectual shades of tone. Pope responds differently to different kinds of stimuli and the perfection of his poetry derives from the perfect adjustment of style to feeling. We cannot say the same about Dryden. To Leslie Stephen and Lytton, Strachey, Pope "seems to be actually screaming with malignant fun". In fact, there is presence of strong personal feelings, the intensity of art is also most striking.

The animal images which abound in the climax of his disgust, the portrait of Sporus are bugs, spaniel, toad and snake. Pope flaps in self-defence. Thus he justifies satire from a man of peace. In the words of Elias F. Mengel. "It is not spiteful or inhuman to slap a mosquito or beat off a mad dog." He suffers fools and knaves with the greatest passions and restraint, but stung beyond endurance, he is forced to lash at them. The self-portrait of Pope is not Alexander Pope alone but the traditional representative of the satirist as well, the descendant of Horace, Juvenal and Boileau. It serves to bring into sharp contrast the characters already described in the poem. He has liked to represent himself as an honest man concerned to see the depravity of the times and anxious to arrest the standards from any further slipping away. The culminating image of apologia for his life and art is Pope, full of love, nursing his aged mother and asking heaven's blessing for his friend. This is at the furthest remove from the popular conception of the satirist as a malevolent man.

18

The Eve of St. Agnes by Keats

Keats was a supremely sensuous poet. He had an exquisite sensibility which was affected by the trembling of the leaf, the ripple in the river and the noiseless noise among the leaves. He had also a melancholy strain within him which enabled him to have a deep insight into "the strife and agonies of the human heart". His poetry reverberates with "the still sad music of humanity".

The Eve of St. Agnes has not the power of *Hyperion*, nor the fire of *Lamia*. It has not the superb and serene mastery of the Odes. But it is the most completely successful narrative poem. With this poem, Keats has at last found the realm of his poetic experience. There is neither fumbling nor insecurity of *Isabella*. It is the perfect expression of a sensuous experience.

Fausset, while defining romance, remarks that "romance has no other aim but the creation of sensuous beauty". *The Eve of St. Agnes* has the delight, the richness and the full bloom of romance. The poem incarnates the aesthetic imagination of the poet. The story is very slight. Porphyro secretly meets his beloved in the castle of a rich, inimical baron and succeeds in eloping with her. But such a paraphrase is reductive of the total impression. The poem releases the rich sensuous powers of Keats's imagination. It is a thing of sensuous beauty.

The very first stanza exhibits the power of Keats in atmosphere building. The epithet in the first line "bitter cold" is the central phrase. The rest of the stanza elaborates the effect of cold in detail. The bird (owl) the beast (hare) and the sheltered domesticated animal (flock) and man "indoors" (the beadman in the chapel) are all numb and silent under the effect of enveloping cold. The climax is reached in the freezing picture of the frosted breath.

Against this atmosphere of cold is set the warmth and glow of chambers ready to receive a thousand guests with its music, dance and festivity. There emerges the scene of some kind of vaguely medieval castle. The main features of the castle are a chapel with aisles, galleries, dusky Gothic windows with stained glass.

The poem has a unique musical beauty and richness of descriptive setting. Each Spenserian stanza is a pictorial unit complete in itself and yet part of the coherent design of the poem. It tends the poetic narrative towards tableau. It is not a dramatic narrative but descriptive narrative rich in beauty of minute details with its gliding musical sweetness which suggests the influence of Spenser. Nowhere such a rich blend of economy and richness is found in the history of English romance.

The heroine of the poem, Madeline is invested with a superb romantic beauty with a unique purity of the body and soul. In this she resembles Lady Una of Spenser whose physical beauty is also symbolic of spiritual beauty. But Madeline is not an allegorical figure. She remains earthly beloved like Imogen. Keats is at the height of his poetic powers in the description of the beauty of Madeline. The romantic beauty of Madeline combines with the magnificence and sphendour of the setting:

> Full on the casement shone the wintry moon
> And threw warm gules or Madeline's fair breast
> As down she knelt for heaven's grace and boon
> Rose-bloom fell on her hands, together prest.
> And on her silver cross soft amethyst
> And on her hair a glory like a saint
> She seem'd a splendid angel newly drest
> Save wings, for heaven: Porphyro grew faint
> She knelt so pure a thing, so free from mortal taint.

This stanza has a unique beauty of detail. It contributes to the richness of setting. The full moon, the symbol of love and romance presides over the drama of love. It throws "warm gules on Madeline's fair breast" who looks like "splendid angel newly drest". She is then "half hidden like a mermaid in a sea-weed". The delicate, sleeping beauty of Madeline finds its exquisite expression in the comparison "as a rose should shut and be a bud again". Keats has here created a supreme paragon of romantic beauty in the image of Madeline. The visual imagination is fused with the imagination of other senses:

> In her dream he melted as the rose
> Blendeth its odour with the violet.

The olfactory, visual, auditory and tactile images combine with the wealth of sensuous impression.

Keats exhibits his great sensuous powers in the poem, *The Eve of St. Agnes.* There is no indulgence in the delight of the senses for its own sake. The sense impressions are subservient to the needs of the poetic narration. They project the nature of the sensuous experience that is at the heart of the poem.

Comment on the imagery in *The Eve of St. Agnes*

Keats was a poet for whom beauty was truth and truth, beauty. His nature was supremely sensuous. It is the essential basis for all poetry. Sensuousness is no more prominent in his early poetry than it was in the early works of Shakespeare. But at the same time he was a poet in whom the strain of melancholy was strong. He was not merely a poet of senses but a poet who was responsive to the sad music of humanity. Sensuousness in the mature poetry of Keats is subservient to the total design of the poem.

The Eve of St. Agnes has not the power of Hyperion nor the superb mastery of Odes. But with this poem Keats has found the realm of his poetic experience. It is the most successful narrative poem. There is "neither fumbling nor insecurity of *Isabella*". It is the perfect expression of a sensuous experience.

Fausset remarks that romance has no other aim but the creation of sensuous beauty. *The Eve of St. Agnes* has also the delight, the richness and full bloom of romance. The poem incarnates the aesthetic imagination of the poet. The story is very slight. Porphyro secretly meets his beloved in the castle of a rich, inimical baron and succeeds in eloping with her. Such a paraphrase is reductive of the total impression of the poem. The story releases the rich, sensuous powers of Keats's imagination. The myth of St. Agnes derived from Ben Jonson and Burton's *Anatomy of Melancholy* is itself charged with romance and stirs the romantic imagination of the poet to create the sensuous beauty that *The Eve of St. Agnes* is.

The very first stanza exhibits the power of Keats in atmosphere-building:

St. Agnes Eve-Ah bitter cold it was;
The owl for all his feathers was a-cold
The hare limped trembling through the frozen grass.
And silent were the flock in the sheltered fold
Numb were the beadsman's fingers while he told
His rosary, and while the frosted breath
Like pious incense from a censer old,
Seemed taking flight for heaven, without a death,
Past the sweet Virgin's picture while his prayer he said.

The epithet in the first line, "Ah, bitter cold" is the central phrase. The rest of the stanza elaborates the effect of cold in detail. The bird (owl), the beast (hare) and the domesticated animal (flock), man in the house (beadsman in the chapel) are all numb and silent in the enveloping cold. The climax is reached in the frosted breath. The second stanza with it "frozen sculptured dead" and "icy hood and mails" further heightens the effect of cold.

Against the cold atmosphere outside is set the warmth of the chambers glowing to receive a thousand guests. The details of the "argent revelry" are richly sensuous with "Plume, tiara and all rich array/ Numerous as shadows haunting fairly, the brain new, stuffed in youth with triumphs gay/ Of old romance." But the real emotional warmth is not to be found here as "came many a tiptoe amorous cavalier and back retired". The music of the chambers is also harsh: "The silver snarling trumpets began to chide." The real emotional warmth is to be identified with Porphyro "with heart on fire" and whose heart is "love's feverous citadel" and Madeline who is "all amort/ save to St. Agnes." This warmth and vitality of Madeline's chamber finds a contrast in the revelry below:

> Full on the casement shone the wintry moon
> And threw warm gules on Madeline's fair breast
> As down she knelt for heaven's grace and boon
> Rosebloom fell on her hands, together prest
> And on her silver cross soft amethyst
> And on her hair a glory like a saint
> She seemed a splendid angel newly drest
> Save wings for heaven, Porphyro grew faint
> She knelt so pure a thing, so free from mortal taint.

Keats is at the height of his poetic powers in the description of the sensuous beauty of Madeline. The poet's eye for minute particular details bathes the whole scene in rare splendour of sensuous beauty. It is the beauty of the romantic heroine reflected in the grandeur of moonlight. The brilliance of the moonlight on the casement reflected on Madeline's breast is described as "warm gules on her fair breast". "Rose blooms", "amethyst", "glory", "splendid angel", "so pure a thing", free from mortal taint" create a superb aesthetic impression of visual beauty. It is further heightened by the description of Madeline "half-hidden like a mermaid in a sea-weed". The visual imagination is mainly at work here.

The visual imagery blends with the images of other senses in the poem:

> Into her dream, he melted, as the rose
> Blendeth its odour with the violet.

The flower imagery with its odours presents, the physical consummation of their love. The rose, the symbol of passion and the violet, the symbol of purity elevate their union to the spiritual level. The feast of "dates and dainties" with its "heap of candied apple, quince and plum and gourd/ With jellies soother than the creamy curd/ From silken samarkand to

Cedar'd Lebanon" emphasizes the richly sensuous nature of love. The sounds of "t" and "th" present the milky smoothness of jellies and the "s" and "t" sounds evoke the stickiness of the dates. Apart from the tactile and olfactory images, the visual, the auditory images also combine with the wealth of sensuous impressions.

> The arras, rich with horseman, hawk and hound
> Fluttered in the besieging winds uproar

The repetition of "r" and "h" sounds in the lines has almost an omatapoeic effect. The auditory and visual imagery combine into the impression of the uproar of the storm.

The Eve of St. Agnes reflects the sensuous beauty of Keats's imagination. It is in perfect harmony with the aesthetic quality of the experience. The sense impressions or the sensuous imagination is subservient to the needs of the poetic narrative.

EXAMINE THE MEDIEVAL AND ROMANTIC ELEMENTS IN *THE EVE OF ST. AGNES*

John Keats holds a special place among the English romantic poets. *The Eve of St. Agnes* is one of the perfect romantic poems. It is fully executed in the spirit of the medieval legend that inspired it. Turning from the magnificence of *The Paradise Lost* which he realized was not suited to his genius in *Hyperion*, he seems to have turned to Spenser under the guidance of Chatterton.

Keats seeks his subject in the medieval legend and invests it with a dream-like atmosphere of enchantment and wonder. The story is based on medieval superstition connected with the eve of St. Agnes that if a maiden performs certain ceremonies or rites on the eve of St. Agnes, she will dream of her future husband. The rites include fasting, not looking back or sideways, prayers and sleeping on the back. Like the medieval romances, the story is laid in the distant past with its Gothic castle. Though at no place there is complete description of the castle but the few details of the structure of the castle here and there evoke the picture of the castle in black massiveness outlined against the sky. Porphyro stands "buttressed from moonlight by portal doors". The window of Madeline is "pale, latticed and chill". It is a casement high, triple arched and carved with images of fruits, flowers and with panes of innumerable stains and dyes. The castle is guarded by horsemen, hawk and hound and is furnished with carpets, arras and chained lamps. There is a chapel attached to it and the level chambers glow to receive a thousand guests. Not only the castle is magnificent, the robes and costumes have the splendour and majesty of a world of old romance:

At length burst in the argent revelry
With plume, tiara and rich array
Numerous as shadows haunting fairly
The brain, new stuffed, in youth with triumphs gay of old romance.

The adjective "argent" unfolds a world of opulent splendour with "plume, tiara and rich array" and introduces us to a world of romantic glamour.

Madeline, the heroine of the poem, eager to test the truth of the belief connected with the eve of St. Agnes, takes no interest in the revelry. She performs the necessary rites of the eve of St. Agnes and retires to her chamber. She is invested with superhuman beauty, unique purity of the body and soul. In this, she resembles Lady Una of Spensor as her physical beauty reflects the beauty, of her soul. But she is not an allegorical figure like Lady Una. She remains earthly like Imogen. Keats is unparalleled in his description of the romantic beauty of the heroine. It merges with the romantic beauty of the setting:

Full on this casement shone the wintry moon
And threw warm gules on Madeline's fair breast
As down she knelt for heaven's grace and boon
Rose-bloom fell on her hands, together prest
And on her silver cross soft amethyst
And on her hair a glory, like a saint
She seemed a splended angel, newly drest
Save wings, for heaven.

The beauty of the setting lends a peculiar romantic charm. The moon, the symbol of beauty, purity and romance presides over the drama of love, when the full moon shines on the casement. It throws "warm gules on Madeline's fair breast" and she looks "free from mortal taint", like an angel "save for wings". As she slips her clothes down to her waist, she is then "half-hidden like a mermaid in sea-weed". In her sleep she is presented "as a rose should shut and be a bud again". The visual and tactile images lend their soft, delicate splendour to the human figure. Keats is at the height of his descriptive power in the creation of Madeline as the paragon of romantic beauty. Similarly, Porphyro is presented as a hermit in the shrine of love and their physical union is presented through the blend of olfactory images:

> Into her dream he melted as the rose
> Blendeth its odour with the violet.

The moon, the symbol of love and romance has "set" as the lovers are threatened by the light of dawn. The poem ends with the following lines :

> And they are gone, ay, ages long ago
> These lovers fled into the storm.

Like romances, the tale is placed in "ages long ago". The Spenserian stanza which Keats employs with marvellous success accords well with the romantic stuff of the poem. Sensuousness is the essential romantic trait which characterises the entire poem as we have already seen. *The Eve of St. Agnes* is unmatchable in the creation of sensuous romantic beauty among the narrative poems of Keats. It has the delight, the richness and the full bloom of romance as no other verse tale of Keats has.

DISCUSS *THE EVE OF ST. AGNES* AS A NARRATIVE POEM

The Eve of St. Agnes is one of the most perfect verse tales of John Keats. John Keats seems to have been influenced by Spenser in his narrative poem, with its medieval atmosphere, employment of the Spenserian stanza and maintaining the spirit of romance. Turning from the magnificance of *The Paradise*

Lost which he realized was not suited to his genius in Hyperion, he seems to have turned to Spenser under the guidance of Chatterton.

The love of Madeline and Porphyro which is set in the background of the family feud is reminiscent of Shakespeare's *Romeo and Juliet* with its background of the family feuds of Montagues and Capulets. The old Angela also resembles Juliet's nurse in the Shakespearian play. While the love of Romeo and Juliet ends in death on account of the family feud, the love of Madeline and Porphyro ends in the death of all others except the hero and the heroine who are able to elope successfully. Shakespeare again seems to have influenced Keats in the description of the entrance of Porphyro in the mansion of Madeline like Romeo.

The Spenserian stanza of the poem frees it from the artificial hurry that was found in the employment of ottava rima in *Isabella*. Each Spenserian stanza of the poem is a pictorial unit complete in itself, yet part of the coherent design of the poem. It tends the poetic narrative toward tableau. The story moves without halt or hurry. The narrative is rich in descriptive beauty which combines with the gliding musical sweetness. Nowhere such a rare blend of richness and economy is found in the history of English romance. The slow movement of each Spenserian stanza with its Alexandrine allows the images to settle down fully in the mind.

Keats is at the height of his descriptive powers in the portrayal of Madeline, the central figure of romance. It combines the magnificence and splendour of the setting:

> Full on the casement shone the wintry moon
> And threw was in gules on Madeline's fair breast
> As down she knelt for heaven's grace and boon
> Rose-bloom felt on her hair a glory like a saint
> She seemed a splendid angel, newly drest,
> Save wings for heaven, Porphyro grew faint
> She knelt so pure a thing, so free from mortal taint.

The stanza has a unique beauty of detail. It contributes to

the richness of the setting which is natural, sensuous and romantic. Madeline appears like an angel in this particular setting. As her rich attire creeps down to her knees in her bed, she is "half-hidden like a mermaid in a sea-weed". The sleeping beauty of Madeline is presented "as a rose should shut and be a bud again". Keats has thus created a paragon of supreme romantic beauty. She resembles Lady Una of Spensor but she is no allegorical figure. She remains earthly and human like Imogen. The visual imagery is dominant but the impressions of the senses blend into a unity of impression.

The word-pictures do not impede the movement of the narration. We have not to put up with the suspension of action while enjoying the passages of rich sensuous beauty: "Into her dream he melted as the rose/ Blendeth its odour with the violet." The olfactory image of the rose blending its odour with the violet is pregnant with rich suggestiveness through which the narration moves forward. The physical consummation is couched in the sensuous imagery. As the story of Porphyro and Madeline runs in the present tense when the movement of the narration is brisk: "They glide, like Phantoms, into the wide hall/ Like Phantoms, to the Porch, they glide." When the story moves to a close, the tense of the poem changes to the past tense: "And they are gone, ay, ages long ago/ These lovers fled away into the storm". The drama of love which the reader was following closely in the present tense, with the change of tense is distanced into the past "ages long ago". The distance in time lends a charm to the story, the charm of distant romance which a few lines earlier the reader was following as if everything were happening before his mental eyes.

The Eve of St. Agnes has not the swiftness of narration of *Lamia* which was written in the heroic couplet. Nor it has the mawkishness of *Isabella.* But here Keats certainly achieves the full expression of his poetic powers. The final impression left by the poem is that of rich sensuousness which fully accords with the romantic experience of the poem.

COMMENT ON THE TREATMENT OF LOVE IN *THE EVE OF ST. AGNES*

The Eve of St. Agnes is one of the perfect verse tales of the romantic poet, John Keats. Love has been the constant source of inspiration to writers of romances in European and other literatures. Malory's *Morte de Arthur* and Spenser's *Fairy Queen* also move round the romance of love. John Keats seems to have been influenced by Spenser in his romantic verse tale, *The Eve of St. Agnes.*

As Keats is inspired by Spenser and Chatterton, the setting of the poem is medieval. The poem opens with the description of a chapel attached to a medieval mansion where the chambers are glowing to receive a thousand guests. The heroine of the poem, Madeline resembles Lady Una of Spenser's *Fairy Queen* as her physical beauty reflects the beauty of her soul. Her beauty is unearthly. She is heavenly and angelic in her beauty except for the wings of an angel. The superstition of the Eve of St. Agnes that Madeline entertains and the rites she performs in order to have a vision of her future husband is itself basically romantic.

The love of Madeline and Porphyro is silhouetted against the background of the family feud in *The Eve of St. Agnes.* Here Keats seems to have been influenced by Shakespeare's *Romeo and Juliet* where the love of Romeo and Juliet buds and blossoms in the background of the family feud of Montagues and Capulets. The old Angela also resembles Juliet's nurse in the Shakespearian play. But there is a difference between the love of Romeo and Juliet and the love of Madeline and Porphyro. The love of Romeo and Juliet ends in their death on account of the family feud. But the love of Porphyro and Madeline ends in the death of others and the hero and the heroine are able to elope successfully.

The moon, the symbol of beauty and purity, love and imagination presides over the drama of love in the poem:

Full on this casement shone the wintry moon
And threw warm gules on Madeline's fair breast,

As down she knelt for heaven's grace and boon
Rose bloom fell on her hands, together prest
And on her silver cross soft amethyst,
And on her hair a glory like a saint.

It bathes the scene of love in the opalescent moonlight. There is great sensuous beauty about the heroine as well as the setting in which the events take place.

Keats again seems to have been influenced by Shakespeare in his description of the entrance of Porphyro in the mansion of Madeline in the face of dangers like Romeo. The scene in which Porphyro with the help of old Angela finds himself in a secret place from where he can see the charms of Madeline is reminiscent of Shakespeare's *The Rape of Lucrece.* The physical consummation of their love is couched in the sensuous imagery of the blending of the odours of the rose and the violet. The olfactory image which has a synaesthetic character adds to the sensuous beauty of the experience:

Beyond a mortal man impassion'd far
At these voluptuous accents, he arose
Etherea, flushed, and like a throbbing star
Seen 'mid the sapphire heaven's deep repose
Into her dream he melted as the rose
Blendeth its odour with the violet
Solution sweet.

The love of Porphyro and Madeline has a religious or spiritual colouring as in *The Fairy Queen* of Spensor:

"And now, my love, my seraph fair awake
Thou art my heaven, I thine eremite.

The images of "heaven" and "eremit" in the language of Porphyro is suggestive of the spiritual content of their love.

As the story of Porphyro and Madeline comes to a close, the tense of the poem changes from the present to the past:

And they are gone: aye, ages long ago
These lovers fled away with the storm.

The drama of the elopement which the reader follows closely with the change of tense is distanced into the past "ages long ago". The distance in time lends a charm to the story which was a little ago happening before the mental eyes of the reader. Though the hero sings the song "La belle dame sans mercy", the story is not the story of a beautiful maid without mercy, but a beautiful maid with pent-up emotion of love in her heart which guides their love to a successful end.

In *Lamia* and *Endymion,* the poet fails to combine beauty and love. Endymion seems to be illusory. No less illusory is Lamia, the serpent woman who cannot escape the gaze of scrutiny and disappears. But *The Eve of St. Agnes* celebrates the consummation of sensuous and successful love.

19

MAC FLECKNOE BY DRYDEN

An epic or heroic poem is a poem which deals with the significant national or human issues. The action of a heroic poem is weighty, the personages are dignified and the style is elevated. Such a poem is *The Paradise Lost* by Milton, Homer's *Odyssey* and Virgil's *Aenied.* A mock-heroic or mock-epic poem is a comical imitation of the serious epic. The elevated style of the epic is applied to the trivial and triffling characters and theme. As a result, the poetic effect is comic and ridiculous.

John Dryden's poem, *Mac Flecknoe* is cast in a mock-heroic form. It presents a deliberate contrast of the form with the content. There is an epical treatment of a trivial theme. It is reminiscent of Pope's *The Rape of the Lock* and *The Dunciad.* The satire of the poem is directed against a contemporary poet, Shadwell. The subject of the poem is the coronation of Shadwell as the monarch of the realm of non-sense. In fact, the subject of the poem is literary. It is a condemnation of Shadwell as a poet and dramatist.

The poem opens with a solemn tone:

All human things are subject to decay
And when Fate summons, monarchs must obey.

The cumulative impression of the words, "All human things", "Fate" and "monarch" is that the poem is concerned with issues of great human significance. But it is a preface to the selection of Shadwell as the successor to the monarch of non-sense and his coronation. Flecknoe, the monarch of non-sense enumerates the qualification of Shadwell as the fittest successor:

Shadwell alone my perfect image bears
Mature in dullness from his tender years,
Shadwell alone of all my sons is he
Who stands confirmed in full stupidity
The rest to some faint meaning makes pretence
But Shadwell never deviates into sense

There is juxtaposition of words of epical association of grandeur with words of trivial significance. The words "mature", "perfect", "confirmed" and "never deviates" build up the impression of grandeur but they are juxtaposed with "stupidity", "dullness" and "non-sense" which deflate the impression of grandeur. Here satire is subtle as it takes the form of praise. The same mock-heroic vein is discernible in the prophecy of Acient Dekker about the reign of a mighty prince like Shadwell, building-up of Shadwell's throne with the worthless plays of Flecknoe and the blessing of his father at the time of coronation. The long speech of Flecknoe imparts a biblical solemnity of tone with its religious imagery:

Heywood and Shirley were but types of thee
Thou last great prophet of tautology
Even I, a dunce of more renown than they
Was sent before but to prepare the way.

The religious metaphor dominates here. But the implications are only ironic. Dryden accommodates classical allusions to Arion, Hannibal, Romulus in an ironic context. The epical reference to vultures by the side of Romulus as the presage of his coronation turns into the flight of owls by side of Shadwell. The classical allusions seem to lend a majestic stature to Shadwell. Dryden has the art of transforming "the small into the great, the prosaic into the poetic, the trivial into the magnificent." But the ironic context of the poem transforms the epical into the mock-epic, the majestic into the ridiculous. The classical allusions, "the metaphors of the prophet and a real artist only represent the standards by which Shadwell is judged and found wanting". Shadwell bears a poor comparison to the figures of classical literature. The nature of the metaphor in the poem is ironic.

The mock-heroic vein is maintained throughout the poem. The gravity of the tone enhances the triviality by contrast. The effect is magnificent at the end which is anticlimatic. Flecknoe seems unwilling to finish his abdication speech. Shadwell sends him down a stage trap-door as in one of Shadwell's own plays. The king's cloak is blown upward by the subterranean wind and falls on Shadwell. T.S. Eliot is not wrong when he says, "Dryden applies vocabulary, images, and ceremony which arouse epic associations of grandeur to make on enemy helplessly ridiculous."

Mack Flecknoe is not a complete imitation of an epic as the action of the heroic or epic poem includes a battle also. *Mac Flecknoe* is concerned with the selection of Shadwell as the monarch of non-sense and his coronation. Pope's *The Rape of the Lock* which is a mock-heroic poem presents a battle with fans and snuff-box. Nevertheless, *Mac Flecknoe* remains essentially a mock-heroic poem in the contrast of its grand form and the trivial subject matter.

COMMENT ON *MAC FLECKNOE* AS A SATIRE OR "MAC FLECKNOE IS A LAMPOON" COMMENT

John Dryden has his place in English literature as a satirist. His satires are directed against contemporary figures but they are still enjoyed as literary works of art as Dryden was able transform the temporal into the timeless, the personal into the impersonal and the particular into the universal.

Mac Flecknoe is the masterpiece of Dryden's art. It is not a lampoon, though it has its origin in Dryden's personal conflict with Shadwell. The poem presents a pen-portrait of Shadwell. Dryden does not make use of invectives. He is in perfect control of his emotion and transmutes Shadwell into the monarch of non-sense, the symbol of the poetaster for all times.

The poem, *Mac Flecknoe* is cast is a mock-heroic framework. It deals with the selection of Shadwell as the fittest successor to the monarch of non-sense and his coronation. Shadwell's succession to the throne is decided in view of his qualifications:

Shadwell alone my perfect image bears
Mature in dullness from his tender years
Shadwell alone of all my sons is he
Who stands confirmed in full stupidity
The rest to some faint meaning make pretence
But Shadwell never deviates into sense.

The emotion of the poet is completely subdued. There is play of wit and humour on the surface. The adjectives, "mature", "confirmed", "perfect" and the phrase "never deviates" suggest a rising tone of praise. But they are juxtaposed with "dullness", "stupidity" and non-sense. Dryden achieves his effects through juxtapositions and irony. Here satire functions by pretending to be praise. This is the characteristic vein of satire in Mac Flecknoe.

The classical allusions to Augustus, Ascanius, Hannibal, Arion and Romulus are accommodated in the ironic context. They seem to suggest a higher stature of Shadwell equal to the classical figures. They bring into sharp focus the insignificance of Shadwell in comparison:

On his left hand twelve reverend owls did fly
So Romulus, 'tis sung, by Tiber's brook
Presage of sway from twice six vultures took.

Allusion is part of the irony here. The twice six owls instead of vultures suggest that the comparison between Shadwell and Romulus is a comparison between owls and vultures. The implications of the comparison are damaging.

The ceremony of coronation is marked by religious solemnity. The blessing speech of Flecknoe at the time of coronation is packed with religious imagery and seems to impart a solemn tone to the poem:

Heywood and Shirley were but types of thee
Thou last great prophet of tautology
Even I, a dunce of more renown than they
Was sent before but to prepare the way

There is a magnificent use of irony. Shadwell is "the last great prophet" no doubt but of "tautology". Dryden has the art of transforming "the small into the great, the prosaic into the poetic, the trivial into the magnificent". But the application of the solemn tone to the trivial material results into a ridiculous effect. Dryden's ridicule is not direct. He subtly suggests the quality of his ironic victim. Criticism is relieved by the lightness of wit and humour.

The poem ends by crowning Shadwell as the monarch of non-sense. The point of the poem is Shadwell is not a poet, a prophet or real artist. The metaphors work ironically. Shadwell is judged by these metaphors and is found wanting. Shadwell is a type as well as a symbol of the poetaster for all times. Dryden restrains his feelings in order to transmute them into art. Dryden does not give vent to the passionate outburst of a lampooner. He himself remarks, "It is easy to call a man rogue and a villain but hard to make a fool, a blockhead without actually using any of these opprobrious terms." Dryden uses this art in *Mac Flecknoe*. His pen-portrait of Achitophel is mainly invective but his portrait of Shadwell is subtle satire.

Dryden's indignation does not break through the surface. He aligns himself with Horace rather than Juvenal. Dryden's satiric intensity is not the intensity of bitterness. It is the intensity of fun generated by wit and humour. In the words of Eliot, "The piece of Dryden which is the most fun which is the most sustained display of surprise after surprise of wit from line to line is *Mac Flecknoe*." Dryden's method here is very similar to parody. "He applies vocabulary, images and ceremony which arouse epic associations of grandeur to make an enemy helplessly ridiculous."

20

The Ancient Mariner by Coleridge

Coleridge, the poet of the supernatural has produced three poems "Kubla Khan", "Christabel" and "The Ancient Mariner" which are purely conceived on supernatural scale. But "The Ancient Mariner" is the "only one which stands a rounded and finished whole". It is the masterpiece of Coleridge not only for its completeness but also for its vivid description. The sailing of the ship, the killing of albatross, the suffering and relief of the Mariner, the gradual disappearance of the landmark and the rest are described in a highly dramatic way. "It is a haunting narrative poem of symbolic adventure in which the handling of visual details, the selection and ordering of incidents, the deliberate varying of mood and tone, the counter-pointing between the factual and the magical, the familiar and the exotic are combined to produce an appeal."

"The Ancient Mariner" deals with the supernatural on a large scale and in a generous sense. It is a spectrum of themes as it has many layers of themes such as the theme of punishment and reward of moral struggle and of love between living creatures. The strange adventure of Mariner takes place not in "the Goethic setting of a medieval castle which was used in 'Christabel' but on a boundless sea with the days of pitiless sun and soft nights". His "machining persons" are not of the same breed as his Geraldine. According to Maurice Bowra the new setting and new persons "with which Coleridge shapes his supernatural poem moves on a wide range of emotion and touches equally on guilt and remorse, suffering and relief, hate and forgiveness, grief and joy."

The poem "The Ancient Mariner" comes from the dream of Coleridge's friend Mr. Cruickshank. As every poet of supernatural has to relate his theme to the familiar experience which touches the heart of his readers, Coleridge did it by exploiting some of the characteristics of dreams because he knew that the dream is the necessary part of human life. Coleridge was much attracted by the strange powers of dream. In "Christabel" he speaks of:

> Such perplexity of mind
> As dreams too lively live behind.

and "The Ancient Mariner" bears the mark of such liveliness. On the surface, it illuminates many qualities of dreams as "it moves in abrupt stages, each of which has its single, dominating character". Its visual impressions are brilliant and absorbing and it clings to the memory as the dream does after waking.

Coleridge uses the atmosphere of dreams to accustom us to his special (supernatural) world and then he proceeds to create freely within his chosen limits. The story moves unchecked doubtless through a world of wonder in a very mysterious way. Each incident and experience is presented clear cut and in a concrete form in which the details are selected for the appeal to the common experience. "Amid all the strange happenings, nature remains itself and its preservance, sometimes comes in the ironic contrast to what happens on the ship as when the Mariner is haunted by the look of his dead comrades after shooting albatross, the moon continues her unchanging course":

> Softly she was going up
> And a star or two beside.

Even when nature breaks into more violent moods it is still itself and each dramatic touch of description makes it more real. Each detail comes from the known world to provide with a firm background to the supernatural events which accompany it.

This realistic treatment of the setting is matched by the appeal which Coleridge makes to our emotions in handling his human persons. The sufferings and agonies of the Mariner and his comrades are simply and universally human. We feel and respond mentally to their misery and pathos just as we do with the tragic heroes of Shakespeare or Marlowe. The scene in which the misery and sterility are symbolised by drought as in "The Waste Land" and "The Grail Legends," and the rain comes to slake the thirst of the Mariner are described with a striking economy of words. Coleridge shows skilfully how it happens and what a wonderful relief this is:

Sure I had drunken in my dreams
And still my body drank.

There is no doubt that physical sensation plays a large part in dream, but Coleridge describes them as we know them in a awaking state and in a lively way to create a powerful emotional effect.

These scenes are portrayed so powerfully that we assume the situations of the Mariner to be real and to have some kind of human feelings. When the supernatural takes command, Coleridge makes it as natural and real as possible, because he forms it from the elements which are in themselves familiar. Coleridge epitomizes "the weird situation in which the deadmen stir and begin to do again what they used to do in life" in one highly significant action:

The body of my brother's son
Stood by me knee to knee.

The habitual profunctory action, now conducted by a deadman and a living man together has an extraordinary horror. When at last the ship comes to the land, the angels standing by the dead bodies give the Mariner infinite relief and fill his heart with hope and joy. "The poem moves between the extreme of despair and of joy and reflects through its variation the light and the shade of human life."

The supernatural elements through which Coleridge conveys the struggle of a man who commits a hideous crime and then is punished by the doom of "Life-in-Death" in such an artistic way that no question of its validity rises in our mind as Coleridge says in his lecture on dream in 1818:

> "In ordinary dreams we do not judge the object to be real: we simply do not determine that they are unreal."

"The Ancient Mariner" leaves its magical impact upon us as the dreams do. "The Ancient Mariner" is merely "a world of dream and fantasy" with the strong appeal to the common experience. Maurice Bowra rightly points out, "By introducing us to a world of dream and fantasy, he suggests how mysterious is the experience which concerns him." No other poet of supernatural in English poetry has quite done this with such abundance of authentic poetry.

Q. 1. There are haunting echoes of moral struggle in "The Ancient Mariner." Discuss.

Q. 2. "The Ancient Mariner" is evidently and specifically Christian. Discuss.

Q. 3. "The Ancient Mariner" is a fine blend of fantasy and moral lesson. Discuss.

Ans. S.T. Coleridge is an isolated figure on the Romantic poetic scene. His achievements are explained in terms of extreme individuality which is characterized by his strong impulse for supernatural. What Worldsworth found in Nature, Coleridge found in supernatural. Amid all his three great supernatural poems; "The Ancient Mariner", "Kubla Khan" and "Christabel", "The Ancient Mariner" is the only one "which stands a rounded and finished whole". As these two poems are fragments, their themes are not on the surface but "The Ancient Mariner" is a spectrum of themes. It has many folds of themes such as the theme of punishment and reward, of love between living creatures and, of guilt and redemption. But all these themes are secondary as they spring from one major theme — the moral struggle.

Here, we cannot but agree with Boris Ford when he says, "There are haunting echoes of moral struggle in 'The Ancient Mariner'." The Mariner's wanton shooting of the albatross who seems to stand for the power of Nature's blessing, breaks the sympathy between nature and voyagers because the killing of albatross is a violation of a deep natural sanctity. And then Mariner's struggle starts as he begins to suffer punishment for what he has done. The world which he faces after his crime is dead and loathsome. The ship is afflicted with the drought of stiffling heat. Natural life becomes hideous and threatening. The death fires dance about the ship at night. The colour of water looks strange and unnatural. This passage and what follows is a powerful symbol of a life cut off from all sympathetic natural forces. It becomes more powerful and horrible when in the terrifying episode of Death and Life-in-Death, Death wins the souls of the rest of the Mariner's comrades and life-in-Death wins that of Mariner himself. The reign of Life-in-Death is more terrifying than that of Death. It is according to Graham Hough "*the misere de l'home sans Dieu* — the consciousness of being abandoned and the utter inability to do anything for oneself towards salvation;"

> I looked heaven and tried to pray
> But or ever a prayer had gusht,
> A wicked whisper came, and made
> My heart as dry as dust.

Here, the complete paralysis of the will is suggested by the motionless ship. In that paralysed state, the Mariner envies the Moon and Stars for their steady progress through the heaven. The guilty soul is cut off not merely from the human intercourse but also from the consoling friends of nature.

After his long suffering and struggle, the Mariner watches water-snakes which appear as a good omen. Though they had been "slimy things", symbol of horror, now they are in a strange kind of beauty. They are in different colours, "blue, glossy green, and velvet black" and their tracks seem as a "flash of golden fire". At this moment his whole feeling changes and "A spring of love gushed" from his heart and then he blesses them. Mariner's recognition of beauty and happiness of water-snakes makes him aware of the oneness of the creation and so he has made some amends even if he does it "unawares" for his wanton destruction of the albatross.

With it a new peace comes in his heart and he is able to sleep again. The misery and sterility of the preceding periods portrayed in the image of a universe dying of thirst as in "The Waste Land" and "The Grail Legend", now disappears as it rains even in the dream of Mariner. A new spiritual power takes hold of the ship to guide it home. The wind begins to blow and the ship to move. Images of the homely land, "I heard the sky look sing", "A noise like a hidden brook/ In the leafy month of June", begin to appear. The regeneration of Mariner starts and though he has still a long way to go his path is now steadily homewards till he comes to his own country.

Though the Mariner is very little guilty but he has broken the bond between himself and life of nature and in consequence, he is spiritually dead. No doubt, "the Mariner is evidently and specifically Christian" as the attitude of the poem is merely based on "Christian values : redemption, equality and universal love". The Mariner believed in confessing his guilt through which he feels "free" and his heart "burns". Here, the verb "burn" is very apt as it suggests atonement for the sin which he committed and forcing others to listen to his story provides him with psychological relief. Through ghastly tale he teaches people:

> "He prayeth best, who loveth best
> All things both great and small
> For the dear God who loveth us,
> He made and loveth all."

In this context, the moral quality of the poem cannot be dismissed as it is noticeable that the entire poem is nothing but an extension of this stanza in which the stress on equality and universal love is laid. Here, Herbert Grierson and J.C. Smith rightly remark, "In truth the moral is embedded in the poem, and gives articulation to what without it would be a phantasmagoria." The moral lesson in the poem is conveyed through a world of fantasy. Coleridge uses the atmosphere of fantasy to accustom us to his special world and then he proceeds freely within his chosen limits. The poem "The

Ancient Mariner" is such a fine blend of fantasy and moral lesson that it leaves its deep impact on our mind and the moral does not seem imposed like that of G.B. Shaw. It comes in a natural way as it is due to the consummate art of Coleridge and for which it is hard to parallel with any other poem in English literature.

21

St. Joan by Bernard Shaw

G.B. Shaw in *St. Joan* is like William Shakespeare in his tragedies. Like Shakespearian tragedies, the originality of Shaw does not consist in the invention of the story which is borrowed from history but in the treatment of his theme in the play. *St. Joan* is not only a historical play, one whose theme is the compelling force of a religious idea. His success as a dramatist consists in the transmutation of a historical figure into the timeless and universal symbol of prophet or a man of genius.

The history of Joan existed before Shaw. But viewed from the traditional angle, the story of Joan has no form and meaning. But Shaw discovers a universal meaning in the pattern of events that leads to the tragedy of Saint Joan. The conflict is presented in terms of the conflict between the person of genius and the society which is represented by the church and the Feudal order.

Unlike Shakespearian tragic protagonists, St. Joan does not represent mankind in general but the extraordinary person of genius. Her treatment at the hands of the Feudalistic and religious society stands for the treatment meted out to an extraordinary man of genius by our human society. The play is a record of what mankind does to its geniuses and saints. In the words of C.B. Purdon man wants neither and the hatred men have for each other flares up intensely against great souls.

Joan of Arc was a farmer's daughter. She could not read or write, though she did and could dictate letters. She was undoubtedly an exceptional woman. She was a visionary and a person of action. She heard voices and saw visions. She believed that her voices and visions were commands of God. She acted upon them. She had exceptional military ability, when the military commanders of her time were confused. She made all the soldiers fight, she made them conquer soldiers by whom they were accustomed to be defeated. Her sexlessness and singleness of purpose was remarkable. She is a saint because she subordinated the facts of her personality in order to accomplish the task of liberating France from the English and crowning the native king as the only deserving ruler of the country. She believed throughout that this task was laid upon her by the divine command.

Saint Joan was one of the first protestant martyrs. She decided to uphold her conscience against the church. She believed that her voices were the voices of God which ran counter to the judgment of the church that they were not. It is a conflict of the genius and the discipline as Shaw states in the preface. But the personality of Joan poses a danger to the church as she affirms that "in case the church should bid me to do anything contrary to the command I have from God, I will not consent to it". She is a danger to the existence of independent barons also as she has established the divine legitimacy of the French king. Therefore the church and the Feudal lord combine in their hatred against her and she is condemned to be burnt at the stake. In the epilogue we hear the despairing voice of Joan, "O God that madest the beautiful earth when will it be ready to receive Thy saints? How long, O Lord, how long?"

Saint Joan is the instrument of life-force or creative evolution. Shaw declares in the preface to *St. Joan* that "There are forces at work which use individual for purposes for transcending the purpose of keeping these individuals alive and prosperous and safe and happy." There is a superpersonal need, an appetite for evolution which uses men of genius to accomplish something that takes mankind a step ahead in its evolution. St. Joan is the medium of life-force to accomplish at that particular stage of history something unprecedented. She tells her judges, "If you command me to declare that all I have done and said and all the visions and revelations I have had, were not from God, then that is impossible. I will not declare it for anything in the world; what God commands me to do I will never go back on; and what he has commanded or shall command I will not fail to do in spite of any man alive. That is what I mean by impossible. And in the case the church should bid me do anything contrary to the command, I have from God, I will not consent to it, no matter what it may be." She further says, "All things that you call my crimes have come to me by the command of God, I say that I have done them by the order of God; it is impossible for me to say anything else. If any churchman says the contrary, I shall not mind him, I shall mind God alone whose command I always follow." St. Joan is fulfilling the divine purpose of evolution. In the Shavian view life-force is perfection hungry and progressive. Joan, like any other genius, serves the evolutionary appetite by iconoclasticism. The law of evolution is the divine law of change. The existing authority, the church is disobeyed as it stands in the way of evolution and stands for the old order which must be changed. Joan represents the new ideologies of nationalism and protestantism. Nationalism may prove ephemeral but protestantism will not die. In the martyrdom of St. Joan who chose to put her conscience against the judgment of the church, Shaw perceives the universal phenomenon. If a genius is far ahead of his time, his capacities for private judgment bring him into disruptive clash with the organised judgment that constitute the warp and woof of social structure. The last speech of Joan, "O God, when will it be ready to receive Thy Saints? How long, O Lord, how long?" suggests the recurring pattern of behaviour with saints and prophets. St. Joan is one such example.

EXAMINE *ST. JOAN* AS A CHRONICLE PLAY

There is a difference between a chronicle and a chronicle play. It is the difference which exists between life and art. A chronicle or life follows a chronological order. Life is not art and the artist has to impose his own order on the chaos or flux of life. It is reordered and refigured in the symmetry of art. In the same way a chronicle or history is not art. Though the dramatist follows the facts of history, the material of history is reorganised from the dramatic point of view. It is the angle of the dramatist which determines the form or order to be imposed on history in order to shape it into drama.

G.B. Shaw's *St. Joan* is a play. It presents the facts of the history as faithfully as possible. As Shaw himself claims, "I have dramatised the original documents. Every one else has romanced about Joan. I have told the story exactly as it happened. It is the easiest play, I ever had to write. All I have done is to put down the facts, to arrange Joan for the stage. The trial scene is merely a report of the actual trial. I have used Joan's very words: thus she spoke, thus she behaved." Shaw presents the main events in the play of Joan exactly as the history presents them. Her interview with captain Bandricourt, her arrival at the court of the Dauphin, the hostility of the nobles at the court, her influencing of the Dauphin, raising of the siege at Orleans, the coronation, her trial, momentary recantation, her burning at the stake and clinging to the cross have been presented with rare fidelity. Voltaire and Mark Twain have presented adorable portraits of Joan and Anatole France does not believe in her miraculous gifts. She presents her as a hard-headed female who fought like any military general. Shaw follows the middle course. He presents her gifted with mystical inspiration as well with sound, calculating, practical common sense which leads to her military victory.

Shaw has preserved the medieval atmosphere in this play, which, according to Shaw, Shakespeare did not maintain in his historical plays. Apart from the historical figures, he has brought in the medieval institutions like the church, the holy inquisition, the Feudalism, the divine inspiration, the torture and execution. Shaw has carefully studied the historical documents available to him so that he has been able to use the words of Joan herself in the trial scene. For example, when Joan is asked whether Michael appears to her as a naked person, Joan replies in the play as well as in historical records, "Do you think God cannot afford clothes for him?" Shaw has kept the spirit and tone of the original speeches of Joan in the play.

Like all writings of chronicle plays, Shaw has preserved the historical authenticity of the events. And like others he has also treated imaginatively. He has not strictly followed the chronological events. He has exercised his judgment and presented his view of historical events. Therefore at points, he has departed from traditional history. For example, Cauchon has been shown in a favourable light. He is shown as a devout, charitable churchman who makes honest efforts to save the soul of Joan. He is not presented as a monster but as a churchman who believes that Joan is a heretic and a danger to the church. The same is applicable to the characterisation of the Earl of Warwick. Shaw's *St. Joan* is not a literal transcription of history. He has added to and subtracted from history in order to present his imaginative view of history.

The history of Joan existed before Shaw, but viewed from the traditional angle, the story of Joan has no form and meaning. But Shaw discovers a universal meaning in the pattern of events that leads to the tragedy of Joan. Shaw presents the conflict between the person of genius and the society which is represented in terms of the church and the feudal order. St. Joan represents not mankind but the extraordinary person of genius. The play is a record of what mankind does to its genius and saints through the martyrdom of St. Joan who chose to put conscience against the judgment of the church. Shaw perceives the universal phenomenon of a genius is far ahead of his time, his capacities of private judgment bring him into disruptive conflict with the organised judgment that constitutes the warp and woof of social structure. The question at the end of the play, "O God who madest the beautiful earth, when will it be ready to receive Thy saints. How long, how long?" suggests the recurring pattern of behaviour with saints and prophets. One such example is St. Joan herself. St. Joan serves the divine purpose of evolution. In the Shavian view life-force is perfection hungry and progressive. Joan like any other genius serves the evolutionary appetite by iconoclasticism. The existing authority, the church is disobeyed as it stands in the way of evolution which stands for the old order which must be changed. The personal history of St. Joan is transmuted into the impersonal and the particular into the general. *St. Joan* is a chronicle play which treats the historical material imaginatively and discovers a universal, recurring pattern in the history of St. Joan.

THE SIGNIFICANCE OF EPILOGUE IN "SAINT JOAN"

The epilogue is generally spoken by a single character at the end of the play. Through this means, the dramatist is able to speak to the spectators directly and communicate his point of view. But the Epilogue in "*Saint Joan*" is not spoken by a single character. Rather it is the extension of the play beyond the burning of St. Joan at stake. Luis F. Lutz compares it to the satyr play in the Greek tradegy which was a comic portrayal of the same theme.

Some critics like Henderson have found fault with the Epilogue in "Saint Joan". In their view, the Epilogue is an unnecessary appendage to the historical tragedy. They find it "a disconcerting, inartistic mixture of force, satire and didactic explanation. But G.B. Shaw holds that "the Epilogue must stand" as it is the essential part of the meaning of the play.

The play, "Saint Joan" will be incomplete without the Epilogue. The play presents the history of Joan of Arc with her burning at the stake. The Epilogue provides the light in which the play is to be interpretted. We will miss the significance of the play, the meaning of St. Joan without the Epilogue. Shaw was himself aware of this necessity as he points out in the preface, "Many a woman has got herself burnt by carelessly whisking a muslin skirt into the drawing-room fire-place, but getting canonised is a different matter and a more important one. "The Epilogue brings to light the face that the burning of St. Joan for heresy was an error.

In the Epilogue, Charles, the king of France is on his bed and all the figures reassemble in his dream. Through it we learn that after her burning in 1431, St. Joan was rehabilitated in 1556, declared blessed in 1904 and finally canonised in 1920. Ladvenu and Dunois who were sympathetic to her depose in her favour at the retrial. John Stogumber touched by her fortitude is her ardent advocate. The king is indifferent this time as he has to establish that he was not crowned by a witch. The Churchman who had now nothing to fear from Joan were united in their support and Cauchon was excommunicated, dug out of his grave and thrown into a sewer. The reputation of Joan was fully rehabilitated and her martyrdom fully established.

The Epilogue drives home to us the fact that St. Joan's tragedy is not a tragedy which ends with the death of the hero or the heroine. It is a continuing tragedy for the intolerance that mankind shows to saints and persons of genius. Joan suffers in her life and is canonized after her death. Mankind is not ready to accept persons of genius in their life and are inclined to lionize them after they are no more. The characters who are opposed to her in life now adore and worship her but none wants her return to life. It shows that humanity is still imperfect. The Epilogue shows that Joan's struggle is the struggle of life force against feudalism and the established church and that her martyrdom is a step forward in the impersonal evolution. Critics like Henderson hold that the tragic effect is diminished by the comedy of the Epilogue but it is Shaw's achievement of reconciliation between the tragedy of personal death and the comedy of impersonal Evolution. The Epilogue further brings about the interpretation of reality and fantasy like the comedy and tragedy. The play is a chronicle and the Epilogue takes the form of the vision of the sleeping Charles in which centuries run into each other and the ghosts from the Hell visit him. The rules of probability have not been discarded as the Epilogue remains just a vision but without which "Saint Joan" will be merely a chronicle without depth or significance.

"SAINT JOAN" AS TRAGEDY OR HIGH TRAGEDY

"Saint Joan" presents difficulties to critics as it is a tragedy but not in the Aristotelian sense. Bernard Shaw himself calls it "high tragedy". The tragic hero, according to Aristotle, is a person of noble character and important position who is ruined by some one flaw of his own character in an action which excites pity and fear. The Greek and Shakespearian tragic protagonists have a definite flaw in their character. The blindness of Oedipus, the ambition of Macbeth and the credulity of Othello are the tragic flaws from which emanate the tragic consequences. In the sound and fury of the consequences, the tragic protagonist is caught and destroyed. Butcher points out the difficulty of writing a tragedy on the life of a saint. The chief difficulty is that the death of martyr presents to us not the defeat but the victory of the individual. The sense of suffering is lost in the moral triumph.

Saint Joan like Eliot's "Murder in the Cathedral" is a tragedy where the tragic protagonist is not Everyman like Shakespeare's Macbeth. Macbeth or Hamlet in conflict with himself as well as in his conflict with fate or external forces represents mankind or humanity at large. But Saint Joan like Thomas Becket in "Murder in the Cathedral" stands on a different plane as she is almost a supernatural character. Her tragedy does not represent the common human situation of life. The other characters do not stand on equal plane. Rather by contrast they highlight the sainthood or the miracle that her personality is. It has a parallel in Thomas Becket's relationship with the chorus which represents common humanity.

Saint Joan is a peasant girl in the French of village of Domremy. There is only superficial resemblance to the Aristotelian concept of tragic hero with her self-confidence, her brashness and her appearance of rash impetuosity. Her superb self-confidence breaks down in the panic of recantation. In fact, those who accuse of pride and error themselves suffer from error and pride of self-righteousness. The hubris which characterises the hero in Greek tragedy does not belong to her. Her only weakness is her brief recantation in the trial scene. But soon realizing the futility of recantation-she tells the representatives of the church, "If you command me to declare that all that I have done and said, and all the visions and revelations I have had were not from God, that is impossible." The response of her judges is that "The old Greek tragedy is rising among us. It is the chastisement of hubris." Joan is burnt as a heretic for declaring that the instructions of her voices take precedence over the instructions of the church.

The conflict as Shaw points out in the play is between genius and discipline. The tragedy lies in the failure of Everyman or average man to recognise the genius. In the Epilogue Cauchon cries, "Must then a Christ perish in torment in every age to save those who have no imagination?" Eliot strikes the same note when the chorus asks in "Murder in the Cathedral, shall the son of Man be born again in the litter of scorn?"

Shaw maintains the play on the level of "high tragedy". It excludes any philosophy of evil in favour of stupidity, ignorance, self-will. Immense care has been taken to present both the sides of the conflict. Her trial by a French court of inquisition is fair as far as the standards of that age go. This is why Shaw calls it "high tragedy" and adds that "the tragedy of such murders is that they are not committed by murderers. They are judicial murders, pious murders". The play arouses pity but not fear.

Shaw extends the tragedy in time and space through the Epilogue in order to perceive the comedy and thus removes at one stroke the possibility of a full tragic response. It resembles the medieval religious drama as the tragedy produced in time is seen from an altitude in which "the angels may weep at the murder but the gods laugh at the murderer".

Comment on the Trial Scene in St. Joan

G.B. Shaw's play "Saint Joan" is a chronicle play. It is based on the history of France and England. It has to be born in mind that it is a play, not a chronicle. Quite naturally fidelity to the details of the chronicle is not essential for a play which exploits the creative ability of the writer or the dramatist. Therefore "Saint Joan," though a chronicle play is quite independent of the shackles of history. G.B. Shaw, the dramatist imposes an artistic pattern on the historical matter.

Dr. Coulton and L.P. Barrett have dug out a good deal into medieval history and brought the evidence against the historical accuracy of the trial scene in "Saint Joan". Shaw has demonstrated through his play that the trial of Joan was fair as far as it was humanly possible. But the scholars referred to above have shown that there was a definite bias against Joan in her actual trial. The Bishop of Beauvis had personal reasons for acting maliciously against Joan. He had joined the English Earl of Warwick who regarded her as his enemy as well as of feudalism. He had himself suffered defeat at her hands. The Bishop of Beauvis who presided over the trial had also appointed other judges of the trial. Therefore fairness and justice was completely out of the question in the trial of Joan. But Shaw has departed from history in his play.

Shaw has sacrificed the historical truth in the interest of his art whereas history shows that the trial was not conducted in a spirit of unbiased search for truth but motivated by the impulse to destroy the enemy. Shaw has stripped the trial of all streaks of unfairness. Shaw has shown Cauchon the Bishop of Beauvis in a new light. He is presented as a devout and pious clergy who spurns all the bias and prejudices of the Earl of Warwick. He does not allow torture to be applied to Joan. The actual trial which spreads over a number of months is compressed and concentrated to a single scene. It, therefore, does not give the impression of a broken spirit or spineless Joan.

Cauchon brushes aside the charge of sorcery, witchcraft and others of political nature. The trial is conducted to prove or disprove the charge of heresy. Ladvenu who is sympathetic to Joan is allowed to speak freely. Though the Earl of Warwick and John de Stogumber are present through the trial, they fail to influence the proceedings. Cauchon acts from a sense of duty to guide the soul of Joan to salvation. He gives her ample opportunity to recant. Both Cauchon and the inquisitor do their best to save the soul of the girl. As the good intentions of the judges are established beyond shadows of doubt, it is also established that Joan's murder was "a judicial murder" not one committed by the villains.

The artistic beauty of the trial scene is the perfect balance maintained between the viewpoints of the two sides. The case of Joan as well as the church has been presented with equal clarity and impartiality. Joan has complete faith in her visions and voices. She tells the judges, "If you command me to declare that all that I have done and said and all the visions and revelations I have had were not from God then that is impossible." On the other hand, Cauchon fears the modern heresy of the strong mind in Europe which "sets up the private judgment of the single erring mortal against the considered wisdom and experience of the church". He honestly believes that such heresy will bring about so much anarchy in Christendom that individual is allowed to undermine the authority of the church.

The trial makes use of some of the words exactly used by Joan. For example, when asked whether Michael appears to her as naked person, Joan replied as in the historical records, "Do you think God cannot afford clothes for him?" The trial has also been compressed to a single scene which spread over months in real life. The trial thus takes away the impression that spirit of Joan was broken by a lengthy trial. The scene arouses pity and fear for Joan. Yet Shaw leaves the impression that Joan got a fair trial, fairer than it is possible in a modern, secular court. Shaw, in fact, succeeded in transforming the history of Joan into the conflict of genius and discipline, individual freedom and authority.

22

Metaphysical Poetry

Metaphysical Poetry is the output of a unified sensibility. Comment.

Metaphysical Poetry is the blend of passion and reason. Discuss.

Metaphysical poetry is the output of the unified sensibility. It has behind it the dramatic vitality of the Elizabethans. It is the expression neither of the heart nor the head but of the whole man. It is different from the cerebral poetry of Dryden or from the ruminative melancholy of the Victorians or the spontaneous overflow of the powerful feelings of the Romantics.

In the words of Eliot, "The metaphysical poets of the seventeenth century possessed a mechanism of sensibility which could devour any kind of experience." They made use of a neutral language neither emotional nor intellectual but based on common speech which is a blend of intellect and emotion. For the metaphysicals, nothing is poetic or prosaic *per se*. It is the craftsmanship of the poet that renders it poetic. It is on account of this attitude that metaphysical poetry is the output of the unified sensibility. There is neither the wit of Dryden nor the romantic sensibility. It is this virtue of the metaphysicals that invigorated the modern poetry of Eliot and Yeats and others.

There is a blend of reason and passion in the poetry of John Donne, George Herbert, Andrew Marvell and Henry Vaughan. John Donne's "Song" is a case in point:

> Yester night the sun went hence
> And yet is here today

He hath no desire nor sense,
Nor half so short a way;
Then fear not me
But believe that I shall make
Speedier journeys, since I take
More wings and spurs than he.

The context of parting from the beloved is intensely emotional. Argument is employed to dispel the fear of the beloved by contrasting the insensible sun and the poet as journeyman. The poet is spurred on by his desire to return to the beloved. In keeping with the metaphysical poetic tradition, the comparison of the poet and the sun has been carried to the farthest possible extent. The elaboration of the comparison is required in order to drive home the forcefulness of logic which is the emotional need of the hour. Here reasoning is tinged with emotion. In the words of Herbert Read metaphysical poetry is "felt thought". It is chiefly in view of the imagery that Eliot remarks that metaphysical poets "feel their thought as the odour of the rose". Apart from Donne's comparison of the lovers to a pair of compass and Marvell's comparison of the infinite and the finite love to oblique and parallel lines, Henry Vaughan's "white celestial thought" in "The Retreat" and Marvell's "green thought in a green shade" in "The Garden" are cases in point. The entire poem "To His Coy Mistress" is the example of close interpenetration of intelligence and passion which blooms in the happy expression of rhythm, sound and images of the poem:

My vegetable love should grow
Vaster than empires and more slow.

The intellectual or reasonable grasp of the amorous impulse which grows impatient with the coyness of love identifies it with the extremely slow growth of "vegetable" against the flying wing of time. A comparison like this excites the remark of a critic like Dr. Johnson, "Metaphysical poets yoked heterogeneous ideas by violence together." A certain degree of heterogeneity of material is the characteristic of all poetry. The metaphysical poet's material is strikingly heterogeneous but it is welded into a unity of impression by the operation of the poet's mind. The remark of Dr. Johnson is justified only where the images fail to fuse into a unity of impression. This criticism illustrates the nature of failure in bad metaphysical poetry. No doubt, such poetry runs counter to the Arnoldian principle of "high seriousness" but it is free from the bane of sentimentality as it blends levity and seriousness by which seriousness is intensified by contrast.

The metaphysical image is not immediately sensuous like the Romantic or the Victorian images. It is not an individual splendour. It is functional. The material is not poetic in itself. It is the craftsmanship of the poet that renders it poetic. The image does not appeal directly to the heart as "O my luve's like a red, red rose." It appeals to the heart through the mind. This is why it does not possess the sensuousness of the Romantic or Victorian poetry. Its content is always logical or intellectual.

It is for this composite character of metaphysical poetry that it is not highly musical or rhythmical like Milton's or Spenser's poetry. It is based on speech rhythm which stirs up the heart and mind of the reader at the same time. The colloquial tone and the dramatic touch in "For God's sake hold your tongue and let me love" is highly appropriate emotional presentment of experience. It is not a matter of surprise that Eliot turned to the tradition of metaphysical poets while struggling towards the achievement of the unification of sensibility in:

> Let us go then, you and I
> When the evening is spread out upon the sky
> Like a patient etherised upon the table.

The functional and scientific imagery, the speaking tone, the wit, the blend of wit and seriousness, emotion and intellect which are associated with Metaphysical Poetry appear to form the shaping spirit behind modern poetry as it has a rich and complex appeal to the mind.

Discuss conceits in Metaphysical Poetry.

Or

In Metaphysical poetry "a conceit is like a spark made by stones striking together." Discuss.

A comparison discovers likeness in things unlike. A comparison becomes a conceit when we are made to concede likeness being strongly conscious of unlikeness. In the words of Helen Gardner, "A conceit is like a spark made by stones striking together. After the flash the stones are just two stones. The Metaphysical poetry abounds in such flashes."

In Metaphysical poetry a conceit is an instrument to persuade the beloved or an argument to prove a point. The Metaphysical conceit or imagery is not condensed but extended to the last point to which the ingenuity of the poet can carry. The reason for this extension is the analogy of the poet, as we see in Donne's "A Valediction" in which the union of the lovers is compared to legs of "compass" and the poet attempts to elaborate the analogy by which he persuades his beloved not to mourn. Similarly, Cowley compares the world to a chess-board through long stanzas in his poem, "To Destiny". Thus Metaphysical poetry acquires an argumentative character through the use of conceit. The metaphysical conceit or image is not sensuous or decorative but functional in character. It is particularly the imagery or the conceit that distinguishes Metaphysical poetry from the rest.

Joan Bennet in her essay, "Five Metaphysical Poets" remarks, "Experience to the metaphysical poets was as it were grist to an intellectual will." Bennet is absolutely correct because the Metaphysical poetry is nothing else but the product of intellect. The Metaphysical poets interact their feelings and thoughts in their poetry. The fusion of thought and feeling makes the poetry intellectual or logical and it extends the tradition of Shakespeare, Chapman, Middleton and Jonson. Metaphysical poets were learned persons who could transmute their erudition into poetry. Geographical and scientific images like globe, hemisphere, legs of compass, oblique and parallel lines abound in Metaphysical poetry. Metaphysical poets felt their thought as the odour of the rose as they possessed a mechanism of sensibility which could devour any kind of experience. This is missing in the Victorian poets like Tennyson and Browning. So, Eliot calls them, "reflective poets" who "think but do not feel their thought as immediately as the odour of a rose."

Metaphysical poetry is "felt thought". No doubt, such poetry seems counter to the Arnoldian principle of "high seriousness" and it is free from the bane of sentimentality as it blends levity and seriousness by which seriousness is intensified by contrast. Metaphysical poets "yoked the heterogeneous ideas by violence together". The remark of Dr. Johnson illustrates the failure of minor Metaphysical poets who failed to fuse the images into a unity of impression. There is no yoking but welding of ideas into a single unity. They are reborn in the heat of creative imagination through the operation of the poet's mind. As we see in "To His Coy Mistress", the comparison of love to "vegetable" seems quite striking and at first sight illogical. But the way the poet persuades his beloved to make most of the opportunity of youthfulness is logical and in this context "vegetable" becomes the most integral part of the logic of the poem as a symbol of slow growth. We cannot but agree with Helen Gardner when she points out, "the first impression a conceit makes is of ingenuity rather than of justice. The Metaphysical conceit aims at making us concede justness while admiring ingenuity". "Vegetable" is the symbol of very slow growth which the fleeting time will not grant to their youth which sits on their skin "like dew". It is in this background that the poet urges his beloved to "make their sun run" if they cannot make it stand.

The peculiar use of conceit or imagery differentiates Metaphysical poetry from all periods except the modern age and some Elizabethan poets like Shakespeare, Chapman, Middleton and Jonson. It paves the way for the modernity in the 20th century as Eliot, Yeats and many others have adopted the Metaphysical style.

DISCUSS THE SALIENT FEATURES OF THE METAPHYSICAL POETRY

Metaphysical poetry has a unique place in English literature. It is completely different from the poetry of all periods except the Modern age and some Elizabethan poets such as Shakespeare, Middleton, Chapman and Jonson etc. The reason for affinity with these mentioned poets is the recreation of thought into feeling. But there is also a difference between these Elizabethans and the Metaphysical poets in the sense that the Elizabethan poetry lacks scientific images while the Metaphysical poetry is full of these images. The Metaphysical poetry paves the way for the modernity in the 20th century. The Modern poets like Eliot, Yeats and many others adopted the Metaphysical style and so, Metaphysical and Modern poetry works in the same way. It touches our heart through intellect while Elizabethan, Romantic and Victorian poetry appeals to our heart directly. So, the poetry in English literature can be divided into two categories — musical and intellectual. Metaphysical and Modern poetry is intellectual as it appeals to us through reason and Elizabethan, Romantic and Victorian poetry is musical because it directly appeals to our heart without reason.

The Elizabethan age is the age of music. This is why F.R. Leavis says, "In an age when music is for all classes an important part of daily life, when poets are along with so large proportion of their fellow-country men, musicians, write their lyrics to be sung, Donne uses in complete dissociation from music a stanza form that proclaims the union of poetry and music." This view represents not only the quality of Donne but reflects the entire Metaphysical poetry. In some Elizabethan poetry there is a gush of feelings which makes it highly musical but in Metaphysical poetry feeling and thought are unified which makes it less musical. In Elizabethan lyrical poetry music is for music's sake while in Metaphysical poetry music is for the sake of meaning. It is true to say that the Elizabethans especially Nashe and Campion sing their feelings while the Metaphysicals speak them. Metaphysical poetry is remarkably famous for its speaking tone and abrupt, dramatic opening in which the poet addresses his beloved and God unconventionally. As the Metaphysicals are unconventional in their love for God and beloved, their language is simple and colloquial. This quality is completely absent from Milton, Dryden and Johnson etc. This is why Eliot says, "While the language became more refined, the feeling became more crude." The best examples of language's simplicity and of speaking tone are in Donne's "Cannonization":

> "For God sake! hold you tongue/ And let me love," and
> in "Good Morrow,"
> "I wonder by my troth what thou and I
> Did till me loved?"

and in Herbert's divine poems:

> "Ah my dear God! Though I am clean forgot
> Let me not love thee if I love thee not."

And

> "You must sit down", says Love "and taste my meat. So
> I did and eat."

Carew's "Ingrateful Beauty Threatened" has also the representative quality of the typical Metaphysical tone. The speaking tone in their poems lends dramatic touch to them and brings them in close affinity with Shakespeare. F.R. Leavis rightly points out, "The dissociation is positive, utterance, movement and intonations are those of the talking voice."

The unification of thought and feeling makes Metaphysical poetry logical. This interaction of thought and feeling is only possible when one's mind works in the logical way. The Metaphysical poets interact their feelings and thoughts. This interaction is absent from the Victorian poets like Tennyson and Browning. So Eliot calls them "reflective poets" and rightly says: "They think but do not feel their thoughts as immediately as the odour of a rose." Metaphysical poetry is "felt thought". The poet transmutes his feeling and experience into logic. This is why Metaphysical poetry is logical or intellectual and not sensuous like that of Shelley, Keats, Tennyson, Browning and

Coleridge etc. The logic in Metaphysical poetry is especially the result of the poet's peculiar use of conceit which is the characteristic feature of this age. Helen Gardner says, "All comparisons discover likeness in things unlike, a comparison becomes a conceit when we are made to concede likeness being strongly conscious of unlikeness [...]. A conceit is like a spark made by stones striking together. After the flash stones are just two stones. Metaphysical poetry abounds in such flashes."

In Metaphysical poetry conceit is an instrument to persuade the beloved, an agrument to prove a point. The Metaphysical conceits are not condensed but extended. And the reason for this extension is the analogy of the poet, as we see in Donne's "A Valediction" in which the union of lovers is compared to the legs of "compass" and the poet attempts to give a proof of their union through analogy by which he persuades his beloved not to mourn. Cowley compares the world to a chess-board through long stanzas in his poems "To Destiny". Helen Gardner rightly points out, "the poem has to say something which the conceit explicates or something to urge which the conceit helps to forward."

In Metaphysical poetry two completely dissimilar things are brought together by the intellectual mind of the poet. This dissimilar comparison makes Metaphysical poetry untraditional, unique and different from the poetry of all ages except the modern. We see in Donne's "A Valediction" the comparison of two lovers to the legs of "compass", the growth of love to 'vegetable' in Marvell's "To His Coy Mistress" and in "Thoughts in A Garden" thought as "green" etc. Apparently all these comparisons have no connection between themselves but the connection between them is forged logically by poets and they are successful in conveying their feelings fully. We cannot agree with Dr. Johnson who says, "the most heterogeneous ideas are yoked by violence together" in Metaphysical poetry. There is no yoking but ideas are connected in a logical way. As we see in "To His Coy Mistress" the comparison of love to the "vegetable" seems quite illogical. But when we study the poem thoroughly, we find that the way the poet persuades his beloved to use the opportunity is logical and so "vegetable" becomes a functional image. Here we agree with Helen Gardner who points out, "the first impression a conceit makes is of ingenuity rather than of justice; the metaphysical conceit aims at making us concede justness while admiring ingenuity". The geographical or scientific conceit in Metaphysical poetry isolates it from the poetry of Elizabethan, Romantic and Victorian periods. It can be said that science was the dominating power during this period. The use of "compass", "globe", "chess board", "Indian Ganges" and many other examples are of scientific or geographical images.

The concentration in Metaphysical poetry, one of the main characteristic feature is also the product of the poet's intellect. Donne in his sermons speaking of psalms says, "such form as is both curious and requires diligence in the making and then it is made, can have nothing, no syllable taken from it nor added to it". It shows that the Metaphysical poets for their logical thinking were able to exploit the traditional rule and regulation of poetry. This is why Helen Gardner remarks, "A stanza of Donne or Herbert is not like rima royal or Spenserian stanza, an ideal mould into which the words have flowed. It is more like limiting frame in which words and thoughts are compressed, a box sweets compacted lie." The concentration and sinewy strength of style is the mark of Ben Jonson as well as of Donne. The Metaphysicals were fond of either very simple verse forms, octasylabic couplets or quatrains in which length of the line and rhyme scheme artfully enforced the sense.

Metaphysical poetry is not only famous for its speaking tone and abrupt, dramatic opening and conceits but also for passionate feelings, sensuous images and fine lyrical grace. Marvell's "To His Coy Mistress" is its best example in which the poet advises his beloved to seize the opportunity in a logical way with the contrast of images, "worms", "time's winged chariot", "preserved virginity", "private place" and "morning dew". The theme is just like "O Mistress mine",

"Gather ye Rose buds" and "Carpe Diem" but this one is superior because it is more sensuous and musical. The images heighten the sensuality and musicality of the poem and the fast moving rhythm is co-operative in conveying the poet's feeling as well as the speed of time. The comparison of the growth of love to the "vegetable" and threatening that the "preserved virginity" will be tried by worms in the grave impart witty turn to the poem. Instead of the fine lyric and wittiness, the reason in the poem through which the poet persuades his beloved not to lose the opportunity "Then worms shall try/ That long preserved virginity" is strong enough. In this condition, we agree with Eliot who says there is "tough reasonableness beneath the lyrical grace".

We see that the characteristic features of Metaphysical poetry: the speaking tone, dramatic opening, concentration, images and peculiar use of conceits all are the product of the intellect of the poet. Joan Benett rightly remarks that "Experience to the Metaphysical poets was as it were grist to an intellectual mill."

23

WORDSWORTH AS A POET

The Wasteland is the "music of ideas". Comment.

Or

Discuss the structure of _The Wasteland._

Or

Consider _The Wasteland_ as an epic.

Or

Comment on the use of myth in _The Wasteland._

I.A. Richards describes *The Wasteland* as "The music of ideas". The phrase suggests the new technique or the organising principle in the poetry of Eliot. The conventional narrative or intellectual sequence is not to be looked for as Eliot has suppressed the connecting matter altogether. Some degree of suggestiveness has always been brought in to bridge the gap of sense between images in the poetry in the past. But Eliot has pushed this technique far beyond the conventional limits which results in "the music of ideas". *The Wasteland* was a far longer poem. It was Ezra Pound to whom Eliot pays his tribute in his dedication as *il miglia fabric* who cut the poem to its present size. One of the sources of the obscurity of the poem derives from it. The poem is a juxtaposition of contemporary scenes, allusions and quotations from literature, myth and religion. Probably, the phrase "music of ideas" is inappropriate. It should be replaced by the term "musical unity", because the word "idea" is abstract and the juxtapositions are concrete scenes and events.

The charge of overintellectualization brought against Eliot is based partly on the new technique or the organising principle that the reader does not anticipate and partly on his use of allusions. The allusions and quotations suggest an impressive range of Eliot's study. The *Waste Land* acquires epical bearings from the use of allusions. It is a device for compression. Each allusion brings its own aura of suggestiveness from its context. In the words of Richards "the poem is equivalent in content to an epic without this device twelve books could have been needed". *The Wasteland* is "a heap of broken images" where you can "connect nothing with nothing" owing to the absence of a narrative sequence. The anticipation of a logical or intellectual thread constitutes the stumbling block for numberless readers whose sensibility has been trained on conventional poetry. In fact, a good deal of conventional poetry consists in juxtaposition of images and it is their suggestiveness that leads the reader to their significance. In "Prufrock" and "The Portrait of a Lady," there is a slight semblance of continuity. But in *The Hollow Man* and *The Wasteland* the poet completely suppresses the connecting matter. *The Wasteland* reflects a point of stasis and the progression is not linear like *The Paradise Lost* but cyclic. From the very beginning, in poem after poem, Eliot tries to capture the stream of consciousness of the individual. He has gone one step further in capturing the comprehensive human consciousness through the symbol of Tiresias, "the old man with wrinkled female breasts" who combines the experiences of both the sexes as well as of the past and the present.

Eliot admired the mythical method of James Joyce in *Ulysses* which accommodated allusions in its texture. Eliot's allusions and symbols have their roots in Jessie Weston's *From Ritual to Romance* and Frazer's *The Golden Bough*. But at the same time, the basic elements of nature — earth, air, water, and fire form the essential pattern of images and symbols in the poem. The significance of the poem lies in the recurrence and repetition of images, personages and references. Eliot in the note attached to the poem himself admits "just as the one-eyed merchant, seller of currants melts into the Phoenician sailor and the latter is not wholly distinct from Ferdinand, the Prince of Naples, so all women are one woman and the two sexes meet in Tiresias". In the same way, the waste land is reflected in "the dead land", "stony rubbish", "dead tree", "dry stone", "the unreal city", "dead" men of "The Burial of the Dead". Robert and Lil with "synthetic perfume" and Philomel and the nightingale in "The Game of Chess" register the waste land in the biological infertility and the emotional sterility. "The Fire Sermon" which echoes with references to Elizabeth and Leicester, Lord Buddha, Fire Sermon, St. Augustine, Carthage, Troy presents the physical liaison of the typist girl and the man carbuncular in terms of "human engine throbbing like a taxi". The water that drowns in "Death by water" turns into "the sound of water" and rock in "the sunken Ganga", "empty cisterns", "dry bone" in *What the Thunder Said.*

The images, allusions and personages of one section appear and reappear in another. Each episode, each allusion builds up emphasis upon emphasis and the result is a deeper exploration of human experience. Each acts like a musical note and they unite into a unity of emotional effect, tone or impression. *The Waste Land* was not meant to achieve logical, intellectual or narrative coherence. It achieves a musical harmony. The allusions which are derived from the Bible, Buddha, St. Augustine, Upnishad, French, Greek, Latin and Sanskrit and English literature of the past impart epical hearings to the poem. *The Waste Land* acquires universality and timelessness through timeless and universal parallels and contrasts drawn from the range of entire human history. The structure is repetitive as it enacts the idea of *The Family Reunion*:

> We do not know very much of the future
> Except that from generation to generation
> The same things happen again and again.

All the allusions, images and symbols form the metaphorical representation of timeless and universal human condition. The Upnishadic reference to "Datta", "Damyatta" and

"Dyadhavam" occur here but no healing water is released to regenerate the Waste Land.

T.S. ELIOT

T.S. Eliot is a modern poet. By his criticism and the kind of poetry he wrote, he brought about a revolution in the literary taste of his times. He gave a new direction to poetry which ran counter to the decadent victorian poetry. His poetry was original in idiom, imagery and rhythm. But his originality lay in intertwining different strands of tradition.

T.S. Eliot came under the influence of Elizabethan dramatists. Metaphysicals, French symbolists and imagists. As a poet-critic, his criticism laid emphasis on impersonality and objective correlative. His early poems "Love Song of Alfred Prufrock", "Portrait of a Lady" etc. present the objective correlative for emotional states of mind. These poems are difficult, allusive, ironic, dramatic and have the rhythm of common speech that reflects the movement of thought or mind. Much of the connecting matter is suppressed in these poems and the poet relies on the suggestiveness of the images to fill up the gap of sense. This remains the permanent feature of Eliot's poetic technique. His early poems present the image of urban life with a sardonic touch and explore the barrenness and hollowness of life in the modern age.

His poem, "*Gerontion*" is a step towards "The Wasteland". "The influence of the imagist poetry is evident in his use of hard, clear and precise images in the poems.

T.S. Eliot is a classicist. In sharp contrast to romantics, he lives in the world around him and shows his deep concern with contemporary society. In his pursuit of giving a realistic portrait of life around him, many a time, he becomes critical of the spiritual degeneration of man and expresses despair over the utter emptiness of contemporary civilization. In "The Wasteland" and "The Hollow Man" he describes the spiritual degeneration of the modern man. "The Wasteland" is a symbolic poem. Its poetic fabric is composed of allusions and quotations from English, Spanish, Italian, Sanskrit and many other languages. The framework of symbolism is derived from Jessie Weston's myth of Fisher King in "From Rituals to Romance" and James Fraser's vegetation myth in his book "The Golden Bough".

Eliot's early poetry is difficult on account of its difficult poetic technique where he *dislocates* language into meaning. But the difficulty in the later poetry has a different nature. For example in "The Four Quartets" the difficulty in the poem does not arise from the technique as much as from the complexity of thought or idea in them. It is a beautiful, moving poem on flux and eternity unlike the early poetry, the images are supplied not from the urban life but from nature. The images and rhythm are moving and have a natural beauty. Eliot once remarked, "Genuine poetry communicates before it is understood." This is the quality of the poetry of "The Four Quartets". Probably this is his finest poetic achievement.

Eliot's rhythm is dictated by the poetic meaning. But his diction is not governed by any metrical law. This accounts for great variety, flexibility in the movement of the lines. The verse is *distinct* from verse *libre*. "It consists of lines of varying lengths, commonly with strong beats pausing midway as if for deliberation." It upholds the most precarious poetic flights in "The Four Quartets". Eliot is a great poet. Apart from the invention of a new style, his achievement lies in his concern with the dominant anxieties and feelings of his age. He restores life and vitality to the English language by bringing it in contact with not only common speech but also with the European tradition. He extended the range and possibilities of the language by writing a kind of poetry which reflects a consciousness beyond which words fail but the meaning still exists. Eliot wrote a number of poetic dramas like "Murder in the Cathedral", "The Family Reunion" and "The Cocktail Party". But he could not revive poetic drama as in the Elizabethan age.

WORDSWORTH AS A POET

The history of English literature presents a see-saw movement of classicism and romanticism. The values of the nineteenth century Romantic poetry came into existence in reaction against the eighteenth century standards. Wordsworth's poetry amply exhibits it, in its shift of emphasis from the social to the personal. Dryden's *Absolom and Achitophel* or Pope's *The Rape of the Lock* is concerned with the events in the external world. But Wordsworth's *The Prelude* is an autobiographical poem as in it he traces the influences on, and the development, of his mind.

Since Wordsworth conceived poetry as "the spontaneous overflow of powerful feelings", he does not use balance, antithesis and paradox as devices to achieve his effects. He eschews the figurative language of Shakespeare which reduces a multitude of images to a single unity. "He makes scenes from actual life rise up before us and if the scenes are rightly chosen and faithful rendered, they carry the sensations and emotions accompanying them into the heart of the reader. The boat stealing incident in *The Prelude* is a case in point where the poet as a boy takes out the boat on the lake without the permission of the owner when the mountain peak, all of a sudden uprears its head:

> And growing still in stature the grim shape
> Towered up between me and the stars
> For so it seemed, with the purpose of its own
> And measured motion like a living thing,
> Strode after me.

The poet hastens to the bank, tethers the boat and runs back home. The emotion of the poet is chastened and purified through fear. It shows how natural objects came to play a role in the emotional and moral life of the poet. Nature emerges as a mother or teacher in Wordsworth. He does not exclude the unpleasant part of nature. Nature is a source of strength and delight as well as terror. The success of poetry depends on the vivid recreation of immediate personal experience where the poet withdraws from it into philosophising, immediate concreteness and vividness give way to abstractions. The poem, "Ode on the Intimations of Immortality" bears it out where he laments the loss of his sensuous delight in natural objects and asserts to have been compensated by other gifts. The early part of the poem is devoid of the immediacy of personal encounter with natural objects:

> The Rainbow comes and goes
> And lovely is the Rose.

It, thus, convincingly brings out the loss. The personification of "Rainbow" and "Rose" in the eighteenth century manner, fails to make up for the particular details of the personal experience. Its further attempt to compensate by what Coleridge calls "mental bombast" is not successful. Yet he achieves a poignant sense of wistfulness in the twelve monosyllables that follow:

> Turn wherever I may
> By night or day.
> The thing that I have seen now I can see no more.

He uses the notion of pre-existence as the glorious home of the soul to explain the gradual loss of his ability to experience the objects of nature. He tries to discount the loss by counting the gains. But gains are not asserted with the forceful poetry. "Tintern Abbey" in which the poet feels a divine presence in nature comes in between the autobiographical poems and those concerned with "the still sad music of humanity".

There is stress on spontaneity but it is expressed in and represented by the tranquil surface of the verse. This is what makes Wordsworth different from Shelley. Shelley's stress on spontaneity implies dissociation from reason and intellect. This accounts for the lack of objective correlative in the poetry of Shelley whereas Wordsworth always presents a situation, a chain of events which faithfully rendered generates the necessary emotion in the reader. When Wordsworth is at his best, there is no emotional comments, but bare facts literally stated. And this situation in Wordsworth is always taken from the rural, humble life. The lines and events of ordinary human life form the raw material of Wordsworth's poetry. "Margaret", "Ruth" and "Michael" are specimens where the poet's creative ability is operating on experiences that are not his own. His portrayal of the figures is psychological. Margaret's husband is gone and she becomes an image of perpetual expectancy:

> I have heard my friend
> That in yon arbor oftentime she sat
> Alone through half the vacant sabbath day
> And if a dog passed by, she still would quit
> The shade, and look abroad. On this old bench
> For hours she sat and evermore her eye
> Was busy in the distance, shaping things
> That made her heart beat quick.

In the same way, in the poem, "Michael" after his separation from his son, Michael "could not raise a single stone" for the sheepfold that he with his son was constructing. Wordsworth's capacities are not Shakespearian but he has a peculiar power of realising human emotions into actions. "Margaret" has surely behind it the memory of Annet Vallon and this is why the image of a forsaken woman recurs in his poems like "Margaret", "Ruth" and "Guilt and Sorrow".

Lucy poems of Wordsworth possess a unique beauty. They are idiosyncratic and some of them have a delicate, almost precarious balance. They present in a bare but suggestive style the imagination of Lucy that was and the loss of this dream with the death of Lucy. Lucy poems have a peculiar emotional force and imaginative beauty.

Though Wordsworth lacked negative capability that Keats admired but his poetry is not merely "egotistical sublime". The Metaphysical wit is not to be found in his poetry but his poetry has a powerful appeal to the human heart for its presentation of simple human emotions and passions in natural surroundings.